STUART BUTLER, OLIVER BERRY, STEVE FALLON,
ANITA ISALSKA & NICOLA WILLIAMS

Contents

PLAN YOUR TRIP

Highlights 6
Best For 12
With Kids.................................... 14
Accessible Trails 16
Essentials.................................... 18
Walking in France.................... 20

BY REGION

BRITTANY & NORMANDY............27
Dinan: Up & Down Town....................30
La Côte de Granit Rose 32
Giverny Impressions....................34
Grouin: Up to a Point 36
Circling the Île d'Ouessant.............38
Omaha Beach....................40
Pointes du Raz & Van 44
Also Try 46

LILLE & THE SOMME 49
Thiepval Loop.................... 52
Beaumont-Hamel
    Newfoundland Memorial....................54
Baie St-Jean.................... 56
Lochnagar Crater 58
Also Try 62

FRENCH ALPS & JURA 65
Lac de Roselend & Lac de la Gittaz ... 68
Grand Balcon Nord 70
Lac Blanc.................... 74
Pic des Mémises 76
Chalets de Bise to Lac de Darbon...... 78

Arbois to Pupillin....................80
Cirque de Baume-les-Messieurs........82
Tête de la Maye....................86
Lac des Vaches &
    Col de la Vanoise 88
Also Try 92

CENTRAL FRANCE....................95
Brantôme Circuit....................98
Lac Chambon & Murol Circuit 100
Beynac Castle Loop 102
The Chemin de Halage.................... 104
Pilgrimage Around Rocamadour.........106
Stevenson's Journey 108
Climbing Puy de Dôme 110
Ascent to Puy de Sancy....................112
Castles of the Dordogne....................114
Also Try 118

PROVENCE &
THE CÔTE D'AZUR.................... 121
Wetlands of the Camargue 124
Lac du Lauzanier.................... 126
Port-Miou, Port-Pin & En-Vau 128
Roussillon Ramble 130
Cap Roux 132
The Blanc-Martel Trail 134
Gordes Loops 136
Les Eaux Tortes 140
Also Try 142

LANGUEDOC-ROUSSILLON....... 145
Gorges d'Héric 148
Cirque de Mourèze 150
Roc des Hourtous 152
Pic St-Loup 154

Cirque de Navacelles 156
Mont Aigoual 158
Also Try 162

THE PYRENEES 165
Plateau de Bellevue 168
Refuge des Oulettes de Gaube......... 170
Lac d'Ayous Circuit 172
Brèche de Roland 174
Cirque de Troumouse 176
Lac Vert 178
Lac d'Oo & Lac Saussat....................180
Pic du Tarbésou &
    the Blue & Black Lakes 182
Marcadau Valley &
    the Cardinquère Lakes 184
Col & Pic de Madamète 188
Also Try 192

CORSICA 195
Cascade des Anglais 198
Capu Pertusato & Bonifacio.............. 200
Sentier des Douaniers....................202
Vallée du Tavignano....................204
Capo Rosso....................206
Lac de Nino....................208
Lac de Melo & Lac de Capitello........ 210
Also Try 214

LANGUAGE....................216
BEHIND THE SCENES 218
BY DIFFICULTY....................219
INDEX 220
OUR WRITERS 224

From Mont Blanc and other alpine giants to the volcanic cones of the Massif Central and the visual poetry of the Pyrenees, France is blessed with wave after wave of beautiful mountain peaks. Traversing these mountain ranges are a network of high-quality walking trails that attract hikers from all four corners of the world.

But walking in France is about more than just cinematic mountain vistas. At its heart, this is a land of gentle woodlands where rivers meander past old villages surrounded by fields of vines, lavender and sunflowers.

Then, there's the salt-brushed coastline where quaint fishing villages, storm-hammered headlands and sweeping sandy beaches are linked by tranquil coastal footpaths.

All of this makes France one of the world's most diverse and inviting walking destinations. And with more than 180,000km of marked trails, you're never going to run out of new routes to explore.

Highlights

**MARCADAU VALLEY &
THE CARDINQUÈRE LAKES,
THE PYRENEES**

A symphony of beautiful lakes, a frosty mountain pass, idyllic valleys and views that stretch forever. This is the walk that just keeps on giving. **p184**

POINTES DU RAZ & VAN, BRITTANY & NORMANDY

Catch ocean breezes while walking over white-sand beaches and watch storm swells unleash their anger on the cliffs at the end of France. **p44**

GRAND BALCON NORD, FRENCH ALPS & JURA

Experience the best of Chamonix en famille: cable-car magic, France's largest glacier, a mountain train ride and big bold Mont Blanc views. **p70**

THE BLANC-MARTEL TRAIL, PROVENCE & THE CÔTE D'AZUR

One of the most iconic walks in France rumbles beneath the textured walls of the 'Grand Canyon' of Europe. **p134**

CASTLES OF THE DORDOGNE, CENTRAL FRANCE

A quiet ramble along the banks of the River Dordogne that takes in hilltop castles, cliffside villages, and beautiful oak and chestnut woodlands. **p114**

BRÈCHE DE ROLAND, THE PYRENEES
Welcome to the high mountain world of glaciers and snow fields. This breathtaking walk takes you to a fabled rock gateway between France and Spain. **p174**

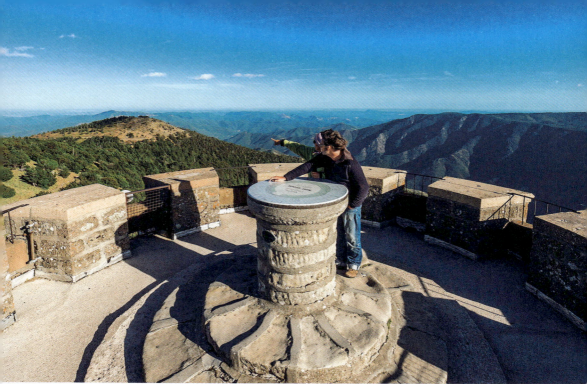

MONT AIGOUAL, LANGUEDOC-ROUSSILLON

A tough, full-day hike up to one of the best viewpoints in the Cévennes – with a historic observatory included too. **p158**

BEAUMONT-HAMEL NEWFOUNDLAND MEMORIAL, LILLE & THE SOMME

Pay your respects to those who made the ultimate sacrifice. This melancholic trail through WWI battlefields is as much a pilgrimage as a walk. **p54**

GROUIN: UP TO A POINT, BRITTANY & NORMANDY
A walk up this stunning headland is the ultimate Brittany experience, with spectacular coastal views, glimpses of Mont St-Michel and seabird life in spades. **p36**

LAC DE MELO & LAC DE CAPITELLO, CORSICA
Twin lakes thrown up against sky-high rocky mountain fingers. This is the Corsica you never knew existed. **p210**

Best For...

ALESSANDRO CRISTIANO/SHUTTERSTOCK ©

MARGOUILLAT PHOTO/SHUTTERSTOCK ©

🐦 WILDLIFE

France is blessed with an incredibly rich diversity of plants and animals, and observant walkers have a good chance of spotting some exotic creatures.

WETLANDS OF THE CAMARGUE
The greatest wetland wilderness in France is home to white horses and very pink flamingos. **p124**

POINTES DU RAZ & VAN
Scan the ocean waves for seals, porpoises and dolphins, plus a bevy of different seabirds from these high cliffs. **p44**

LAC DU LAUZANIER
Cuddle up to the tame marmots (pictured above) in this alpine valley and watch the choughs circle in the breeze. **p126**

LAC D'AYOUS CIRCUIT
The western Pyrenees is renowned for its raptors: griffon vultures, golden eagles and even formidable lammergeier can all be seen. **p172**

CHALETS DE BISE TO LAC DE DARBON
Spot majestic ibex on this wild alpine walk where wildlife is as much an attraction as scenery. **p78**

⛰ ESCAPING THE CROWDS

Clear the mind on these walks that take you far from the madding crowd.

ROC DES HOURTOUS
Deep in the heart of the Parc National des Cévennes, this walk veers on the quieter side of life (pictured above). **p152**

PILGRIMAGE AROUND ROCAMADOUR
Follow this trail to Rocamadour and you'll likely have only the ghosts of pilgrims past to walk with. **p106**

LAC DES VACHES & COL DE LA VANOISE
Spectacular lakes and gargantuan glaciers are the reward for those who venture out here. **p88**

GIVERNY IMPRESSIONS
Who would have thought that busy, touristy Giverny could hide such undisturbed countryside? **p34**

CAP ROUX
From this silent coastal massif, peer down on the glam crowds of the Riviera. **p132**

12/PLAN YOUR TRIP

BRINGING THE PAST TO LIFE

Walk on routes where the past is ever present.

OMAHA BEACH
Site of one of the bloodiest WWII D-Day battles. **p40**

THIEPVAL LOOP
The Thiepval Memorial (pictured above) is the most moving tribute to the tragedy of the Battle of the Somme. **p52**

CIRQUE DE BAUME-LES-MESSIEURS
Visit a 7th-century abbey. **p82**

BEYNAC CASTLE LOOP
When this fairy-tale castle swings into view, you can imagine knights going into battle. **p102**

STEVENSON'S JOURNEY
Retrace the route of *Treasure Island* author Robert Louis Stevenson. **p108**

COASTAL VIEWS

Some of the best walks in France are by the sea.

CIRCLING THE ÎLE D'OUESSANT
Feel the raw power of the Atlantic Ocean on this remote, weather-beaten isle (pictured above). **p38**

SENTIER DES DOUANIERS
Walking this route takes you from beach to headland to beach. **p202**

PORT-MIOU, PORT-PIN & EN-VAU
Be stunned by lucid clear waters and butter-coloured cliffs. **p128**

GROUIN: UP TO A POINT
This nature reserve juts out on a windblown promontory. **p36**

LA CÔTE DE GRANIT ROSE
Secluded bays and a milky-blue sea linked by orange-pink granite boulders. **p32**

PRETTY VILLAGES

Mother Nature is a great artist, but some French villages can give her a run for her money.

GORDES LOOPS
The village of Gordes might be the most heavenly in southern France. **p136**

DINAN: UP & DOWN TOWN
Dinan is one of the loveliest old towns in northern France. **p30**

CAPU PERTUSATO & BONIFACIO
Snap that perfect shot of Bonifacio huddled onto the side of high coastal cliffs. **p200**

THE CHEMIN DE HALAGE
Walk through oak woodlands to magical St-Cirq-Lapopie. **p104**

BRANTÔME CIRCUIT
The impressive abbey (pictured above) is the centrepiece of enchanting Brantôme. **p98**

PLAN YOUR TRIP/13

With Kids

Walking with children can be incredibly rewarding for both you and them. It's time together as a family without the distractions and pressures that day-to-day life brings.

TRAILS & TRIBULATIONS

As wonderful as walking with children can be, it does bring challenges and requires careful planning. The most important thing is to pick your route wisely.

It's important not to be over ambitious. If your children consistently find the walks you choose too difficult, then they'll quickly be put off walking for good. On the other hand, the shortest and easiest walks are not always the best ones for children either. If it's too easy then many a child loses interest. Throw in some boulders to climb up, summits (achievable ones) to conquer and streams to jump across, and you'll probably find your kids can't get enough of it.

It's a good idea to go through the different trail options with your children the night before and let them know what's in store. When it comes to walk times, keep in mind that the times written in this book are for walking only and don't include stops. With children, you'll stop much more than if you were only with adults. It's best to double all walk times. For most children under the age of 12 a five-hour walk will take most of the day. Start early and take a torch just in case it takes more than all day!

Don't take a risk with the weather. Trudging up the side of a mountain in sheets of rain will not endear you to your children. Ideally, choose only dry, sunny days but ones that aren't too hot either. If it is hot then choose a walk that involves a lake, stream or beach and let them cool off in the water.

BEST WALKING REGIONS

There are good walks for children in every corner of France, but the coastline of Brittany and Normandy has some real kid-friendly classics. Another great region for family walking holidays is Central France. The Dordogne and Lot region has the scenic variety to keep mums and dads happy

Walking with Babies & Toddlers

Walking with children below the age of about four or five presents a unique set of issues.

If your child is still a baby and hasn't yet found their feet, then walking with them is generally pretty easy. You just need to wrap them up warm and put them in a baby backpack (on most walking trails you can forget about pushchairs) and off you go.

Toddlers and young children are a different matter. Chances are they're not going to want to spend too long strapped to your back. But they can't generally walk very far either. You might find that getting more than a few hundred metres from the car park is something of a struggle. But don't let that put you off entirely. Instead, try and find a walk that has interest within the first kilometre (such as a beach or a river). If children start associating walking with fun outdoors then you'll have them hooked for life. La Côte de Granit Rose in Brittany and Lac du Lauzanier in Provence both have a lot of interest within a few hundred, easy, metres of the parking area.

as well as castles and rivers to keep children's minds inspired.

All the mountain areas can be superb, but it's important to pick the right walk and not attempt something too ambitious.

WHAT TO PACK

Make sure your children have good-quality, comfortable walking shoes. You really don't want them getting blisters because of ill-fitting shoes.

Bring plenty of warm clothes as well as spare clothes (because if there's a stream they will fall in it). Most importantly, bring lots of food, snacks and water. Bring at least twice as much as you think they might want. You'll be amazed at how much children can eat while walking.

TOP TIPS

Make things a little easier for all of you by following these tried and tested tips.

- Let the kids map-read or use a compass (but keep an eye on progress yourself!).

- Take a plastic container to collect identifiable wild berries, including blueberries and raspberries. In many mountain areas, there are lots of unusual things for children to collect.

- Ask them to find their own walking stick.

- Bring or download a field guide to the animals, birds and flowers of an area and see how many they can identify. Searching for animal footprints is also a good way of keeping children interested.

- Bring a friend for them. It's amazing how much better children walk if they've got friends along.

- In the Alps (and occasionally elsewhere), it's often possible to combine a walk with a cable car or mountain train (to both kill off some of the steep climb up and inject some extra fun into the day).

PLAN YOUR TRIP/15

Accessible Trails

ACCESSIBLE TRAVEL IN FRANCE

On the whole, France presents constant challenges for those with *mobilité réduite* (reduced mobility) and *visiteurs handicapés* (visitors with disabilities) – cobblestones, sidewalks crowded with cafe tables, a lack of kerb/curb ramps, budget hotels without elevators/lifts. On the plus side though, the French government is making significant strides to improve the situation.

When it comes to travelling across France to reach your chosen destination, many SNCF train carriages are accessible to people with disabilities. If you use a wheelchair, you and a person accompanying you may qualify for discounts. For information in English on all aspects of accessible rail travel in France, see www.sncf.com/en/passenger-offer/travel-for-everyone/accessibility.

Tourisme et Handicaps issues the blue 'Tourisme et Handicap' label to tourist sites, restaurants and hotels that comply with strict accessibility and usability standards. Different symbols indicate the sort of access afforded to people with physical, mental, hearing and/or visual disabilities.

Further general information on accessible travel in France is available on the following sites:

• Jaccede.com (www.jaccede.com) is an excellent interactive accessibility guide; before arrival download the phone app to search for accessible hotels, cinemas and so on.

• Gîtes de France (www.gites-de-france-var.fr) can provide details of accessible *gîtes ruraux* (self-contained holiday cottages) and *chambres d'hôte* (B&Bs); search the website with the term 'disabled access'.

• The French Government Tourist Office website (www.france.fr) has lots of info for travellers with disabilities.

Download Lonely Planet's free Accessible Travel guide from https://shop.lonelyplanet.com/categories/accessible-travel.com.

CHOOSE YOUR REGION WISELY

Although many trails in France are challenging for people with reduced mobility or for the older or less fit walker, there are some routes that are at least partially accessible, and highly rewarding, to everyone. Throughout this book, any of the walks marked as Easy can be conquered by almost anyone, although some are still on partially uneven paths or involve gentle climbs and descents. Note that a walk

Resources

The following websites have useful information on accessible-for-all routes.

The best adapted hiking routes in France (www.sunrisemedical.fr/blog/randonnees-adaptees-france)

Vanoise National Park (www.vanoise-parcnational.fr/fr/des-decouvertes/un-parc-accessible-tous/nos-partenaires-pour-le-tourisme-et-handicap)

Mercantour National Park (www.mercantour-parcnational.fr/fr/des-actions/sensibiliser-eduquer-et-accueillir/accessibilite-et-handicap/randonnees-accessibles-tous)

marked as Easy in the Alps or the Pyrenees is not the same as a walk marked Easy in Central France.

Less fit walkers should add plenty of rest time to the standard walk times listed (the walk times in this book do not include any stoppage time). Walking poles are useful for walkers of all abilities in mountain regions, but less fit walkers will also appreciate them on flatter walks as well.

It's always worth contacting the local tourist board of your chosen region and asking their advice on accessible trails.

The following gives a rundown on the plus and minus points for every region of France included in this book.

BRITTANY & NORMANDY

Brittany and Normandy are a pretty good choice for less fit and less experienced walkers. Most of the walks here are coastal and follow obvious cliff-side trails. However, these trails can be rough and narrow, which makes them difficult for wheelchair users. Elevation gains are not generally enormous, but there's still plenty of up and down.

LILLE & THE SOMME

This is a great area for less fit walkers, and some trails are at least partially suitable for wheelchair users. There's very little in the way of elevation gain and many routes are at least partially on quiet country roads. Route marking can be less clear here though than in some popular mountain areas.

FRENCH ALPS & JURA

It hardly needs stating that the Alps and Jura Mountains are not friendly to wheelchair users, and stiff climbs and big elevation changes on narrow trails can be difficult for less fit walkers.

CENTRAL FRANCE

This is another good region for less fit walkers. Many routes are at least partially along quiet country roads or fairly smooth farm tracks. There's a reasonable amount of up and down but most climbs and descents are fairly short. Trail marking can be a bit unclear in places.

PROVENCE & THE CÔTE D'AZUR

With everything from coastal rambles to high mountain trails, there are lots of options in this sun-soaked region – some of the trails are suitable for older or less experienced walkers and wheelchair users.

LANGUEDOC-ROUSSILLON

There's a lot of variety in this region including some lower level village walks that can be accomplished by most people.

THE PYRENEES

The mountainous terrain in the Pyrenees means that there are very few options for wheelchair users, and only a couple of routes are suitable for less fit walkers.

CORSICA

Corsica is famously rugged and there are very few options that can really be described as being wheelchair friendly. There are, however, some good bets for the less fit walker.

PLAN YOUR TRIP/17

Essentials

WHEN TO WALK

There is some form of walking available year-round in France.

Spring and autumn are great seasons to hike in Corsica and other non-mountainous parts of southern France, which swelter in summer. Many of the lower routes in these areas can even be walked throughout the winter.

Up high, the season is short and sweet in the Alps and Pyrenees, running from mid-May to late October. The central regions of France are excellent from March to late October but if you get a dry spell then you can stroll along most of these routes right through the year.

Winter should be avoided in northern France. Spring can be great, summer is near perfect, but autumn can be stormy.

Further details on the best time to walk in each area are given in the relevant chapter.

RESPONSIBLE WALKING

By its very nature, walking is an activity with a low environmental footprint and most walkers are keenly aware of their impact on the environment. Below are some pointers:

Park regulations National parks and other protected areas often have very strict regulations that are clearly marked on signboards near parking areas. Stick to these rules.

Camping Wild camping is generally forbidden in protected areas except at designated spots, often in the immediate vicinity of mountain *refuges* (huts). Bivouacking however, is normally allowed for a night. Outside of protected areas the rules can be a little less clear. Camping is always forbidden on beaches, but in rural areas putting up a small tent for the night well away from houses is often tolerated. Make sure you obtain the permission of landowners if on private land.

Trails Always stick to marked trails and never try to create your own shortcut. This can not only be potentially dangerous but it also leads to erosion.

Fire Campfires are prohibited in protected areas, on beaches and almost all other public lands. In certain areas (primarily the Mediterranean), some walk areas can be closed in summer because of the high risk of forest fires.

Water Avoid buying bottles of mineral water and instead invest in a portable water filtration system. There are many different types on the market.

Disturbance Don't pick wildflowers and avoid disturbing wildlife.

Rubbish Remove all of your rubbish. It's a good idea to bring a small bag to use as a waste bag.

Safety

Walking in France is generally a safe affair, especially in non-mountainous areas. Walking in the Alps, Pyrenees, Massif Central and other mountain regions does present extra risks. Follow these tips for a pain-free day on the trail:

- Check the weather forecast before you go (www.meteo.fr) but be prepared for it to change suddenly for the worse.
- Inform someone of your intended route and when you expect to be back.
- Set your pace and objective to suit the slowest member of your group.
- Carry a mobile phone for emergencies, but don't rely on it for navigation.
- Pack for all weathers even if the forecast is fine. Bring enough food to get you through a night. And always have a torch.
- Dial 112 in case of an emergency. Operators speak English.
- France's hunting season is September to February: if you see signs reading *'chasseurs'* or *'chasse gardée'* tacked to trees, enter the area with caution.

WHAT TO PACK

The number one rule when it comes to packing for a French walking holiday is bring less than you think you might need. Bring too much and half your gear will inevitably remain unused at the bottom of your bag. If you do forget something then well-stocked outdoors shops are common in bigger towns throughout France.

Some essentials that nobody should come without:
- quality hiking boots
- comfortable backpack
- walking poles
- sun cream
- sunglasses and hat
- torch/flashlight
- wet-weather gear (including waterproof trousers)
- relevant maps (IGN produce superb 1:25,000 hiking maps to almost every corner of France)
- water filtration system and bottle (tap water is fine to drink, but it's sensible to filter water you pull out of a lake passed on the trail)
- fleece and other warm clothing (nights in the mountains can be cold even in high summer and snow can fall as early as September and as late as May).

WAYMARKING

Official walking trails almost always have some kind of waymarking to help with route finding (although on some remoter mountain routes the waymarking can be so minimal as to not really be worthwhile).

These waymarkings come in a confusion of styles. Long-distance walking tracks across France are called Grandes Randonnées (GRs) and have red and white waymarking. Such routes are invariably very well marked throughout their length. Trails that stick to a particular region are called Grandes Randonnées du Pays (GRPs) and have yellow and red waymarking. These are also normally very clearly marked.

Shorter local trails are called Promenades et Randonnées (PRs) and are marked in a range of colours, although yellow is the most common (blue or green are other frequently used colours). Waymarking on these can be a bit hit and miss.

In some regions there are frequent, very clear markings, but in others the waymarking can be indistinct and sometimes even wrong.

In mountain areas where the waymarking can be limited, keep an eye out for rock cairns (small piles of rocks) that serve the same purpose.

Walking in France

The *terroir* (land) of France weaves a varied journey from northern France's sand dunes to the piercing blue sea of the French Riviera and the great mountains in between. Whether you end up walking barefoot across wave-rippled sands in Brittany, striding beside glacial panoramas above Chamonix or ambling between castles in the Dordogne, France does not disappoint, and the next walking trail is always just a step away!

LYRICAL LANDSCAPES

Walking in France doesn't just take you to the country's most beautiful corners. The very act of moving across the countryside by foot means that a walking holiday in France is slow travel at its very best and gives you a chance to get under the skin of the country – and in particular its rural soul – in a way that darting by car from one honeypot tourist site to another doesn't. It's not just possible, but highly likely, that being out on a walking trail means that you can go for days without encountering another foreign tourist or hearing any language but French. If you thought that holidaying in France meant dealing with short-tempered, and less than welcoming, Parisian waiters, by walking through the French countryside, stopping in village bars and overnighting in mountain *refuges* (huts) or at farm homestays, you're going to see a whole new side of France. And it's one that will leave you infatuated.

NATURAL WALKERS

With so many diverse landscapes and so many quality walking trails, it won't come as a surprise to learn that the French are natural walkers, and that hiking is one of the most popular activities in the country with people of all ages. It's not at all unusual to see people aged over 70 striding up the side of a Pyrenean mountain slope as if they were just taking a quick stroll around the park. There are walking clubs and groups in most towns and, at weekends, it's common to see large groups of club members out walking together. There are numerous walking magazines, with many dedicated to very specific areas, and an endless number of websites, blogs and apps covering walking in France. Many French people travel, both within the country and further afield, solely for the purpose of hiking, and there are numerous walking-holiday companies to cater to this demand.

All of these are fairly new developments that have occurred over the past few decades. But many of France's thousands of kilometres of walking trails are actually ancient paths that, before the invention of the car, were once the main routes between villages, towns and cities. Vestiges of days past are often still visible alongside these trails: old water fountains that still spurt forth delicious cool clear water, ancient dry-stone walls lining the paths, stone route markers with distances carved by hand into the rock. Sometimes, you may even find yourself walking along an old cobbled or paved road laid by Roman hands. If you know where to look, it would be fair to say that any countryside walk in France is a walk through history.

WHERE TO WALK

With around 180,000km of walking trails, there's always somewhere new to walk in France. And that's only the trails that are properly marked.

Hikers have a high time of it in the Alps, with mile after never-ending mile of well-marked trails. Lifts and cable cars take the sweat out of hiking here in summer. Chamonix is the trailhead for the epic 10-day, three-country Tour de Mont Blanc, but gentler paths, such as the Grand Balcon Sud, also command Mont Blanc close-ups. Some of the finest treks head into the more remote, glacier-capped wilds of the Parc National des Écrins, with 700km of trails – many following old shepherd routes – and the equally gorgeous Parc National de la Vanoise.

But the Alps are tip-of-the-iceberg stuff. Just as lovely are walks threading through the softly rounded heights of the Vosges and through the forest-cloaked hills of Jura spreading down to Lake Geneva. The extinct volcanoes in the Auvergne, interwoven with 13 Grandes Randonnées (GR; long-distance footpaths), and the mist-shrouded peaks and swooping forested valleys of the Parc National des Pyrénées offer fine walking and blissful solitude. In the Cévennes, you can follow in Robert Louis Stevenson's footsteps on the GR70 Chemin de Stevenson from Le Puy to Alès – with or without a donkey.

Corsica is a hiker's paradise – the GR20, the multiday trek that crosses the island north to south, is one of France's most famous, but there are dozens of shorter, easier walks. Or combine walking with swimming on the *sentiers littoraux* (coastal paths) in Alpes-Maritimes. More bracing hikes await on the GR21 skirting the chalky cliffs of Côte d'Albâtre in Normandy, the Côte d'Opale's GR120 taking in the colour-changing seascapes of La Mance (the English Channel), and Brittany's Presqu'île de Crozon peninsula with 145km of signed trails woven around rocky outcrops and clear ocean views.

Local and regional tourist offices almost always have booklets outlining walks in the vicinity.

PREVIOUS PAGE: MOUNTAIN WALK, PARC NATIONAL DU MERCANTOUR
THIS PAGE
TOP: SHORT-TOED SNAKE EAGLE; BOTTOM: ALPINE IBEX

NATIONAL PARKS

France's protected areas are invariably excellent places to walk. The scenery is almost always superb and the parks are laced with well-marked trails. However, the proportion of protected land in mainland France is surprisingly low: eight *parcs nationaux* (www.parcsnationaux.fr) fully protect just 0.8% of the country. But the government is making a push to get 30% of its land territory under special environmental protection, and lands in metropolitan France and its overseas territories are also protected by 56 *parcs naturels régionaux* (www.parcs-naturels-regionaux.fr).

The two most recent to be protected, in 2020, are Baie de Somme on the coast of Picardy and Mont Ventoux in Provence. A further 321 smaller *réserves naturelles* (www.reserves-naturelles.org), some of them under the eagle eye of the Conservatoire du Littoral, protect a fraction of the land. While the central zones of national parks are uninhabited and fully protected by legislation (dogs, vehicles and hunting are banned and camping is restricted), their delicate ecosystems spill over into populated peripheral zones in which economic activities, some of them environmentally unfriendly, are permitted and even encouraged.

Most regional nature parks and reserves were established not only to maintain or improve local ecosystems, but also to encourage economic development and tourism in areas suffering from hardship and diminishing populations (such as the Massif Central and Corsica).

Select pockets of nature – the Pyrenees, Mont St-Michel and its bay, part of the Loire Valley, the astonishingly biodiverse Cévennes, a clutch of capes on Corsica and vineyards in Burgundy and Champagne – have been declared Unesco World Heritage Sites.

For walkers the best national parks include the following:

Parc National des Pyrénées
Protecting a 100km-long strip of mountains along the France–Spain border, the Parc National des Pyrénées is crisscrossed with superb walking trails and is home to a diverse range of wildlife including the only brown bears in France and a healthy population of griffon vultures.

Parc National du Mercantour
Provence at its most majestic, with 3000m-plus peaks and dead-end valleys along the Italian border. There's a lifetime of walking trails here and this southern part of the Alps is home to marmots, mouflons, chamois, ibex, wolves, and golden and short-toed eagles. Bronze Age petroglyphs can be seen in the south.

Parc National des Écrins
Home to some of the most soul-stirring scenery in France, the Parc National des Écrins is a walkers' paradise of glaciers, glacial lakes and mountaintops soaring up to 4102m.

 Pilgrim Trails

France is crisscrossed by pilgrim routes, many of which date back to the Middle Ages. In recent years, there has been a surge of interest in such routes, but most people walking them today are doing it simply for the challenge and the history rather than for religious reasons.

The most famous pilgrimage route is the Camino de Santiago (Chemin de St-Jacques in French), which leads to the holy city of Santiago de Compostela in northwest Spain. There are several different 'Camino' routes across France but most of them meet up in the small town of St-Jean Pied de Port in the French Basque Country. The most popular of the routes across France begins in Le Puy in eastern France.

Parc National de la Vanoise
A stunning postglacial landscape of alpine peaks, beech-fir forests and 80 sq km of glaciers forming France's first national park (530 sq km). There's diverse wildlife and some of the finest walking trails in Europe.

Parc National des Cévennes
The inspiring landscapes here consist of wild peat bogs, granite peaks, ravines and ridges bordering the Massif Central and Languedoc. Look out for red deer, beavers, vultures and wolves. The park is known for trekking with donkeys.

Parc National des Calanques This gorgeous coastal park abutting Marseille might be small (20km), but with spectacular promontories, sheer cliffs, hidden coves and sublime beaches as well as a staggering 900 plant species, it never fails to entice walkers.

WILDLIFE

France has more mammal species (around 135) than any other European country. Couple this with around 500 bird species (depending on which rare migrants are included), 40 types of amphibian, 36 varieties of reptile and 72 kinds of fish, and wildlife-watchers are in seventh heaven. Of France's 40,000 identified insects, 10,000 creep and crawl in the Parc National du Mercantour in the southern Alps.

High-altitude plains in the Alps and the Pyrenees shelter the marmot, which hibernates from October to April and has a shrill and distinctive whistle; the nimble chamois (mountain antelope and known as the izard in the Pyrenees), with its dark-striped head; and the *bouquetin* (alpine ibex), seen in large numbers in the Parc National de la Vanoise. Mouflons (wild mountain sheep), introduced in the 1950s, clamber over stony sunlit scree slopes in the mountains, while red and roe deer and wild boar are common in lower-altitude forested areas. The alpine hare welcomes winter with its white coat, while 19 of Europe's 29 bat species hang out in the dark in the alpine national parks.

The *loup* (wolf), which disappeared from France in the 1930s, returned to the Parc National du Mercantour in 1992 – much to the horror of the mouflon (on which it preys) and local sheep farmers. It's now spreading very quickly across large parts of France. Dogs, corrals and sound machines have been used as an effective, non-lethal way of keeping wolves from feasting on domesticated sheep herds.

A rare but wonderful treat is the sighting of an *aigle royal* (golden eagle): 40 pairs nest in the Mercantour, 20 pairs nest in the Vanoise, 30-odd in the Écrins and some 50 in the Pyrenees.

Other birds of prey include the peregrine falcon, the kestrel, the buzzard and the lammergeier (bearded vulture) – Europe's largest bird of prey, with an awe-inspiring wingspan of 2.8m. More recently, the small, pale-coloured Egyptian vulture has been spreading throughout the Alps and Pyrenees, and distinctive-looking black-winged kites (a native of northern Africa) are increasingly turning up in southern and southwestern France.

Even the eagle-eyed will have difficulty spotting the ptarmigan, a chicken-like species that moults three times a year to ensure a foolproof seasonal camouflage (brown in summer, white in winter). It lives on rocky slopes and in alpine meadows above 2000m. The nutcracker (with its loud, buoyant singsong and larch-forest habitat), the black grouse, rock partridge, the very rare eagle owl and the three-toed woodpecker are among the other 120-odd species keeping birdwatchers glued to the skies in highland realms.

Elsewhere, there are now around 2700 pairs of white storks; 10% of the world's flamingo population migrates through the Camargue; giant black cormorants – some with a wingspan of 1.7m – reside on an island off Pointe du Grouin on the north coast of Brittany; and there are unique seagull and fishing-eagle populations in the Réserve Naturelle de Scandola on Corsica. The *balbuzard pêcheur* (osprey), a migratory hunter that flocks to France in February or March, today only inhabits two regions of France: Corsica and the Loire Valley.

OPPOSITE: SNOW SHOEING, FRENCH ALPS

❄ Snow Shoeing

If you're in the snow-bound mountains of France in winter then you might think that hiking is out of the question. But then along came snow shoeing (known as *raquettes* in French), and suddenly mountain hiking became a year-round activity. Snow shoes aren't shoes at all but more akin to tennis-racquet-shaped 'skis' that strap onto hiking boots and enable you to walk through deep snow that you'd otherwise sink into. For your first attempts start by renting gear at a ski station and walking one of the clearly marked snow-shoe trails found in many ski resorts.

BRITTANY & NORMANDY

01 **Dinan: Up & Down Town** An easy stroll past ramparts, cobbled squares and half-timbered houses. **p30**

02 **La Côte de Granit Rose** Admire this stunning coastline of pink-and-russet granite. **p32**

03 **Giverny Impressions** Experience the classic landscapes that inspired the impressionist painter Claude Monet. **p34**

04 **Grouin: Up to a Point** Wide-ranging vistas from a sublime and stormy headland. **p36**

05 **Circling the Île d'Ouessant** Hike the storm-tossed island that feels far from anywhere. **p38**

06 **Omaha Beach** View D-Day's most brutal battleground from on high. **p40**

07 **Pointes du Raz & Van** Unforgettable sunsets from France's westernmost cliffs. **p44**

Explore
BRITTANY & NORMANDY

Normandy is blessed with a wonderfully varied and intensely historic coastline. The dunes and forested hills above Omaha Beach, site of the D-Day landings' most ferocious fighting, offer superb walks, while the hinterland around the impressionist village of Giverny is an easy outing. Brittany's coastline is crumpled into innumerable bays, beaches and estuaries separated by rocky headlands. There are many dramatic walks here and – most importantly – they are easily accessible.

ST-MALO

Jutting out from the Channel waters like a honey-stoned super-tanker, the walled city of St-Malo cuts one of northern France's most unforgettable silhouettes. With a plethora of great hotels and restaurants, it makes an excellent base for walks along the rugged Côte d'Émeraude and gentler Baie du Mont St-Michel. But visit in season and you won't have the streets to yourself.

The nearby (and impossibly picturesque) town of Dinan offers a slightly more chilled vibe.

PAIMPOL

The busy commercial harbour of Paimpol hosts one of the area's largest fish and produce markets every Tuesday morning. It's also the launch pad for walks along the Côte de Granit Rose, where the boulders blush pink in profusion.

BAYEUX

The very attractive and historic town of Bayeux may be synonymous with the World Heritage–listed Bayeux Tapestry, which vividly depicts the dramatic story of the Norman invasion of England in 1066, but it's also a wonderfully picturesque base from which to explore the D-Day beaches, especially Omaha Beach.

It has a wide choice of places to stay and eat, and good transport links.

GIVERNY

Synonymous with Monet, this small village gets swamped by visitors queuing to visit the artist's famous gardens and to pay their respects at his resting place in the little churchyard. Despite more than 600,000 visitors teeming down its one main street annually, the surrounding countryside offers gentle walks that are never overly subscribed.

QUIMPER

The capital of Finistère (or 'Land's End'), village-like Quimper is the troubadour of Breton arts and culture. For walkers, it's the ideal base for the rugged trails of the Presqu'île de Crozon and the Pointe du Raz.

28/BRITTANY & NORMANDY

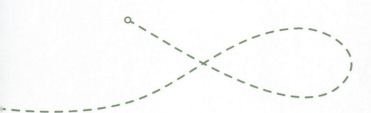

WHEN TO GO

Villages and towns like Giverny and Dinan, where each season has its own particular beauty, are rarely quiet outside winter, though weekdays may be less crowded than weekends.

During May and June, before the crowds arrive along the coasts of Brittany and Normandy, there's a good chance of settled weather, although some camping grounds don't open until June.

Good weather is also likely in September. Spring – April and May – can be pretty wet and the days grow shorter (and the temperature drops) from October. Avoid July and August at all costs.

WHERE TO STAY

Whether you're looking to camp under the stars, take a room by the sea or live the high life in your very own château, you'll find something to suit in Brittany and Normandy.

Both are chock-a-block with lovely hotels and campsites, but if you really want to get under the skin of either region, *chambres d'hôte* (bed and breakfasts) are worth considering; staying with a local family is a great way of immersing yourself in the culture, and the owners are usually a great resource for local restaurant tips, sights and secret spots. Best of all, breakfast is often included in the room price.

WHAT'S ON

Festival de Cornouaille (www.festival-cornouaille.com; late Jul) Quimper's six-day celebration of traditional Celtic music, costumes and culture.

Festival du Chant de Marin (www.paimpol-festival.bzh; early Aug) Biannual music festival celebrating sea shanties in Paimpol.

Fête des Remparts (www.fete-remparts-dinan.com; late Jul) Medieval festival in Dinan.

Festival Interceltique de Lorient (www.festival-interceltique.bzh; early Aug) A 10-day pan-Celtic festival in Lorient, 30km northwest of Carnac.

Fêtes d'Arvor (www.fetes-arvor.org; 13-15 Aug) Three-day celebration of Breton culture in Vannes.

Les Transmusicales de Rennes (www.lestrans.com; early Dec) France's biggest indie-music festival.

Médiévales de Bayeux (http://lesmedievales.bayeux.fr/en; Jul) Middle Ages–themed parade and other events.

TRANSPORT

Cities and major towns in Brittany and Normandy have good rail connections, including TGV trains to Rennes in Brittany and towards Le Havre in Normandy, though the interior remains poorly served. The bus network is extensive; however, services between smaller towns are infrequent at best.

With gently undulating, well-maintained roads, an absence of road tolls and relatively little traffic outside the major towns, driving in both regions (but especially in Brittany) is a real pleasure. Cycling is also popular, and bike-rental places are usually easy to find.

BRITTANY & NORMANDY/29

01

DINAN: UP & DOWN TOWN

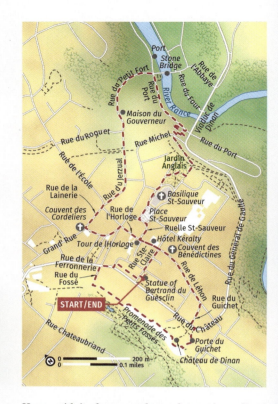

DURATION	DIFFICULTY	DISTANCE	START/END
2½hr return	Easy	3km	Place du Guesclin, Dinan
TERRAIN	Paved, packed-earth trail, some steps		

Picturesquely perched high above the fast-flowing River Rance, Dinan is one of the loveliest old towns in northern France. This muddle of cobbled squares, creaking half-timbered houses and snaking ramparts tumbling down to the old port, where barges and riverboats still putter along beside the old town quays, is best explored on foot.

From the **statue of Breton hero Bertrand du Guesclin** in the square of that name, walk north along rue de la Ferronerie and turn left onto the short but steep rue du Fossé. Walk along the Promenades des Petits Fossés – erstwhile moats – with the ramparts of the **Château de Dinan** on your left. Between the castle's tower and keep, pass under the **Porte du Guichet** and walk up to rue du Guichet.

Head left along rue de Léhon and past the 17th-century **Couvent des Bénédictines**. Further along on the right is the **Hôtel Kéralty** (1559), or Maison de la Harpe, with its dozen wooden sculptures in medieval dress. Further to the left is the 15th-century **Tour de l'Horloge** clock tower. At rue de l'Apport, turn left to enjoy some of the most wonderful overhanging **half-timbered houses** in Dinan.

A right onto rue de la Lainerie will take you past the sprawling **Couvent des Cordeliers** and down rue du Jerzual and its extension rue du Petit Fort, an astonishing cobbled street lined with medieval houses (pictured; don't miss the **Maison du Gouverneur**). It leads steeply downhill to the River Rance and its little port.

At the foot of the **stone bridge**, turn right on rue du Port and, just below the soaring Viaduc de Dinan, climb the switchback path (and steps) up to the lovely **Jardin Anglais**, a former cemetery behind the soaring **Basilique St-Sauveur**. Have a look at its 12th-century western portal then slip down narrow ruelle St-Sauveur and passage de l'Horloge to return to place du Guesclin.

30/BRITTANY & NORMANDY

Best for
PRETTY VILLAGES

02
LA CÔTE DE GRANIT ROSE

DURATION	DIFFICULTY	DISTANCE	START/END
2hr return	Easy	5.5km	Parking du Petit Port de Ploumanac'h
TERRAIN	Road, walking trail		

This walk is one non-stop succession of secluded bays and milky-blue sea waters linked together by orange-pink granite boulders piled one upon the other like squashed strawberries. It's an ideal family walk. On a warm day, pack your swimming gear.

Walk north along the **waterfront**, and turn right along a cobbled path when you see signs for the **Sentier des Douaniers** (Customs Trail). Almost immediately, you'll be rewarded with views over melted pink-granite rock and mirror-blue waters. Meander along the clear headland path and drop down to and across the superb **St Guirec** beach.

Go uphill past an old **Breton cross** and into a giant puzzle of orange-tinted, butter-smooth boulders. Veer left off the main trail towards the **Phare de Men Ruz** (Men Ruz Lighthouse; pictured). Return back to the main route and continue eastward around the headland, where you will quickly come to a small bay with a **lifeboat station**. The lifeboat is launched by sliding down a railway track and into the sea.

Continuing east and then more south, you'll pass two **rocky coves** with tempting snorkelling at high tide. At the trail junction go right, away from the coast, following red and white trail markers. Walking through gorse heath and woodland, go straight ahead at all junctions until you reach the **Parc des Sculptures**, where humanity's attempt at moulding rock is no match for nature's.

Leave the park and follow the road to the right for 100m. Turn sharp left down rue Traverse, then right at rue du Moulin. A few minutes later, you'll reach your start point.

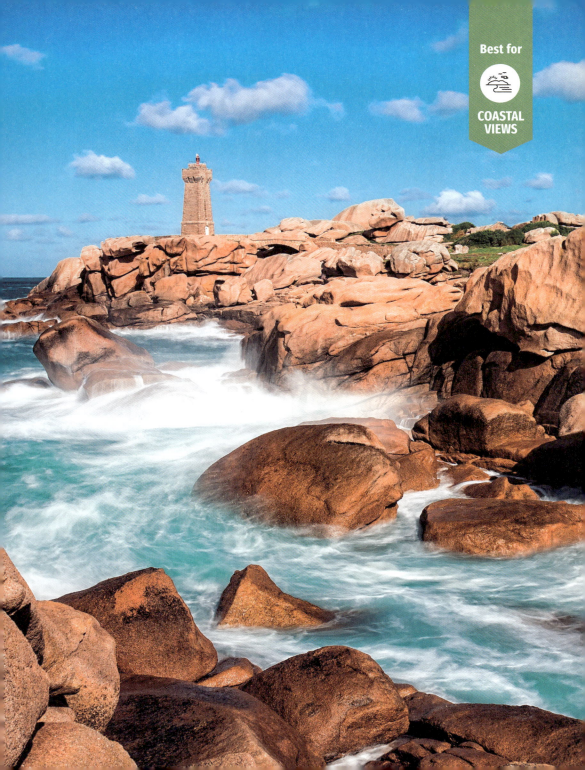

03

GIVERNY IMPRESSIONS

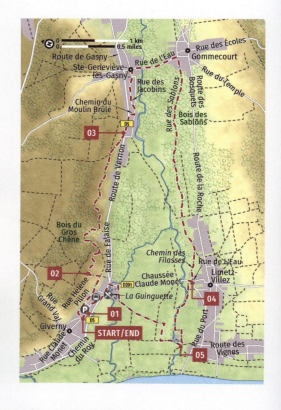

DURATION	DIFFICULTY	DISTANCE	START/END
3-3½hr return	Moderate	12.5km	Fondation Claude Monet car park
TERRAIN	Paved & packed earth, some steep sections		

Giverny owes its fame to Claude Monet, who was captivated by its rustic charm and peaceful atmosphere. The village has retained much of its allure, as has the surrounding countryside. Hills rise steeply from the plains through which threads the narrow Epte River, one of the painter's sources of inspiration. You'll pass through woodlands, fields and typical Normandy villages – before or after a visit to Monet's beautiful house and gardens.

GETTING HERE

The springboard for Giverny is Vernon, a town 5km to the northwest served by SNCF train travelling between Paris' Gare St-Lazare (50 minutes) and Rouen (40 minutes) A *navette* (shuttle bus; €5 one way, 20 minutes) meets four to five trains a day from Easter to October.

STARTING POINT

From the (free) Fondation Claude Monet car park it's a short walk to the start of the trail.

01 With **Monet's house** (pictured) behind you, walk left along rue Claude Monet for 200m then right along chemin Blanche-Hoschedé-Monet. Immediately veer right along rue Hélène Pillon; beyond a road diverging downhill to the right you pass villas and sloping fields. A grassy track leads uphill for about 220m; leave it to ascend a steep path with a hedge on its right.

02 After about 150m, swing right along a path through the hedge that takes you on a contouring route through woodland and into **Bois du Gros Chêne** (Big Oak Wood). Measuring from Waypoint 02, you'll come to junctions at 240m, 500m and 830m; at each, take the path that maintains your elevation. About 1.2km from

34/BRITTANY & NORMANDY

Giverny, Monet & Impressionism

In 1883 Claude Monet, the father of impressionism, established his studio in Maison du Pressoir in Giverny. He died there in 1926.

Inspired by the surrounding landscapes and gardens, he embarked on an immense artistic and botanical project in his garden. He painted his famous *Nymphéas* here, combining water and plants in a marvellous play of light and colour.

The house and gardens were bequeathed to the Académie des Beaux-Arts in 1966 by the painter's son and, after extensive renovation guided by the Fondation Claude Monet, opened to the public in 1980.

Best for

ESCAPING THE CROWDS

Waypoint 02, you'll get **views of the Epte valley** below and you'll exit the woodland in another 500m. Continue another 750m to a track crossing then bear right downhill.

03 Cross the D5; turn left along the verge for 250m. Turn right down chemin du Moulin Brûlé then left on rue des Jacobins in the village of **Ste-Geneviève-lès-Gasny**. Continue to a crossroads with a church on the left; turn right along rue de l'Eau and cross two **bridges** over the Epte River. The road leads 450m into the village of **Gommecourt**, where you turn right along narrow rue des Sablons. This leads eastwards for about 3.5km, initially through the **Bois des Sablons**.

04 With vegetable plots at the village of **Limetz-Villez** on the left, turn right and follow the rue de l'Eau (D201) for 70m, then turn left down a narrow track leading west. After about 500m, the track skirts a fenced empty lot. Turn left at a road in Le Moulinet for 50m, then turn right at a T-junction to cross a small **bridge** over a branch of the Epte River

05 Past an **old communal laundry** on the left, keep right and follow the track north for 320m, then turn right into fields. After 280m, turn left and head north. Follow the track across fields for 750m, then turn right, soon reaching the D201. This road runs 150m, crossing the **Epte River** before meeting the D5. Here turn left towards Giverny and then right up rue Claude Monet to the car park.

TAKE A BREAK

La Guinguette (06 72 76 03 66; www.laguinguettedegiverny.com; 6 rue de Falaise, Giverny; mains €15-20; noon-2.30pm Tue-Sun, 7-9pm Thu-Sat) is idyllically situated on a branch of the Epte River.

04

GROUIN: UP TO A POINT

DURATION	DIFFICULTY	DISTANCE	START/END
3½hr return	Moderate	11.5km	Plage du Verger car park

TERRAIN	Sand, packed earth, some steps

At the northern tip of the wild coast between Cancale and St-Malo, the Pointe du Grouin nature reserve juts out on a windblown promontory and into the foaming sea. It's an area begging for exploration, and one well-marked trail in particular is worth the effort. You'll be rewarded with views of the Île des Landes, a long barren outcrop and now a bird sanctuary, and on a clear day the distant outline of Mont St-Michel.

GETTING HERE

Most visitors arrive by car to make the trip up to Pointe du Grouin, though **MAT** (Malo Agglo Transports; 02 99 40 19 22; www.reseau-mat.fr) coastal bus 9 between St-Malo and Cancale will drop you off here in July and August (€1.35, 10 minutes, every 45 minutes).

STARTING POINT

The trail literally begins at the Plage du Verger car park (free).

01 Head east along the sandy track parallel to the beach, passing a lake on the right. At the first junction, turn left and continue along a packed-earth ascending trail. The path narrows through undergrowth and then gains height; enjoy the **spectacular views of the beach** below. The path leads east and then due north.

02 After passing **Pointe de la Moulière**, the path levels off and descends. Veer to the left on a narrow path and climb up to the D201. Continue for 50m, turn left and go up to **Pointe de Rochefroide**.

03 Follow the path to a car park. Turn left and arrive at Pointe du Grouin (pictured), with views of **Île des Landes** and distant **Mont St-Michel** to the east. You'll pass a **decommissioned**

36/BRITTANY & NORMANDY

Île des Landes

Separated from Pointe du Gouin by narrow Chenal de la Vieille Rivière, the wave-pounded lozenge of Île des Landes is temptingly close but has been inaccessible to the public since 1961 when it was declared a bird sanctuary.

In addition to attracting the largest colony of great cormorants in Brittany, it is also home to crested cormorants, various types of gulls, pied oyster-catchers and Belon sheldrakes, the only marine duck native to Brittany. From August to October, puffins, gannets and other seabirds also flock here. Explanatory signboards near the tip of the Point du Grouin let you know who's who. Don't forget your binoculars.

Best for
COASTAL VIEWS

lighthouse (1861), a WWII-era **German bunker** with graffiti and **ornithological signboards**.

04 From the point head south and take the first left to join the coastal path, always keeping to the left. You'll pass pine groves, an RV campground, a school, a well-preserved WWII gun battery and cottages with pretty gardens.

05 At **Port Mer**, walk along the beachfront promenade and turn left, at a sign reading 'Le Port', onto rue du Chatry, which follows the outline of Pointe du Chatry as far as Port Picain.

06 With a youth hostel on your right, walk along rue de Port Picain and follow this inland to the right. About 250m up from the port, veer left, go under a road bridge and take the second gravel path over the D201 called La Basse Cancale (the first path is confusingly called Impasse de la Basse Cancale). This merges into Impasse de la Hisse before bending right to become chemin de Clairette. Zigzag across rue de la Vieille Rivière and continue ahead on a lane leading uphill. About 650m along this lane, pass a riding school on the left and cross the D201 again onto a paved lane, keeping the **wooded picnic area** to your left.

07 Carry on straight ahead through the quiet hamlet of **La Gaudichais**. The path doglegs and rejoins the sandy path where you first turned left on the western coastal path. Then trace your steps in the sand back to the Plage du Verger car park.

TAKE A BREAK

Both St-Malo and Cancale have any number of superb seafood restaurants, crêperies and cafes, but there are also a few places on the promontory itself, including, along the beach at Port Mer, **Les Pieds dans l'Eau** (📞 02 99 89 81 59; 1 rue Eugène et Auguste Feyen; seafood buffet €33).

BRITTANY & NORMANDY/37

05

CIRCLING THE ÎLE D'OUESSANT

DURATION	DIFFICULTY	DISTANCE	START/END
6hr return	Moderate	19.5km	Lampaul

TERRAIN	Road, walking track, clifftop trail

The Île d'Ouessant is a storm-tossed and wind-battered island that feels a long way from anywhere. Covered in heathland and bounded by a magnificent coastline, at one moment it can be an inviting picture of white-sand beaches lapped by calm blue waters and the next be dark, rocky and imposing. Although you can walk around the entire length of the coastline in two long days, the majority of visitors only come here as a day trip. The full-day walk (make sure you get the first ferry over and the last one back) described here will show you the best of the island.

GETTING HERE

Ferries for Île d'Ouessant depart from Brest and the town of Le Conquet. **Penn Ar Bed** (📞 02 98 80 81 60; www.pennarbed.fr; return adult €30-35, child €20-25) has multiple daily sailings in summer from Brest (2½ hours), Le Conquet (1½ hours) and Camaret-sur-Mer (50 minutes). In low season, services are more infrequent. **Finist'mer** (📞 0825 135 235; www.finist-mer.fr; adult/child return €34/24) runs high-speed boats from Le Conquet (40 minutes), Lanildut (35 minutes) and Camaret (1½ hours) one to three times per day, with more sailings in July and August.

STARTING POINT

The walk starts from the church in the centre of tiny **Lampaul**, the island capital. Minibuses meet the ferry and will shuttle you to Lampaul for €2.

01 With your back to the church doors, turn left and walk downhill through the village. Turn right by the large cross. A moment later, you'll draw near to the **tiny port**. Just before this, turn left onto a grassy track, walk over the headland and past

Musée des Phares et des Balises

The black-and-white-striped Phare du Créac'h is one of the world's most powerful lighthouses. At its base is a highly educational **museum** (Lighthouse & Beacon Museum; 02 98 48 80 70; www.pnr-armorique.fr/destination-parc/nos-maisons-de-parc/musee-des-phares-et-balises; adult/child €6/4; 10.30am-6pm plus 9-11pm 2 nights a week Jul & Aug, 11.30am-5pm or 6pm Apr-Jun & Sep, 1.30-5pm Tue-Sun Oct-Mar), which tells the story of these vital navigational aids. There are also displays devoted to the numerous ships that have been wrecked off the island.

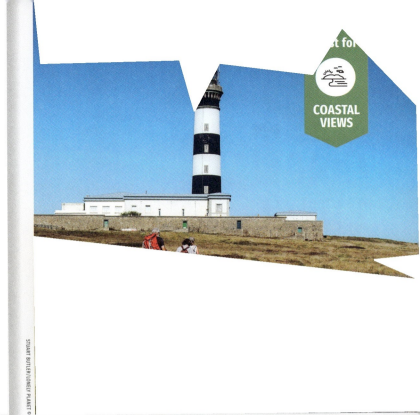

COASTAL VIEWS

STUART BUTLER/LONELY PLANET ©

Plage de Corz (Corz beach). At the end of the beach, follow the road around (southwest) a short way where a minor footpath heads left (south) off the road.

02 Just before arriving at the dinky little **port**, turn right (west) and follow the trail along low cliffs and past **small coves** that – on a sunny day at least – look like they could be straight out of the Mediterranean. You'll eventually arrive at the **Penn ar Viler** headland.

03 Follow the path around the northern side of the peninsula. You'll pass a couple of stunning white-sand, blue-water beaches. **Plage du Prat**, the second of these beaches, is particularly noteworthy. When you reach Plage de Corz retrace your steps back into Lampaul.

04 Turn left at the church and follow the road to the point where it bends to the right. Take the small road that continues straight ahead and, a moment later, you'll find yourself on a **coastal footpath** again. It takes an hour to get to the **Pointe de Pern**. The most westerly point of the island (and indeed of all of France) is a rough-edged, storm-lashed place where even the solid rock has been weathered into surreal nightmare shapes

05 Follow the trail around to the exposed northern side of the peninsula and head to the **Phare du Créac'h** (Créac'h Lighthouse; pictured). Continue along the coastline as far as the tiny **Port de Yusin**. Turn right and walk along a quiet road back into Lampaul.

TAKE A BREAK

There are innumerable spots suitable for a picnic. If you have more time, **Ty Korn** (02 98 48 87 33; Lampaul; mains €16-22, platters from €42; 11am-3pm & 5.30pm-1am Tue-Sat;) is a decent seafood restaurant.

BRITTANY & NORMANDY/39

06

OMAHA BEACH

Best for

EXPLORING HISTORY

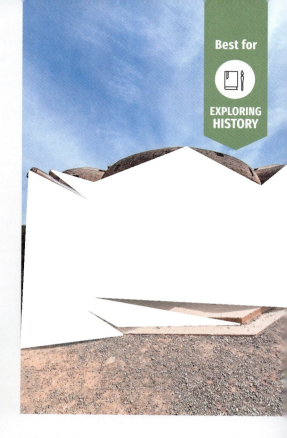

DURATION	DIFFICULTY	DISTANCE	START/END
4½-5hr return	Hard	17.5km	Overlord Museum car park

TERRAIN	Packed earth, some sandy & steep sections, steps

Omaha Beach, which saw some of the heaviest fighting and highest casualties during the D-Day landings in June 1944, may seem an unusual choice for a recreational walk. But the cliffs and the dunes running parallel to the coast offer some excellent (and sometimes challenging) trails, the views are magnificent, and the history is unforgettable. Additional bonuses include a world-class D-Day museum at the start and one of the largest American war cemeteries in Europe at the finish.

GETTING HERE

Bayeux is served by trains from Caen (€6, 15 to 20 minutes, at least hourly), Cherbourg (€20, one hour, 15 daily Monday to Friday, eight to 10 daily Saturday and Sunday) and Pontorson for Mont St-Michel (€24, 1¾ hours, three daily). To and from Paris' Gare St-Lazare and Rouen, you may have to change at Caen. Bus 70 of the **Nomad** (09 70 83 00 14; www.nomadcar14.fr) line links Bayeux' train station and place St-Patrice with Colleville-sur-Mer (€2.50, two to four daily Monday to Saturday, more frequently and on Sunday and holidays in summer, 35 minutes).

STARTING POINT

Begin the walk in the car park (free) of the Overlord Museum in Le Bray, just west of **Colleville-sur-Mer**. The bus stop is at the foot of the hill up to the museum on rue des Chemins de la Liberté.

01 We recommend visiting the **Overlord Museum** (www.overlordmuseum.com; adult/child €8.40/6.10; 10am-5.30pm mid-Feb-Mar, Oct & Nov, to 6.30pm Apr, May & Sep, 9.30am-7pm Jun-Aug, closed Jan-mid-Feb) before setting out. It has an astonishing

40/BRITTANY & NORMANDY

collection of restored WWII military equipment from both sides, and the photos, letters and personal recollections bring the human dimension of the war to life. Then, walk down to the roundabout to rte du Cimetière Militaire Américain. Follow along the verge of this road north past open fields for just under a kilometre to the cemetery's main entrance.

02 Just past the second roundabout and with the **cemetery** straight ahead, turn left onto a paved track and then right at the silos. After a few minutes' walk, passing orchards on your left and houses on your right,

you'll enter the **Bois Guillaume**, a protected forest, where a packed-earth track begins.

There are a few obstructions on this stretch, including a massive tree stump lying on its side in the middle of the path. At the first fork, veer right, follow the trail as it descends and turn left. This soon brings you to a small **bridge** over a stream. Turn right here and begin your ascent. When you reach open fields turn right. The trail continues under forest cover, veers right to join another path and ascends to a clearing with wonderful views. Just ahead is a roundabout and an old aerodrome.

03 From the **plaque** commemorating the Advanced Landing Ground here in WWII, head east and turn immediately left (north) onto a dirt trail. Go through the stile labelled 'Coteau du Ruquet' and continue walking with trees on the right and fields to the left. Soon you'll enjoy **panoramic views** of the ocean and beach. Ignore the waymark indicating a right turn down the hill. Instead go left, passing an **anti-aircraft gun memorial**, until you reach a set of steep and narrow wooden stairs. These lead down to rue Bernard Anquetil and the seafront in the village of **St-Laurent-sur-Mer**.

6 June 1944

The most brutal fighting of the allied invasion of continental Europe, code-named 'Operation Overlord', on D-Day took place on the 7km stretch of coastline around Colleville-sur-Mer, St-Laurent-sur-Mer and Vierville-sur-Mer, 15km northwest of Bayeux, known as 'Bloody Omaha' to US veterans.

More than seven decades on, little evidence of the carnage unleashed here on 6 June 1944 remains, except for the harrowing American cemetery and concrete German bunkers, though at very low tide you can see a few remnants of the Mulberry Harbour.

For an idea of what it was like along this coast on D-Day, visit the Overlord Museum in the Le Bray section of Colleville-sur-Mer.

BRITTANY & NORMANDY/41

04 From the **'Bloody Omaha' explanatory tablets** that describe the invasion of 6 June 1944, walk along the beach promenade for about 600m to the hamlet of **Les Moulins**. Along the way you'll pass rows of holiday homes and bungalows before reaching a modern memorial called **Les Braves** jutting out of the water offshore and a larger and older granite one fronting the roundabout. From here, follow ave de la Libération (rte D517) south for a short distance and turn right at a raised path called chemin de Fossé Taillis. On your right are trees and fields; on the left, you'll pass the back of the **Musée Mémorial d'Omaha Beach** (📞02 31 21 97 44; www.musee-memorial-omaha.com; adult/child/student €7.20/4.20/5.80; 🕐9.30am-6.30pm Apr, May & Sep, to 6pm Oct & Nov, to 7pm Jun-Aug, 10am-5pm Feb, to 6pm Mar, closed Dec & Jan). At the first junction, 650m after leaving the D517, turn right and walk up the trail, passing endless fields, till you reach a T-junction.

05 Turn left onto rue du Hamel aux Prêtres, with the sound of crashing waves harmonising with that of the whispering pines. In the centre of the **Hamel au Prêtre** hamlet, you'll join up with rte du Port (rte D514) for a short while before turning right at rue de la Linière and then left at rue des Écoles, passing some provincial cottages with pretty gardens.

Turn right on rue de la Mer, which runs parallel to the D517 – along the way you'll pass the remains of an enormous **landing ship bridge** that enabled armoured vehicles to reach the shore. Rue de la Mer will lead you to the beachfront promenade in **Vierville-sur-Mer**.

06 Begin walking east along the promenade from the cluster of **monuments** at the intersection of rue de la Mer and the D517. One is to the British RAF and another to the Americans (Secteur Charlie & Dog Green). Along the way to Les Moulins (about 2km), you'll pass several more **WWII memorials** along the promenade, while sheep graze on the grassy cliffs above on the right. Continue along the promenade for about 1.3km until you reach **Hôtel La Sapinière**, turn right and walk up the steps to the **2nd US Infantry Memorial**. Behind it is a switchback trail of wood shavings leading back up to where you turned left to descend the steps to Omaha Beach.

07 You're now back on familiar turf so just redo your steps in reverse. Carry on under the trees until you veer slightly to the right to join a new path; there will be open fields visible to your right. In a short while, you'll reach a T-junction. Turn left and continue till you come to that small bridge over a stream. Cross it and continue upward. At the first fork go right and follow the trail as before, climbing over that tree trunk again, before reaching the Bois Guillaume then orchards and farmhouses. Turn left at the silos and, within minutes, you'll be at

Bayeux Tapestry

'Operation Overlord' was not the only cross-Channel invasion that gave Bayeux a front-row seat. An equally pivotal moment took place here some nine centuries before. The Norman invasion of England in 1066 changed the course of European history, and the dramatic and bloody story is told in 58 vivid scenes by the astonishing Bayeux Tapestry, embroidered just a few years after William the Bastard, Duke of Normandy, became William the Conqueror, King of England. Particularly incredible is its length – nearly 70m – and fine attention to detail. See it in all its glory at the **Bayeux Museum** (La Tapisserie de Bayeux; 02 31 51 25 50; www.bayeuxmuseum.com; 15bis rue de Nesmond; adult/child €9.50/7.50; 9.30am-12.30pm & 2-6pm, closed Jan) in Bayeux.

the roundabout with the main entrance to the cemetery on the left.

08 The **Normandy American Cemetery and Memorial** (www.abmc.gov; 9am-6pm Apr-Sep, to 5pm Oct-Mar) FREE is well worth a visit. The visitor centre on the eastern side has an excellent multimedia presentation on the D-Day landings, told in part through the stories of individuals' courage and sacrifice.

On the western side, Stars of David and white-marble crosses (pictured) stretch off in seemingly endless rows on a now-serene bluff overlooking the bitterly contested sands of Omaha Beach. Some 9387 American soldiers, including 33 pairs of brothers, are buried here.

Between the graves and the visitor centre is a large colonnaded memorial centred on a **statue** called *The Spirit of American Youth*, maps explaining the order of battle, and a wall honouring 1557 Americans whose bodies were not found. A small, white-marble chapel stands at the intersection of the cross-shaped main paths through the cemetery.

09 After your visit, walk south along rte du Cimetière Militaire Américain to the roundabout, the Overlord Museum and the start of the walk.

TAKE A BREAK

Bayeux has some superb restaurants and cafes; one of our favourites is **Au Ptit Bistrot** (02 31 92 30 08; www.facebook.com/auptitbistrot; 31 rue Larcher; lunch menus €18-21; noon-1.30pm & 7-9pm Tue-Sat).

But if you require sustenance on the walk, **Domaine Hostréière** (02 31 51 64 64; www.domainehostreiere.com; rue du Cimetière Américain; crêpes €6-15, lunch menu €12; noon-5.30pm, plus 7-9pm Apr-Sep) is a hotel and crêperie opposite the Overlord Museum and perfectly situated for a bite at the start or finish of the walk.

BRITTANY & NORMANDY/43

07

POINTES DU RAZ & VAN

DURATION	DIFFICULTY	DISTANCE	START/END
6hr return	Hard	20km	Parking de la Baie des Trépassés

TERRAIN	Road, walking track, clifftop trail

The most westerly point of mainland France, Pointe du Raz and its neighbour just to the north, Pointe du Van, are places of elemental beauty. On every side, gorse-cloaked cliffs plummet to the waves far below and gulls trace lazy arcs overhead. On a stormy day, with giant waves hurling themselves at the cliff faces, it feels like the end of the world. But on a warm and clear day it can feel more like heaven.

GETTING HERE

In high season only, BreizhGo bus 53 from Quimper goes to the Baie des Trépassés (€2.50, three daily Monday to Saturday, 1¼ hours), but it's easier and more sensible to visit with your own wheels.

STARTING POINT

The walk starts in the Baie des Trépassés car park for which there is a fee of €6.50.

01 Walk south along the back of the beach and at the **war bunkers** turn left and follow the yellow waymarkers signed for La Tour de la Pointe du Raz. When you reach the dirt road, turn right and carry on uphill into the village of **Kerherneau**. Continue to follow yellow waymarkers around and then back into the village. Eventually, you will come to a small **stone chapel**. Turn left here and walk through countryside of low hedges and stumpy trees. When you come to a road and a big grey wall turn right. After a couple of hundred metres turn right again.

02 When the road ends, veer left onto a walking trail and head towards the edge of the cliff. You will meet another trail, this one with red and white GR markers. Turn right and it's now simply a

44/BRITTANY & NORMANDY

Best for

WILDLIFE

case of following this cliff-edge trail all the way up to the end of France. It's a dramatic hike with the high cliffs crashing down into the **turbulent ocean** below. Watch for **dolphins and seals** playing in the waters below. It takes around an hour to walk to the **Pointe du Raz**.

03 Walk back along the northern side of the headland (pictured), following the red and white waymarkers. The views of the **Baie des Trépassés** keep getting bigger and brighter. You'll arrive back where you started. You could call it a day here, which makes for a three-hour walk.

04 Walk north towards the **Relais de la Pointe du Van Hotel**, and turn right down a track leading from the beach to the road. Follow the road to the point where it bends left and goes uphill. Take the trail leading left (north). At the **farmhouse** turn right, cross the main road and follow small farm roads signed with yellow waymarkers. Take the track to the left of the Breton and cross into woodland. Emerging from the woods go straight, past an **old windmill**, and then left as you enter the village of **Kerléodin**. Walk for 10 minutes to the busy D7 road. Turn right and 15m later turn left onto a small side road.

05 Passing a car park continue straight to the cliffs. Turn left and follow red and white waymarkers to **Pointe du Van**. On the way, you'll pass several glorious but forbidding-looking bays. From the point, bend south and pass a lonely **chapel** on a heather-stained headland. Take the right trail fork behind the chapel and follow the dramatic coast past several bays to the car park.

TAKE A BREAK

There are two hotels offering full meals by the Baie des Trépassés, but rather than eat inside have a picnic while you take in glorious sea views.

BRITTANY & NORMANDY/45

Also Try...

JULIA KUZNETSOVA/SHUTTERSTOCK ©

MONT ST-MICHEL

The renowned rock-top abbey of Mont St-Michel beckons continuously on an unusual route along the shores of Baie du Mont St-Michel, past vast grazing meadows and historic towns.

This walk starts at Avranches in the northeast corner of the bay and follows the shore of the estuary of the Sée and Sélune Rivers, making use of quiet roads and paths on the edge of the grassland, part of the waymarked GR223 trail. It ends at the Mont itself (pictured). Although the open grasslands seem to offer easy walking, they're riven by surprisingly deep, soft-sided channels; finding safe crossings can be time-consuming.

Take very seriously notices warning about venturing onto the tidal flats around the bay.

DURATION 7½hr one way
DIFFICULTY Moderate
DISTANCE 30km

CÔTE D'ALBÂTRE

Quiet rural roads lead to breathtaking paths above sheer white limestone cliffs, extraordinary natural arches and slender wave-washed pinnacles of Normandy's remarkable Côte d'Albâtre (Alabaster Coast).

The walk described here links the two popular coastal towns of Fécamp and Étretat, and includes a vertigo-inducing clifftop path past the finest examples of geological fantasy. The route follows part of the waymarked GR21 trail, making use of quiet roads, tracks and footpaths.

A scenic side trip that takes you from Étretat to a prominent lighthouse offers some quieter paths, which were originally used by customs officers chasing smugglers.

DURATION 4-4½hr one way
DIFFICULTY Moderate
DISTANCE 15.5km

CARLOS MARTIN DIAZ/SHUTTERSTOCK ©

CARNAC MEGALITHS

The countryside around Carnac contains the world's largest gathering of more than 3000 ancient standing stones.

Starting from the edge of the coastal town of Carnac, the route, which is well marked with yellow waymarkers and direction panels, takes you first to the famed Ménec standing stones (pictured) and then to the Kermario collection. You'll also visit a couple of ancient water fountains and a chapel as well as walk through a charmed rural landscape of fields and forests. The Carnac tourist office can provide detailed maps and route descriptions.

DURATION 3½hr return
DIFFICULTY Easy
DISTANCE 10km

PRESQU'ÎLE DE CROZON

The coastline between Morgat and Cap de la Chèvre on the Crozon Peninsula is striking. Beyond the marina at the southern end of Morgat's beach, the coastal path (part of the GR34) follows the sea cliffs to scenic Cap de la Chèvre.

The route takes you past an old fort and pine forests overlooking numerous little coves. Be sure to pause at Plage de l'Île Vierge, an idyllic cove lapped by turquoise waters and framed by lofty cliffs. Finish at Cap de la Chèvre on the windy western side of the peninsula.

DURATION 5hr return
DIFFICULTY Moderate
DISTANCE 13km

ÎLE DE BATZ

Lying in the Channel waters just offshore of Roscoff, the Île de Batz is a low-lying and lightly inhabited island fringed by searing white-sand beaches and crisscrossed by quiet country lanes and walking tracks.

A delightful half-day walk, beginning and ending by the ferry dock from Roscoff, allows you to circumnavigate the island. There are no signed waymarkers but it's simple to just follow the coastal trails around the island. With minimal elevation gains and plenty of beachy excuses to stop, it makes for a good family walk.

DURATION 3½hr return
DIFFICULTY Easy
DISTANCE 10km

LILLE & THE SOMME

08 **Thiepval Loop** A walk through the Somme battlefields surrounding the Thiepval Memorial. **p52**

09 **Beaumont-Hamel Newfoundland Memorial** A melancholy amble through some of the last surviving WWI trenches. **p54**

10 **Baie St-Jean** Varied coastal walk along windswept beaches and unusual dune habitats. **p56**

11 **Lochnagar Crater** Ponder the waste of war as you walk through no-man's land. **p58**

Explore
LILLE &
THE SOMME

There are two sides to a walking holiday in this northern region. The first gives the enjoyment of striding through the wide horizons of beaches washed by giant tides. But where there is pleasure, there is also sadness. And inland, away from the beaches, are the bloodied WWI Somme battlefields, and walking here is nothing less than a pilgrimage.

BOULOGNE-SUR-MER

The beautiful Opal Coast – named for the interplay of greys and blues in the sea and sky – features lofty chalk cliffs, rolling green hills, windswept beaches, scrub-dotted sand dunes and charming seaside towns that have been a favourite of British beach lovers since the Victorian era.

The largest – and most enticing – of these seaside towns, and an ideal base for walks in this region, is Boulogne-sur-Mer. Its largely redeveloped waterfront is home to **Nausicaá** (03 21 30 99 99; www.nausicaa.fr; bd Ste-Beuve; adult/child €26/19; 9.30am-6.30pm, closed 3 weeks Jan), one of the world's largest aquariums.

ALBERT

The small town of Albert was almost totally destroyed in WWI, but today it's a bustling little place with reasonable facilities for walkers taking on the trails around the nearby war memorials.

Albert is linked by train to Amiens (€7, 25 minutes, up to two per hour) and Arras (€8, 25 minutes, every two hours). You'll need a car to reach most of the village trail heads.

AMIENS

One of France's mightiest Gothic cathedrals is reason enough to visit Amiens, the former capital of Picardy. The mostly pedestrianised city centre, tastefully rebuilt after WWII, is complemented by lovely green spaces along the Somme River.

Amiens is an ideal base for visits to many of the Battle of the Somme memorials, although you definitely need your own car to get from Amiens to most of the villages where the walks begin.

The St-Leu Quarter is lined with riverside restaurants and pubs, many with terrace views of the cathedral.

WHEN TO GO

With no high mountains covered in winter snows and no punishing summer heat, you can walk in the Somme region at any time of the year. However, the coast of England is within eyesight and like that famously drizzly and wet country, this far-northern corner of France can sometimes feel as if the drizzle will never ease off.

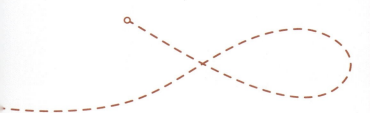

Winter is, of course, the wettest, coldest and darkest time of year to visit, but if you hit a rare dry period then it can be a pleasant time to walk (though be aware that many rural hotels might be closed). Autumn is similar to winter.

On paper summer (June to August) should be the driest, sunniest time, but it can vary wildly from year to year. Some summers can have wall-to-wall sunshine and the mercury in the thermometers can soar; other years, it can blend into autumn in an unceasing curtain of rain.

Spring is an often overlooked time to walk here but, in recent years, it's often been graced by long periods of dry, stable weather and ideal walking temperatures.

Whatever time you come though, do yourself a favour and pack an umbrella!

 **WHERE TO STAY**

Boulogne-sur-Mer has plentiful accommodation options. One highly recommended bed and breakfast is **Les Terrasses de l'Enclos** (📞03 91 90 05 90; www.enclosdeleveche.com; L'enclos de l'Évêché, 6 rue de Pressy; r/f from €90/150; 📶), which has five spacious rooms with hardwood floors and contemporary furnishings.

In Amiens there are lots of hotels aimed at business travellers. A wonderful place to thank aching après-walk muscles is the **Hôtel Marotte** (📞03 60 12 50 00; www.hotel-marotte.com; 3 rue Marotte; r from €175; P ❄ 📶), where modern French luxury is at its most romantic.

 **WHAT'S ON**

ANZAC Day Ceremony (🕐around 25 Apr) Held at the New Zealand Memorial in Longueval.

Ceremonies of the Battle of the Somme (🕐1 Jul) Commemorating the start of the Battle of the Somme. Events are held in numerous places including La Boisselle, Contalmaison, Thiepval, Beaumont-Hamel and Fricourt.

Ceremony at the South African Memorial (🕐5 Jul) Held in Longueval.

Armistice Day (🕐11 Nov) 'Lest we forget' ceremonies marking the signing of the Armistice are held at war memorials throughout the region.

 TRANSPORT

Transport connections from Paris, Lille and other big northern cities to Boulogne-sur-Mer and Amiens are generally good with frequent trains and some buses. To get from these towns to village and beach trailheads using public transport is considerably more challenging. We would highly recommend hiring a car in Amiens or, better, Paris or Lille.

The coastal roads around Calais can be very busy, but otherwise most roads are quiet and the driving much less frenetic than in southern parts of France.

08

THIEPVAL LOOP

DURATION	DIFFICULTY	DISTANCE	START/END
2½hr return	Easy	8km	Thiepval Memorial

TERRAIN	Farm track, road

The imposing red-brick Thiepval Memorial is perhaps the most powerful memorial to the waste that was the Battle of the Somme. It is dedicated to the estimated 72,000 British and South African soldiers who died in the fields of France during WWI and have no known grave. This short circular walk starts and ends at the memorial and heads past battle sites, along pretty riverbanks and over fields that once rang with violence, but today stand silent and peaceful.

We recommend visiting the **Thiepval Memorial & Museum** (www.historial.org; memorial free, museum adult/child €6/3; 9.30am-6pm Mar-Oct, to 5pm Nov-Feb) before you start this walk, but save the memorial itself for afterwards. From the car park outside the museum, walk down to the village, past the church and along the D151 signed Grandcourt. Around 400m later, turn left by the village cemetery and follow yellow markers across fields. This area is the **Schwaben Redoubt**, a German defensive line that was the scene of a bloody battle on the first day of the Battle of the Somme.

Turn left at the village of **St-Pierre Divion** and follow the river to the junction of the D73. Cross straight over and follow the trail into broadleaf woodland. Eventually, you will hit a dirt road. After 200m, take the very discreet turn-off right and head back into forest (there are faded orange markers and two metal poles). Continue to the church in the village of **Authuille** (look for the peacocks in village gardens!). Cross the D151 and follow signs for **Lonsdale War Cemetery**. At the crest of the hill, turn left and walk through a copse of woodland and then over fields for a dramatic approach back to the memorial.

52/LILLE & THE SOMME

Best for

EXPLORING HISTORY

09

BEAUMONT-HAMEL NEWFOUNDLAND MEMORIAL

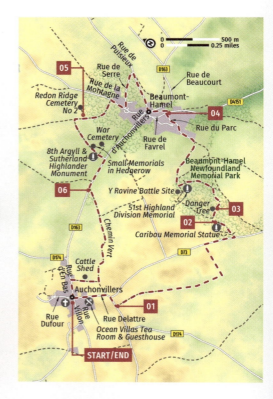

DURATION	DIFFICULTY	DISTANCE	START/END
2¾hr return	Easy	9km	Auchonvillers

TERRAIN	Road, walking trail

On the morning of 1 July 1916, the volunteer Royal Newfoundland Regiment, made up of 780 men, climbed out of their trenches and advanced towards the German lines. Within 30 minutes almost the entire regiment had been wiped out. The next day the commander of the 29th British Division said, 'The assault only failed of success because dead men can advance no further.' This walk takes you through melancholic battlefield sites, where the trenches are still visible, through now quiet and peaceful farming villages, and past numerous war memorials.

GETTING HERE

The walk begins in Auchonvillers, 35km northeast of Amiens along the D919. Public transport is very limited.

STARTING POINT

There are no shops in the village but there is a guesthouse and tearooms.

01 From the village **church**, cross the main road and follow signs to the Beaumont-Hamel Newfoundland Memorial. At the far end of the village, swing right down the D174 at the junction signed for Mesnil-Martinsart (the Newfoundland Memorial is left); 100m later, a **farm track** veers left across fields before a sharp left turn leads to a quiet road. Turn right here.

02 A moment later, you will reach the **Beaumont-Hamel Newfoundland Memorial** (pictured p49). It's one of the few places where the web of **trenches** still exists (pictured). The no-man's land that separates the Allied and German lines is still a blistered mess of **bomb craters**.

54/LILLE & THE SOMME

03 Walk towards the far northern end of the site, past the **Danger Tree**. Sitting in the middle of no-man's land, this shattered tree was used as a landmark and gathering point for the Newfoundland Regiment as they marched towards their death. Continue over to the **51st Highland Division Memorial**, which commemorates those who died here in a fierce battle on 13 November 1916. Just past this is the **Y Ravine battle site**, and next to this is a gate and exit from the memorial site. Follow the trail across fields and down into Beaumont-Hamel village.

04 Turn right in front of the **memorial** dedicated to villagers killed by the Germans. Almost immediately afterwards turn left and follow the farm road. You will soon come to a road junction. Turn right and head uphill. At a fork, swing left, re-enter the village and turn right at the junction.

05 Follow the trail signed **Redon Ridge Cemetery no 2**. After a few minutes, you'll see the cemetery off to your right. Our route bends left and heads downhill. At the bottom of the hill is a **hedge**: look for small crosses and **poppies** left by those paying their respects to the 165 men who died here on 1 July 1916. At the base of the hill, just past a **memorial** to the 8th Argyll and Sutherland Highlanders, is the D163 road. Turn right here.

06 One hundred metres later, veer left down a waymarked **farm track**. Where the gravel track bends left, take a small grassy trail heading straight (southwest). A few hundred metres later, leave the main track and take a smaller trail that passes a grey **cattle shed**. When you reach the road, turn left back into Auchonvillers and the village church.

 **TAKE A BREAK**

The **Ocean Villas Tea Room & Guesthouse** (📞 03 22 76 23 66; www.avrilwilliams.eu; 10 rue Delattre; mains €8-12; ⏰ 9am-5pm), on the edge of Auchonvillers, serves English breakfasts, cakes and soup.

LILLE & THE SOMME/55

10

BAIE ST-JEAN

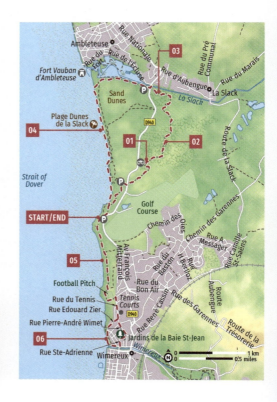

DURATION	DIFFICULTY	DISTANCE	START/END
3hr return	Moderate	10km	Pointe aux Oies car park
TERRAIN	Road, walking trail		

This varied coastal walk takes in lofty clifftop views, an unusual dune habitat, wetlands, a beautiful wide beach dotted with war bunkers and an enjoyably old-fashioned seaside resort. Generally flat, and with plentiful opportunities for little people to dunk their toes in the sea, this is a good family walk for older kids.

GETTING HERE

The small seaside town of Wimereux is 7.5km north of Boulogne-sur-Mer. Multiple trains connect the two towns (€1.80, five minutes). Buses (€1, 11 minutes) run less frequently.

STARTING POINT

The walk begins from the Pointe aux Oies car park, a couple of kilometres north of the town centre.

There are hiking information boards here but no other facilities. You could also start the walk from outside the tourist office in Wimereux, but the advantage of starting from the Pointe aux Oies car park is that it turns the walk into a neat figure-of-eight route with your car at the centre, which means that you could easily do just half the walk.

01 Walk north along headland following yellow trail markers. Veer right at the first junction. Slide through low, scrubby dunes to the next junction where you again turn right at a car park, cross the busy road and then go left a few metres before veering off into the dunes by the yellow waymarker. A moment or two later you will come to a raised wooden **viewing tower**.

02 The trail soon snuggles down into a woodland of **stunted trees**. Around 45 minutes from the start, you reach a raised **wooden viewpoint** overlooking a large pond covered in water plants.

56/LILLE & THE SOMME

03 The trail carries on through a mix of open dunes and woodland (pictured) before bending to the west along a raised **boardwalk** through a marshy area. Cross the main coastal road and head down the **cobbled track** towards the sea. Next to you are extensive **reed beds** that are good for birdwatching. Up ahead is the **Fort Vauban d'Ambleteuse**, which sits on a small island in the bay.

04 When you reach the **beach**, turn left and walk down its length back to the car park. You can either call it a day (two-hour walk) or carry on to Wimereux.

05 The yellow trail markers lead south from the car park along the edge of **80m-high cliffs** with memorable sea views. After 20 minutes you will come to the football pitch on the northern edge of Wimereux. Turn left at the far end of the pitch, then right and down rue du Tennis.

At the road junction by the mini-golf, go straight ahead down rue Pierre-André Wimet and then right into the **Jardins de la Baie St-Jean**. After passing the duck pond and exiting the gardens, turn left and descend to the town centre.

06 Turn right and walk towards the **seafront**, where you turn right again and pass lots of wooden **beach huts**. At the end of the row of huts, veer off to the right and up a set of steps. At the top of the steps, go right and meet up with rue du Tennis. You now simply retrace your steps back along the cliffs to the car park.

 **TAKE A BREAK**

Grab an ice cream from one of the seafront places in Wimereux and enjoy it while building a sand castle on the beach.

LILLE & THE SOMME/57

11
LOCHNAGAR CRATER

DURATION	DIFFICULTY	DISTANCE	START/END
3½hr return	Moderate	12km	Fricourt

TERRAIN	Road, walking trail

This walk takes you straight through the heart of a WWI battlefield. As well as the vast crater that still marks the spot where the mine that started the Battle of the Somme exploded, you will walk quietly down the no-man's land that once separated the opposing sides, along the now buried Allied trenches, past a number of war cemeteries and through some attractive farming countryside.

This walk is best done before or after the crops are planted in the fields. Just after harvesting in late summer is a good period, and if the fields have been ploughed keep an eye peeled for war debris, which is frequently dug up (but don't touch anything that might still be live!).

GETTING HERE
The walk starts from the car park next to the church in the small red-brick village of Fricourt, which is 6km east of central Albert. There's just one bus a day in either direction between Albert and Fricourt, and it's really just a school bus. It's better to bring your own car!

STARTING POINT
There are no special facilities for walkers at the start point of this walk and not much in the way of facilities for passing travellers of any type in Fricourt, although there is a bakery just down the road from the church.

01 Walk north uphill along the small road to the right of the church. Continue to rue du Haut Bois. Turn left (west) here, and go past the water tower. Turn right at the bigger D147 road.

There are occasional yellow waymarkers. Continue a couple of hundred metres uphill and go into the **German War Cemetery** on your right. The German flying ace, Manfred von Richthofen, or '**The Red Baron**', who shot down 80 allied aircraft between 1916 and 1918, was buried here. Today, his remains are in Germany.

02 Descend back down the D147 towards Fricourt. Just at the entrance to the village, turn right (west) down rue de la Boisselle following the signs for the **Fricourt New Military Cemetery** (pictured) and Peake Wood Cemetery. You're now on a farm track. Two hundred metres later, at the trail junction, go right (ignoring the sign left to the cemetery). Then turn right again at the next trail junction and follow the trail through cropland (you're likely to startle plenty of pheasants as you walk down here).

03 You'll reach a small **copse of woodland**. Technically the public right of way continues straight ahead, but the farmer often plants crops over the trail. If you can, carry on straight ahead, until the trail bends right and joins the D147. If the trail is blocked then cut straight down to the D147 where you can.

04 Turn left and walk 50m up the road. You'll see a clear farm track on your left. Head down this. There are yellow waymarkers. You will soon see a **Commonwealth War Cemetery** to your right, but it can't be reached from this trail.

After walking for 20 minutes you will come to the D20 and the village of **La Boisselle**. Turn left (south) and descend downhill through the village. At the far end of the village turn left by the road sign for Becordel-Bécourt, then immediately left again following the sign for the Grande Mine.

📖 Lochnagar Crater

The Lochnagar mine was a huge underground explosive charge secretly planted just in front of the German trenches by the Tunnelling Companies of the Royal Engineers. It was one of 19 mines that were planted by the British and set to go off early on the morning of 1 July 1916.

At the time, these were the largest mines ever detonated but, although they did wipe out a section of the German trenches, for all their flash and bang, they failed to neutralise the German defences. The British were supposed to capture the village of La Boisselle within 20 minutes, but by the end of the day, there were 11,000 Allied casualties on the battlefields around La Boisselle.

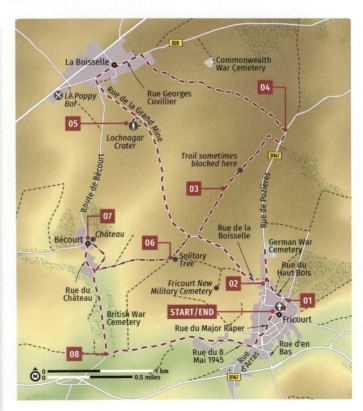

LILLE & THE SOMME/59

05 Take your time exploring the **Lochnagar Crater** site (pictured). It's more than just a huge hole in the ground; there are the graves of some of those who died here and numerous information panels reveal the moving stories of those involved in the battle.

06 Leaving the crater, follow the road downhill. It becomes a farm track after 100m. You are now skipping, carefree, right down the middle of the **no-man's land**. When you get to the trail junction, turn right and walk towards the **solitary tree** that marks the line of the **Allied trenches**. Turn right and you are now walking through the mud where men once fought and died.

07 Ten minutes later you will arrive on the edge of **Bécourt village**. Turn right by the statue of Christ and a small war memorial, wander through parkland for a few minutes and up to the village **château**, and then descend back down the hill via the rue du Château. At the road junction turn right. After a few minutes, you will come to a **British War Cemetery**, which is worth a visit.

08 Continue on down the road, then take the first left up a minor road that climbs slightly and bends to the right before turning into a gravel farm track. Follow this for 10 minutes back towards **Fricourt**. At the road junction, carry on straight and back uphill to the church.

STUART BUTLER/LONELY PLANET ©

60/LILLE & THE SOMME

 The Battle of the Somme

With close to a million people losing their lives over the space of four and a half months, it's hardly a surprise that the Battle of the Somme has become a byword for the waste of war.

The First Battle of the Somme (1 July to 18 November 1916) was an Allied offensive designed to relieve pressure on the beleaguered French troops at Verdun. On 1 July 1916, Allied troops 'went over the top' along a 34km front. But German positions proved virtually unbreachable and instead of the predicted fast gains, the battle dragged on for four and a half months.

When this particular act of WWI came to a close, the British had advanced just 12km and the French 8km.

 TAKE A BREAK

Just south of the turn-off for the Lochnagar Crater, **Le Poppy Bar** (03 22 75 45 45; 4 rte de Bapaume, La Boisselle; menus from €17; noon-2pm & 7-9pm Mon-Fri) looks very basic from the outside, but it actually serves pretty decent, traditional French dishes that are good value.

LILLE & THE SOMME/61

Also Try…

ARTERRA PICTURE LIBRARY/ALAMY STOCK PHOTO ©

LES CROCS

To understand the vast Somme estuary (which has some of the world's biggest tides), march through this long, loop walk.

Along the way you'll experience an impressive array of environments, from towering desert-like sand dunes (known as *crocs* in Picard, the local language), to a beach as wide as the horizon at low tide, a fertile water-logged bird reserve, and gentle rural countryside. Keep your eyes peeled and you might spy seals, herons, spoonbills and a wealth of other wildlife.

The walk begins at the beach car park near St-Quentin-en-Tournon. Follow the sandy path through the dunes for 3.6km to the beach. Turn left (south) and march all the way down the beach and then follow the banks of the estuary inland until you hit the road again. At this point, head north to the village of Le Bout des Crocs and then carry on back to where you parked.

DURATION 5½hr return
DIFFICULTY Hard
DISTANCE 16km

THE ARMISTICE MEMORIAL CIRCUIT

When, after four long years, WWI finally came to an end, it did so at the 11th hour of the 11th day of the 11th month inside a train carriage in an obscure wooded corner of northern France. This walk, which meanders through those woods and along the banks of the pretty Aisne River, will show you where that most momentous of moments happened and is the perfect place in which to finish off a walking holiday in the Somme.

The walk begins at the Mémorial de l'Armistice (pictured), not far from the little town of Compiègne. Following a clear trail waymarked in yellow and red and white, you will walk in a roughly circular route down small farm tracks to take in the best of this countryside. Save visiting the replica train carriage (the first was destroyed in Germany in the closing stages of WWII) until the very end of the walk.

DURATION 3hr return
DIFFICULTY Easy
DISTANCE 8½km

MAELICK/SHUTTERSTOCK ©

CAP BLANC-NEZ

This is an enjoyable, family-friendly walk to the summit of the 158m high Cap Blanc-Nez cliffs.

These chalky-white cliffs (pictured) mark the closest spot between mainland Europe and the British Isles, and are an ideal spot from which to watch the ferries crisscross between the two lands. The walk begins from the village of Escalles and follows a clear trail down to the beach. The hard part is the haul up the slopes of the cliff before an easier descent and then a loop back via the villages of Mont d'Hubert and Haute Escalles.

DURATION 2½hr return
DIFFICULTY Easy
DISTANCE 7½km

LE HOURDEL

Walking the exposed sandspit of Le Hourdel, between sea and lagoon, can feel like you're at the end of the world.

But there's life at the world's end: masses of seabirds and lots of grey seals. In fact, this is one of the better places in France to commune with these playful aquatic mammals. This walk, which begins from the Somme village of La Mollière, sweeps through bleak, sandy countryside and then down the long narrow sandspit in one enjoyable half-day walk. Don't forget your binoculars!

DURATION 2¾hr return
DIFFICULTY Easy
DISTANCE 8km

FAŸ: THE LOST VILLAGE

In the summer of 1916, the village of Faÿ found itself right on the front line between opposing sides in a chilling example of the destruction of WWI.

At the end of the war, Faÿ had been almost completely destroyed. All that remained was part of the church and a bit of a farm building. rather than rebuilding, the inhabitants chose to leave the old village as a memorial of what had happened. This easy stroll (marked with yellow waymarkers) around what remains of Faÿ will certainly live long in the memory.

DURATION 3hr return
DIFFICULTY Easy
DISTANCE 9km

FRENCH ALPS & JURA

12 **Lac de Roselend & Lac de la Gittaz** An easy walk for all ages in the tracks of Tour de France cyclists. **p68**

13 **Grand Balcon Nord** France's largest glacier bookended with a cable-car and mountain-train ride. **p70**

14 **Lac Blanc** Gaze at Europe's highest peak reflected in Chamonix' celebrated turquoise-blue lake. **p74**

15 **Pic des Mémises** Scale a 12m-high ladder for panoramic views of Lake Geneva. **p76**

16 **Chalets de Bise to Lac de Darbon** Track wild ibex in Haute-Savoie's cheese-filled Vallée d'Abondance. **p78**

17 **Arbois to Pupillin** A serene vineyard trail for gourmets in the French Jura. **p80**

18 **Cirque de Baume-les-Messieurs** Explore Jurassien waterfalls, forests and bat-filled caves in a glacial corrie. **p82**

19 **Tête de la Maye** A challenging walk with rock climbs in the national-park-protected Massif des Écrins. **p86**

20 **Lac des Vaches & Col de la Vanoise** Memorable high drama in the flora-and-fauna-rich Parc National de la Vanoise. **p88**

Explore
FRENCH ALPS & JURA

No part of France is more synonymous with walking than the French Alps. The Golden Age of Alpinism was born here amid Europe's highest mountain peaks in the 1850s. The region's iconic hamlets and alpine pastures, soul-soaring cols (mountain passes) and glacier-carved valleys, shark-toothed summits and spellbinding blue lakes have seduced visitors ever since. Nearby are the gently rolling Jura Mountains.

CHAMONIX

Mountains loom large everywhere you look in Chamonix, the mythical heart and soul of the French Alps dominated by Europe's highest peak, snowy domed Mont Blanc (4808m). A packed schedule of seasonal events in the small, dynamic town ensures ample off-trail entertainment: outdoor yoga, forest baths, guided walks and trail runs, traditional alpine arts and crafts, and so on. Dining, drinking and shopping options in town are equally generous and varied.

BESANÇON

An important stop on Gallo-Roman trade routes linking Italy, the Alps and the Rhine, laid-back Besançon is today a springboard for the brooding landscapes of the sparsely populated Jura Mountains. Tucked in a bend of the Doubs River, the town is capped with a museum-filled citadel built by Vauban in the 17th century, and enjoys active contemporary arts and local music scenes.

WHEN TO GO

The walking season is short in the French Alps. Snow can linger on high mountain passes, summits and steep, serpentine access roads well into May and return again in October. This makes June to September the best time to hit the trail: daylight hours are at their longest, weather conditions are warm and sunny with little risk of storms, uneven mountain footpaths are dry and subsequently less slippy, and views as you climb – of soaring mountain peaks blitzing a cloudless, crystal-clear horizon – simply don't get better. Lower elevations in the Jura Massif extend the walking season by a few weeks.

Popular walking routes get busy on July and August weekends; set out early or overnight in a *refuge* (mountain hut) on the trail to bag ethereal views of mirror lakes, icy summits and sunbathing ibex all for yourself.

In larger resorts cable cars and chairlifts take out some of the legwork between late June and mid-September. Bureaux des Guides (mountain guide offices offering guided walks) in resorts share the same seasonal hours.

Alpine wildflowers are at their most exquisite in June, although each summer month sports its own distinctive

blooms. Crocuses and snowbells are among the first to emerge from winter hibernation, carpeting grassy pastures in a blaze of white and purple. Tiny blue forget-me-nots pepper hillsides well into July, as do yellow archangels and blue bugles. Eye-catching blue and yellow gentians flower June to August, alongside wild orchids. August and early September is the time to forage for wild blueberries, strawberries and raspberries.

WHERE TO STAY

From campgrounds, tree houses and self-catering *gîtes* in remote valleys to pleasure-palace hotels in celebrity ski resorts, the French Alps sport every stratum of accommodation. The choice in the Jura is more low-key.

Summer accommodation is easier to bag than in winter's ski season; hotels open mid-June to mid-September. Advance booking is essential for *refuges*, strategically located on long-distance GR trails and other walking routes.

Tourist offices in major ski resorts run an accommodation service with online booking.

WHAT'S ON

Cosmo Jazz Festival (https://cosmojazzfestival.com; late Jul) Open-air jazz concerts on village and town squares, up mountains and at other exhilarating outdoor venues for nine days in the Chamonix Valley.

Fête du Lac One of Europe's largest pyrotechnic displays showers Annecy's lake in magic, 'oohed' and 'aahed' at by some 200,000 spectators. Spectacular music, lighting and special effects accompany the one- to two-hour firework display on the first Saturday in August.

Le Tour de France (www.letour.fr; Jul) The world's most famous cycling race always zips up and down a couple of torturous cols in the French Alps during its mammoth three-week, 3500km journey around France.

TRANSPORT

Car is the easiest way of getting around. Many walkers fly into Lyon (www.lyonaeroports.com), Grenoble (www.grenoble-airport.com) or Geneva (www.gva.ch) in Switzerland and rent a car.

Resources

Savoie Mont Blanc (www.savoie-mont-blanc.com) Walking itinerary suggestions, accommodation links and mountains of other practical information for Savoie and Haute-Savoie.

Isère Tourisme (www.isere-tourisme.com) Practical trail information for Grenoble and surrounding mountain resorts.

Jura Tourisme (www.jura-tourism.com) One-stop shop for information on the French Jura, including 55 suggested walks with trail maps.

Chamonix Tourist Office (04 50 53 00 24; www.chamonix.com; 85 place du Triangle de l'Amitié; 9am-7pm mid-Jun–mid-Sep & mid-Dec–Apr, shorter hours rest of year;) Excellent source of information on accommodation, activities and mountain conditions for the entire Chamonix Valley.

Within France, train services to the Alps are decent. Buses link railhead Moûtiers with Les Trois Vallées and Bourg St-Maurice with Val d'Isère. Modane is the rail stop for the Vanoise, linked by bus to Bonneval-sur-Arc. For Chamonix, change to the Mont Blanc Express at St-Gervais-les-Bains. Besançon is the main railhead for the Jura Mountains, with services to/from Paris-Gare de Lyon and Dijon.

12
LAC DE ROSELEND & LAC DE LA GITTAZ

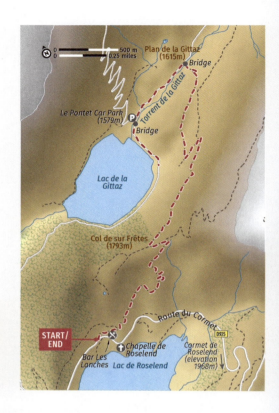

DURATION	DIFFICULTY	DISTANCE	START/END
3hr return	Easy	10.5km	Lac de Roselend

TERRAIN	Gravel road, forest & field footpaths

The road trip to Lac de Roselend – over the 1968m-high mountain pass of Cormet de Roselend – is as stunning as the lake views accompanying walkers on this lake-to-lake walk. Find the trail (min/max altitude 1562/1793m) in Savoie's eminently peaceful, pastoral, Beaufortain region.

Park by Chapelle de Roselend on the northern shore of **Lac de Roselend** (pictured). Tour de France cyclists whizz around this **3** wedged between mountains, and **views** are picture-postcard. Walk downhill past Bar Les Lanches to the roadside 'La Gittaz' waymarker. Follow the gently winding, gravel road uphill, past fields of bell-clanging cows. North, the craggy peak of **Roc du Vent** (2360m) looms large. Lake views get dreamier, the higher you climb.

After 40 minutes (1.6km), the gravel road flattens onto **Col de sur Frêtes** (1793m) – actually a grassy cow field. Continue straight, traversing a short section of enclosed pasture (duck beneath the electric wire) before dropping down to the 'Col de sur Frêtes' waymarker on the right. The milk from these red Tarentaise cows goes into AOP Beaufort, Tome des Bauges and Reblochon cheese.

Now narrow and cowpat-splattered, the footpath weaves downhill to farmland. Views of artificial **Lac de la Gittaz** from above steal the show. Lower down, the path circumvents a hillock and crosses **Torrent de la Gittaz** over a footbridge to arrive on a tarmac road at **Plan de la Gittaz** (1615m). Turn left to 'Le Pontet & Col de la Gittaz' and follow the road for 700m to **Le Pontet car park** (1579m). Bear left, recrossing the river, and follow the road for 500m to a lay-by with footpath plunging to the shore. Return to Roselend the same way.

13

GRAND BALCON NORD

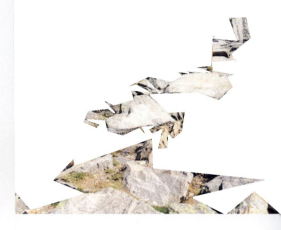

DURATION	DIFFICULTY	DISTANCE	START/END
3hr return	Easy	6.75km	Chamonix

TERRAIN	Softly undulating mountain path

No visit to Chamonix is complete without an up-close peek at France's largest glacier – the climax of this scenic, family-friendly walk. Mont Blanc views are second-to-none, and a cable car to climb up and vintage mountain train to get down cuts out the heavy legwork. Several unique sights at the end of the trail turn this relatively short walk (min/max altitude 1913/2317m) into a memorable day out.

GETTING HERE

Park in open-air Parking du Grépon, opposite the Téléphérique de l'Aiguille du Midi (cable-car station) at the southern end of Chamonix. Buy a return ticket to Plan de l'Aiguille du Midi (adult/child €34/28.90, valid for your return by train from Montenvers) at the ticket desks and ride the cable car to its mid-station at 2317m.

STARTING POINT

Exit the cable car and follow signs on the left for 'Plan 2317m'. Upon stepping out onto the mountainside, feast on dramatic views of high-altitude peaks close-up: to the left (north), a breathtaking line of dark, rocky *aiguilles* (needles) including Aiguille du Plan (3673m), Aiguille de Blatière (3522m), Aiguille du Grépon (3482m) and Les Grands Charmoz (3445m); directly above, Aiguille du Midi (3842m) crowned by a rocket-styled cable-car station; and to the right (south), the dazzling snow-white summits of Dôme du Goûter (4304m) and – drum roll – the mightiest of all, Mont Blanc (4808m), a mere 8.2km away as the crow flies.

01 Walk towards the **Buvette du Plan de l'Aiguille** cafe-bar, follow the steps down (left of mountain hut), and head left downhill following the 'Refuge du Plan de l'Aiguille du Midi' trailhead.

70/FRENCH ALPS & JURA

02 After about 10 minutes, approaching a haphazard grouping of **monumental boulders**, the narrow downhill path forks. Turn right (northeast) here to effectively begin traversing the mountainside horizontally along Chamonix's famous **Grand Balcon Nord** trail.

03 The scenic footpath now gently undulates its way north, ducking and diving across mountain streams and the sinister grey rocks and rubble of the dramatically receded **Glacier de Blatière**. Straight ahead, admire Aiguille de l'M (2844m) – named after its M-shaped twin summit – and the pale red-rose peak beyond of Chamonix's Aiguille Verte (4122m) or 'Green Needle'. This mythical peak was conquered by English climber Edward Whymper on 29 June 1865, two weeks before his fateful first ascent of the Matterhorn in neighbouring Switzerland (when four of his party died). It remains one of Chamonix's most revered mountaineering icons.

04 After about one hour or 2.5km of easy walking, the path arrives at a yellow sign for **Alpages de Blaitière** – lower altitude pastures where ink-black Hérens cows and Savoy goats graze. Ignore the sign and push on straight ahead (north) towards 'Montenvers Mer de Glace' and the dirty black moraine of Chamonix's decimated **Narnillons glacier**.

05 The footpath morphs into a strip of stone slabs as it drops down towards the forest. Across the valley, admire the **flaming red rocks** of the protected Aiguilles Rouges nature reserve. At the 4km marker, take the right fork signposted 'Le Signal' and 'Montenvers Mer de Glace'.

Mer de Glace

The blackened tongue of Chamonix's 7km-long 'Sea of Ice' glacier might be a shadow of the silver-white 'sea' it was, but it remains spellbinding. **Panoramic terraces** in front of Gare de Montenvers provide bird's-eye views of crevasses formed by the immense pressure of the glacier's 50m- to 90m-per-year movement.

To get up close, follow a footpath (40 minutes) downhill, or ride the free cable car from opposite the train station. At the bottom, 580-odd metal steps descend to the glacier and its **Grotte de Glace** (ice cave). Plaques indicate the glacier's fast-diminishing height between 1985 and 2018; the ice is now melting 5m in thickness and 30m in length a year.

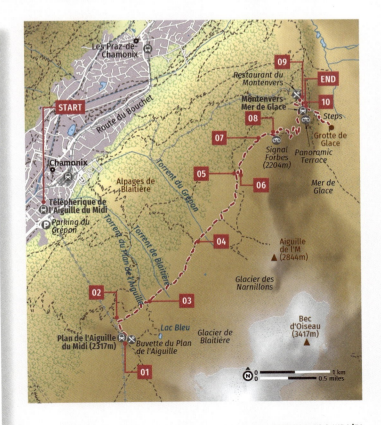

FRENCH ALPS & JURA/71

06 Brace yourself for a short, sharp, stiff zigzag for 300m uphill along a narrow footpath. Catch your breath between hairpins over **magnificent views** of snowy Mont Blanc. As the path flattens, in the distance, spot Switzerland's Lac d'Emosson (1931m) cradled in the Swiss Alps.

07 As the trail reaches its highest point, the dirt path morphs into one chiselled from rocks, slabs and boulders – some meticulously stacked, others precariously strewn across the mountainside by glacial flow thousands of moons ago. Round the final bend and gasp at the razor peak of **Petit Dru** (3733m) with its perilous, feared-and-revered, 1000m-high granite wall of a summit.

08 Follow the stone path to the 'Le Signal' viewpoint, also known as **Signal Forbes**, at 2204m – 5km into the walk – from where you can pick your way across the apocalyptic field of ancient glacial till and modern walkers' cairns to peer down on Chamonix's famous **Mer de Glace** – France's largest glacier (pictured p65). The viewpoint is named after Scottish glaciologist James David Forbes (1809–68) who spent time here studying how glaciers move (about 90m a year in the case of the Mer de Glace). Many walkers picnic here. Beyond the iconic tongue of ice, the majestic Grandes Jorasses peak (4208m) stands sentry; its north face is one of the Alps' three 'greats'.

Adreneline Highs

Every winter thousands of intrepid skiers swarm to Chamonix to fly down the snow-covered Mer de Glace as part of **La Vallée Blanche** off-piste descent (pictured). The world-famous ride of a lifetime involves a hair-raising, 2800m vertical descent from Aiguille du Midi (3842m) to Chamonix (1046m).

Come summer, Chamonix town morphs into a honeypot for walkers and climbers. The historic Grand Hôtel (now glam hotel-hostel Refuge du Montenvers), built in 1853, served as base camp in the 19th century for pioneering ascents of Les Drus, Grandes Jorasses and other mythical peaks. The very air breathed by early alpinists attempting to summit Mont Blanc in the late 18th century remains trapped inside air bubbles in the Grotte de Glace.

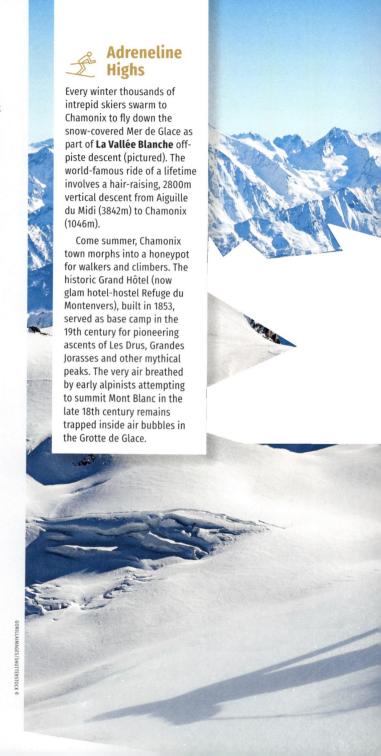

09 Backtrack to the 'Le Signal' marker and follow the signed footpath for 1.75km down the hillside to **Refuge du Montenvers** or Grand Hôtel (1913m) – a traditional alpinists' stop since 1853. A pyramid marker celebrates famous visitors, including Napoleon III and the Empress Eugenie, who trekked up to Montenvers from Chamonix assisted by 60 mountain guides and several mules. The party continued on foot to the edge of the glacier.

10 Count another five minutes to walk from Refuge du Montenvers to **Gare du Montenvers**, serviced by a cherry-red cog-wheel train to/from downtown Chamonix since 1909. The bone-rattling, 5km-long journey through centurion larch forest – brilliant green in spring and golden yellow in autumn just before the deciduous trees shed their needles – is a highlight.

TAKE A BREAK

A picnic amid diabolical rock formations with glacier views is an inviting option; another is a post-walk lunch with magnificent views from the terrace of **Restaurant du Montenvers** (04 50 53 87 70; www.refugedumontenvers.com; mains €18-32; Montenvers). Savoyard dishes include cheese fondue, *diots* (pork sausages) simmered in local white wine, and chicken with *matouille Savoyarde* (oven-baked potatoes, garlic and white wine smothered in gooey Tome des Bauges cheese). End with blueberry tart or a decadent Mont Blanc (vanilla and chestnut ice-cream sundae).

FRENCH ALPS & JURA/73

14

LAC BLANC

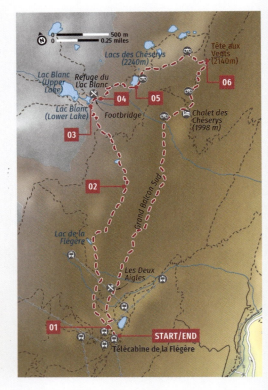

DURATION	DIFFICULTY	DISTANCE	START/END
3½-4hr return	Moderate	8.5km	Top of Flégère cable car
TERRAIN	Rocky footpath with steep ascent			

Admiring razor-sharp reflections of Europe's highest peak in Chamonix's famous lake is what this classic loop is about. The celebrated trail (min/max altitude 1877/2352m) gets packed on summer weekends, so plan ahead – start early or overnight in Lac Blanc's lakeside mountain hut to gorge on sumptuous sunrise views in splendid isolation.

GETTING HERE
From Chamonix, follow the Martigny road 3km north to Les Praz-de-Chamonix. Park at the bottom station of the Télécabine de la Flégère and ride the gondola (single/return €15/19) up to 1877m.

STARTING POINT
Exit the cable car's top station and bear right to pick up the trailhead clearly signposted 'Lac Blanc'. A gravel road briefly dips downhill before morphing into a mountain path.

01 Soon after the Lac Blanc trailhead, the rocky path steepens as it zigzags between blueberry bushes and limestone boulders coloured lime-green with lichen.

02 Wooden walkways ensure dry feet across the occasional stream and metal handrails assist walkers on a tight but short rocky corridor. Turn back to admire **snowy Mont Blanc** (4808m) across the valley – a hypnotic constant throughout the 3.2km, 1½-hour ascent.

03 **Postcard views of Lac Blanc** (2352m) reward at the top (pictured). Cross the **footbridge** and follow the lakeshore path directly beneath Refuge du Lac Blanc's terrace deck to marvel at Mont Blanc reflections in the lake.

74/FRENCH ALPS & JURA

Wild Swimming

Buried in snow for some eight months of the year, high-altitude Lac Blanc (White Lake) seduces summertime walkers with its startling turquoise water and occasional pale-pink-breasted water pipit foraging for food on the lake shores. The lake comprises two bodies of glacial water split by a narrow channel. Even in July and August the larger upper lake, 9m deep, retains a chilly polar vibe with its year-round patches of snow. The shallower, crystal-clear water of the smaller, lower lake, 3.2m deep, is the one to dip in – if you dare.

04 Avoid the late-morning crowd labouring up to Lac Blanc by returning to La Flégère cable-car station via Lacs des Chéserys – a 5km descent. From Lac Blanc, continue past Refuge du Lac Blanc and follow the 'Sentier Piétons' sign between rocks. Almost immediately the path turns into a series of steep but unchallenging wooden steps and metal ladders. Leave 20 minutes to reach the first of several tiny lakes known as **Lacs des Chéserys** (2240m).

05 Take the path around the lake's eastern shore, following signs for Chalet des Chéserys and La Flégère. In summer, **violet rhododendrons** and **yellow cinquefoils** carpet the mountainside here.

06 Skilfully crafted stone cairns mark the **Aiguilles Rouges nature reserve**, named after the ginger crags shaped like 'red needles' that dominate here. About 1km after the first lake, the trail arrives at **Tête aux Vents** (2140m) – the furthest point north on this walk, from where you head back south to La Flégère along a section of Chamonix's **Grand Balcon Sud trail**. A magnificent panorama of (left to right) the Tour, Argentière, Mer de Glace and Boissons glaciers dominates the return walk.

TAKE A BREAK

Refuge du Lac Blanc (📞06 02 05 08 82; www.refugedulacblanc.fr; dm incl half-board adult/child €56/50; 🕙mid-Jun–Sep), with dorms and cafe terrace sensationally overlooking Lac Blanc, serves drinks with Mont Blanc view. Lunch at mountain restaurant **Les Deux Aigles** (📞07 67 15 23 37; 🕙mid-Jun–Sep; 👶), on the trail 10 minutes from the end of this walk. *Croûte au fromage* (oven-baked bread smothered in ham and gooey Comté and raclette cheese) is the house speciality, while *tartelette aux myrtilles* (blueberry tart) and ice cream (fiery *génépi* (herbal liqueur), honey, blueberry) are local sweet temptations.

15

PIC DES MÉMISES

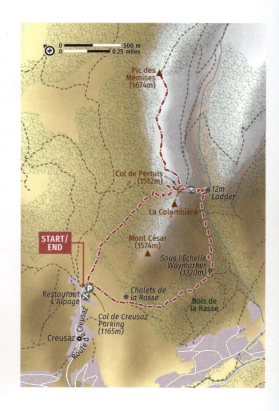

DURATION	DIFFICULTY	DISTANCE	START/END
3hr return	Moderate	6.5km	Col de Creusaz, Bernex
TERRAIN	Forest/mountain tracks & a 12m-high ladder		

Grassy pastures and coniferous woods bookend this circular walk in Haute-Savoie's Bas-Chablais region. Panoramic views of Europe's largest alpine lake – Lake Geneva – and a vertiginous ladder are highlights (min/max altitude 1165/1674m).

From Bernex, drive 4km northeast to Creusaz. Park in the **Col de Creusaz parking** (1165m) in front of Restaurant L'Alpage. From the yellow waymarker at the end of the car park, follow the footpath right to 'Sous l'Échelle'.

Enjoy rural views of the tiny ski resort of Bernex as the wide gravel track gently climbs past grassy pastures along the southern flank of craggy **Mont César** (1574m). The path narrows as it winds through **Bois de la Rasse** (1250m) – forest stitched from conifers and boulders cloaked in emerald-green moss.

At the **Sous l'Échelle** waymarker (1320m), fork left to 'Échelle'. The stream-side trail dives sharply uphill between rocks and tree roots. The final 10m to the foot of this walk's famous **12m-high iron ladder** (*échelle*) is an agile clamber across boulders. At the top of the ladder, follow the path up to **Col de Pertuis** (1512m), with sweeping views. Continue straight to Pic des Mémises – a 25-minute walk along a scree slope then grassy ridge path.

A 5.5m-tall oak cross signals **Pic des Mémises** (1674m; pictured). Picnic over a sublime panorama of subalpine peaks (including Dent d'Oche, Cornettes de Bise and Mont Billiat in France, the Swiss Jura across the lake and the snowy Swiss Alps). The big blue waters of Lake Geneva shimmer far below. For the descent, backtrack to Col de Pertuis then turn right to follow a well-signed path downhill for 45 minutes back to Col de Creusaz.

16

CHALETS DE BISE TO LAC DE DARBON

DURATION	DIFFICULTY	DISTANCE	START/END
3½hr return	Moderate	6.5km	Chalets de Bise, Vacheresse
TERRAIN	Rocky mountain path with several mountain climbs		

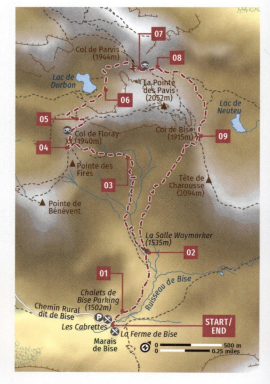

This spectacular circular walk climbs from grassy alpine pastures to a trio of mountain passes peppered with sunbathing ibex in summer. Find it in Haute-Savoie's cheese-fuelled Val d'Abondance (min/max altitude 1500/1955m).

GETTING HERE

From Châtel in ski area Les Portes du Soleil, drive 19km west along the D22 to Vacheresse. Turn left in the village towards 'Site de Bise', left again after 4.4km, then follow the wiggly, single-paved road to the end (another 4.7km).

STARTING POINT

From Chalets de Bise parking, stroll with serenading goats past chalet-restaurant Les Cabrettes to the farm shop and *refuge* La Ferme de Bise. Swing through the wooden gate in front to pick up the trailhead.

01 Follow the path uphill, admiring (right) the natural stone masonry of **Cornettes de Bise** (2432m), Val d'Abondance's highest peak.

02 Clanging cow bells will entertain as you traverse alpine pastures peppered with monk's rhubarb, yellow gentians, purple harebells and alpine crocuses. At the **La Salle** waymarker (1535m), take the left fork towards Col de Floray.

03 The uneven footpath becomes rockier as it zigzags up towards the crags of **La Pointe des Pavis** (2052m), looming large ahead. Listen out for – and spot – whistling marmots at the foot of the huge rocks. In August linger to pick wild petrol-blue bilberries.

04 The final leg up to **Col de Floray** (1940m) is steep and can be slippy when wet. At the top turn right, enjoying head-spinning **360-degree mountain views** as you walk along the ridge towards **Lac de Darbon** (1813m).

78/FRENCH ALPS & JURA

Alpage de Bise

A protected nature reserve at the foot of the imposing Cornettes de Bise (2432m), this remote alpine hamlet – snowed in and inaccessible in winter – is inhabited for just four months of the year by farmers who bring their Abondance cows up from the valley in June to graze here on higher summer pastures. Their milk goes into the valley's signature Reblochon, Abondance, Tome de Bauges and Beaufort cheeses, which have Appellation d'origine contrôlée (AOC; certification of origin).

Best for

WILDLIFE

NICOLA WILLIAMS/LONELY PLANET ©

05 **Bird's-eye lake views** come into view as the crest path drops off to the left and snakes downhill towards the crystal-clear water. Enjoy lake reflections of surrounding rocks and the spiky, needle-like **Aiguilles de Darbon** (2043m). Snow patches linger around the shore until June and, in early summer, **herds of shaggy ibex** lounge lakeside and in the rocks.

06 Follow the footpath (signposted Col de Parvis) around the eastern side of **Lac de Darbon** and bear right (east) uphill along the narrow footpath to **Col de Parvis** (1944m). Ibex often laze on steep sun-baked slopes here.

07 Cross the col's grassy plain sprinkled in late summer with **violet crocuses** and, on clear days, admire the **magnificent panorama of Lake Geneva** languishing far below.

08 The path, washed away in parts, swiftly descends to Montagne de Neuteu Est (1870m) and, five minutes further, Montagne de Neuteu Sud (1834m). Brace yourself for more visual high drama as it climbs gently back up past tiny **Lac de Neuteu** to **Col de Bise** (1915m).

09 Take a breather on the col's grassy banks over sweeping views of the tooth-like **Tête de Charousse** (2094m) and **Dent du Velan** (2087m).

Leave 45 minutes for the straightforward descent down to La Salle (1535m) and beyond to Chalets de Bise.

TAKE A BREAK

Grab an ice cream made with fresh cow's milk at the local farm (known as **La Ferme de Bise**) or reserve a table at **Les Cabrettes** (📞 09 88 18 47 77; Chalets de Bise; 🕐 Jun-Sep; 🅿️ 👪). Deep-fried *beignets de pommes de terre* (potato fritters) with local cheeses and charcuterie is the restaurant's wildly popular house speciality.

FRENCH ALPS & JURA/79

17

ARBOIS TO PUPILLIN

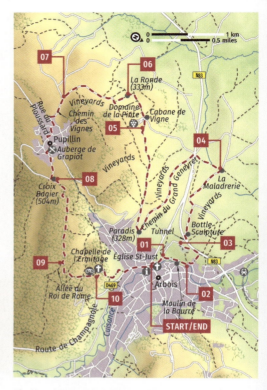

DURATION	DIFFICULTY	DISTANCE	START/END
4-5hr return	Moderate	13km	Arbois

TERRAIN	Paved lanes, vineyard tracks & forest footpaths

This serene vineyard loop in the Jura is for gourmets. Tasting opportunities at *caves* (wine cellars) in honey-coloured Arbois and yellow-brick Pupillin are highlights.

GETTING HERE
Arbois is a 50-minute drive (40km) southwest of Besançon along the N83. SNCF trains also link the two towns (€10, 40 to 50 minutes, hourly).

STARTING POINT
The trail begins by **Église St-Just**, opposite the tourist office on main street rue de l'Hôtel de Ville. Leave 20 minutes on foot from Arbois train station.

01 From the 'Arbois St-Just (293m)' sign by the church, follow rue du Souvenir Français to the cemetery, then turn right onto chemin de la Platière (signposted 'Sentier Pédestre') – a riverside footpath with **sweet views** of the Cuisance River and the 18th-century **Moulin de la Bourre** mill.

02 After 500m the path veers left onto rue Pointelin. At the next fork, turn left onto chemin des Loups and follow the road uphill onto a grassy footpath between vines. As the N83 pops into view, turn left.

03 Follow the cemetery wall, turn right through a tunnel under the N83, then turn left to follow a paved lane past vineyards for 1.2km to La Maladrerie. The **wrought-iron sculpture** of a glass and 6m-long bottle of *vin jaune* mid-pour (2012) is by Arbois artist-winemaker Freddy Wood.

04 From **La Maladrerie** enjoy 1.9km of mellow vineyard walking along country lanes to **Paradis** (328m). At the Paradis waymarker, fork sharp right to Pupillin, 4.1km south. Vineyards and fruit orchards groan with grapes, cherries, pears,

80/FRENCH ALPS & JURA

🍷 Vin Jaune

Arbois wines were France's first to gain an AOC in 1936.

Vin jaune (literally, 'yellow wine') – a slowly fermented, golden wine – is legendary. Savagnin grapes – unique to *vin jaune* – are harvested late and their sugar-saturated juice left to ferment at least six years and three months in oak barrels: 100L of grape juice ferments down to just 62L of *vin jaune*, then is bottled in a chubby 0.62L bottle called a *clavelin*. Prime vintages keep for more than a century.

apples and autumnal quince – *paradis* (paradise) for France lovers.

05 The lane climbs gently up to **Domaine de la Pinte**, one of the first estates to plant savagnin grapes in the 1950s. Admire the *cabane de vigne* (vineyard hut), used to store tools. At the road junction, continue straight to spaghetti downhill through vineyards.

06 At **La Ronde** (333m), continue straight ahead uphill – still between vines – and after 200m, at the top, turn sharply right. The vineyard panorama remains joyous now for the next 2km.

07 When the vineyard trail hits the tarmac road, turn left and climb up to **Pupillin village**. Several winemakers offer *dégustation* (tasting). From the main street, rue du Ploussard, walk 200m north, turn right uphill along rue Bagier, and further uphill along rue de la Croix Bagier into woods.

08 Arriving amid fields at the **Croix Bagier** (504m) waymarker next to a wooden cross, turn left towards Allée du Roi de Rome and follow the grassy footpath into the **forest**.

09 At the **Allée du Roi de Rome** waymarker, turn left towards Ermitage and Arbois–St-Just. Tramp through woods for

another 300m, then turn left downhill along the road (D469).

10 Arriving on Plateau de l'Ermitage, savour the village panorama from the lookout platform in the park. Continue 150m downhill to 17th-century **Chapelle de l'Ermitage** (closed), then follow stone steps and a forest track back to Arbois–St-Just, 1km away.

☕ TAKE A BREAK

Reserve a table at **Auberge de Grapiot** (📞 03 84 37 49 44; www.legrapiot.com; 3 rue Bagier; menus €25-75; ⏰ noon-1.30pm & 7-9.30pm Thu-Mon) in Pupillin. Chef Samuel Richardet cooks up an inventive cuisine from local produce.

FRENCH ALPS & JURA/81

18

CIRQUE DE BAUME-LES-MESSIEURS

Best for

EXPLORING HISTORY

DURATION	DIFFICULTY	DISTANCE	START/END
5-6hr return	Moderate	13km	Abbaye de Baume-les-Messieurs
TERRAIN	Forest footpaths, rocky steps with 2 short steep sections		

The thickly forested Jura is known for its *réculées* or *cirques* (steep-head or blind valleys), formed 200 million years ago by glacial erosion – and Cirque de Baume-les-Messieurs is the region's finest specimen. This circular day walk (min/max altitude 307/510m) takes you from Baume-les-Messieurs, sunken in the imposing limestone amphitheatre, up to its vertiginous limestone cliffs, and through fields and forests atop its horseshoe brow. Crashing waterfalls and bat-filled caves provide high-drama entertainment.

GETTING HERE

Leave 90 minutes to drive from Besançon to Baume-les-Messieurs (pictured), 82km south via the N83 and N193. En route, drive through cheese-fuelled Poligny and wine town Château-Chalon. The final approach, from the northwest along the D70, brings you past Baume's village cemetery, right across the bridge (D70E1), left along the left bank of the River Seille to Pont de l'Abbaye, and back across the river to Parking de l'Abbaye by Baume's iconic abbey (p84).

STARTING POINT

From the abbey car park, walk into the village along main street rue Guillaume Poupet, past the 'Fontaine (308m)' waymarker in front of the tourist office. After the *mairie* (town hall), turn immediately left down chemin du Gyp Bega, cross the river, and when you hit the tarmac road, turn left. Continue for about 10 minutes, past Pont de l'Abbaye, until you reach the 'Échelles de Sermu (Bas) 307m' waymarker.

01 Head uphill for 700m to **'Échelles de Sermu (Haut)'** – not an *échelle* or ladder at all, but several short flights of steep, irregular stone steps interspersed with scrubby footpaths fringed by wild blackberry bushes and piles of fallen rock.

As you climb **lovely village views** unfold – of Baume's 13th- to 16th-century Benedictine abbey and its surrounding patchwork of ancient stone-tiled roofs. Arriving on the plateau atop the limestone cliff, turn left towards Sermu.

02 The footpath – now delightfully flat and tree-shaded – snakes along the crest of Baume's trademark cliffs for 1.1km. Admire the sheer drop down to Baume-les-Messieurs on your left and grassy fields of grazing cows divided by crumbling dry-stone walls on your right.

After about 10 minutes, the path emerges from the trees to unveil a **180-degree panorama** of rocky limestone cliffs holding spectacular sentry on the other side of the deep blind valley – a mirror image of those you're standing on!

03 A line-up of beehives and tractors parked up in a barn herald your arrival in the tiny farming hamlet of **Sermu**. The footpath now joins a tarmac road; carry on straight, following signs for Belvédère des Roches (1.6km) and Grottes de Baume (2.4km).

04 Where the road forks to the right, continue straight and enjoy the peace and quiet of the country for another 10 to 15 minutes until you reach **Belvédère de Crançot** – a viewpoint at the valley's southern end. Bear left, following the road for another 100m to **Belvédère des Roches**

Grottes de Baume

Spawned during the Jurassic period, the spectacular **Grottes de Baume** (Baume Caves; 03 84 48 23 02; www.baumelesmessieurs.fr; adult/child €9/5.50; tours 10.30am-12.30pm & 1.30-5pm, 6pm or 7pm Apr-mid-Oct) were uncovered in 1610.

In the 19th century music concerts were held in the stalactite-laced cave chambers with soaring 71m-high ceilings.

Today niphargus (blind white cave shrimps with no eyes) swim in the cave lake and 5000 bats hibernate here for six months in winter. Watching 800-odd resident summer bats circle wildly overhead is a tour highlight.

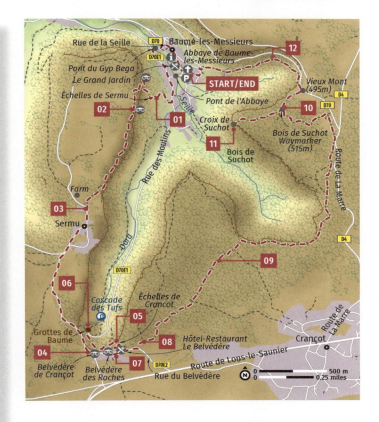

FRENCH ALPS & JURA/83

(507m), where more dramatic views of the cliff-ensnared, horseshoe valley unfold.

05 Turn left, following signs to Grottes de Baume (800m) and Échelles de Crancot (400m). The trail now leaves the road and descends sharply between trees to caves hidden in the cliffs via the **Échelles de Crancot** (irregular stone steps) slicing through woods. Mules laboured up and down here in the 19th century, carrying grains and freshly milled flour between farm and mill.

06 Break for a 55-minute **guided tour** of a 450m stretch of the sprawling 3km-long caves followed by a picnic perhaps – at tables in front of the cave ticket office or on the grass overlooking the neighbouring **Cascade des Tufs**, a huge mushroom-shaped waterfall where the Dard River dramatically crashes down over bulbous tuff beds. Later, retrace your steps up the Échelles de Crancot and back to the Belvédère des Roches waymarker by the road (D70E2).

07 Turn left towards Croix de Suchot, 3.6km away, and walk about 100m along the road (the D70E2), past **Hôtel-Restaurant Le Belvédère**, then turn left onto a gravel road marked with a small 'Croix Suchot' sign nailed on a tree.

08 When the road forks, bear right into the forest. At the next fork, continue straight, always following the single yellow horizontal stripe painted on trees that now marks the leafy forest trail (actually part of the GR59). At the next couple of forks, simply follow the yellow stripe – ignore forks marked with a yellow cross.

09 Enjoy a mellow amble along the shaded forest path, flat and carpeted with golden leaves in autumn. The occasional picnic table in a sun-dappled clearing encourages lingering. Watch out for the odd mountain biker tearing along the same dirt track.

10 After about an hour don't be surprised to hear the faint rumble of motorised traffic as the path strays towards the forest edge. Arriving at the **'Bois de Suchot (515m)' waymarker**, turn left towards the Croix de Suchot, 400m away. Almost immediately the footpath forks – bear right.

11 At the **Croix de Suchot** – a large wooden crucifix atop a hillock at 510m – the 11km you have walked are rewarded with a beautiful panorama of Baume village and its rock amphitheatre spreadeagled far below.

12 The final 2km to the village is a well-posted stroll back through the forest and past a field of beehives. Upon hitting the road (D70) after 700m at **Vieux Mont** (495m), turn left downhill, round the bend and pick up another forest footpath on your left (look for the same single yellow stripe and a sign indicating horses are forbidden to use the path). Zigzag along the narrow path between trees until the the stone-spired abbey pops into view. End with a serene walk around the abbey's elegant trio of historic courtyards. In 16th-century **Cour du Cloître**, dip your hands in the central fountain.

Abbaye Impériale

Baume-les-Messieurs' Benedictine **abbey** (Imperial Abbey; ☎ 03 84 44 99 28; www.baumelesmessieurs.fr; adult/child €8/5; ⏰ tours 10am-noon & 2-6pm Apr-Sep) grew in the 7th century. In 910, its abbot, Bernon (c 850–927), set out with six monks from Baume to establish western Europe's most influential monastical abbey at Cluny in Burgundy.

Guided visits at the abbey include the church, with its 15th-century sculpted doorway, 71m-long arched nave and exquisite polychrome Flemish altarpiece in the choir (pictured) dating from the 16th century (the period when the abbey was at its apogee). In 1759, Pope Clement XIII signed a bill turning the abbey into a secular chapter house.

TAKE A BREAK

Footsteps from the main abbey entrance in the village, **Le Grand Jardin** (☎ 03 84 44 68 37; www.legrandjardin.fr; 6 place Guillaume de Poupet; menus €22-40; ⏰ closed Tue & Wed Sep-Jun; P) serves regional dishes prepared with a personal touch, such as rabbit stuffed with *saucisse de Morteau* (sausage) and char (a type of fish) with absinthe. The artisanal ice cream (absinthe, apricot or violet anyone?) is among the Jura's finest. There are a handful of B&B rooms above for overnighting in style.

84/FRENCH ALPS & JURA

19

TÊTE DE LA MAYE

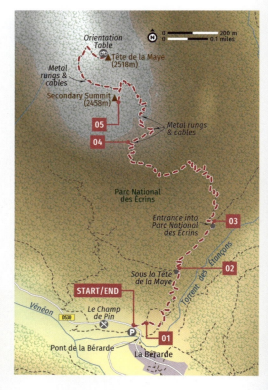

DURATION	DIFFICULTY	DISTANCE	START/END
4hr return	Hard	7km	La Bérarde

TERRAIN	Steep rocky path; vertiginous sections with cables

It isn't the highest peak in the park, but on clear days the 2518m-high summit of Tête de la Maye rewards with a 360-degree panorama of France's second-largest national park. The way up is steep (min/max altitude 1719/2518m) and challenging rock faces make it unsuitable for children.

GETTING HERE
From Grenoble it is a 1½-hour drive (85km) southeast, via Le Bourg d'Oisans, to La Bérarde. This wildly remote hamlet lies at the end of the narrow, sinuous D530 in the dead-end Vénéon Valley.

STARTING POINT
Follow the only road (D530) through the hamlet to the car park immediately before the green bridge across the crashing glacial water of Torrent des Étançons. The yellow **Pont de la Bérarde** (1719m) trail marker is on the left.

01 The rocky footpath up to Tête de la Maye – signposted 2.8km but a little over 3km – climbs mercilessly from the second it leaves the roadside. Basic chalet huts with metal-sheet roofs and scant decorative frills hint at how harsh life is in this remote alpine valley. Dangerous rockfalls in winter force the few who live here to abandon the valley from October to May.

02 As the path zigzags up the mountain past pine, birch and mountain ash trees that **blaze with cherry-red berries** in late-summer, admire the forbidding 3421m-high peak of **Grande Aiguille de la Bérarde** across the valley. This is the giant of a mountain that the low winter sun fails to eclipse, depriving the hamlet of direct sunlight for several

86/FRENCH ALPS & JURA

Parc National des Écrins

Glacial action and the thrashing Durance and Drac rivers carved out France's second-largest national park (www.ecrins-parcnational.fr). An awe-imposing 918-sq-km expanse of mountains and steel-grey moraines stretching between the towns of Le Bourg d'Oisans, Briançon and Gap, the Écrins National Park showcases 100-plus peaks, climaxing with the Barre des Écrins (4102m). Some 700km of walking trails follow in the footsteps of shepherds and yesteryear smugglers, passing en route glaciers, beech forests, waterfalls, wild blueberry fields and summer meadows sprinkled with flowers.

months of the year. After 10 minutes, at the **'Sous la Tête de la Maye'** waymarker, follow the path around to the right.

03 Ten minutes on (or 800m into the walk), a French flag painted on a boulder and information panel marks your entrance into the **Parc National des Écrins**. About 30m further, at the fork, bear left to **'Tête de la Maye'**. Peer down to see gushing **Torrent de Bonne Pierre** fed by the Bonne Pierre glacier.

04 At the 1.85km mark, **metal rungs and cables** drilled into the rock help walkers safely cross a 250m-long wall on the mountain's austere south face. Three more sections of steps and cables follow. The final assisted rock climb up a short dramatic gully rewards with **dizzying views** of the glacier-gouged valley below.

05 After two hours of walking Tête de la Maye's **secondary summit** (2458m) appears, recognisable by its flat stoney dome. Continue for almost another kilometre to the **summit** – red-and-white stripes on the rocks and cairns left wayside by other walkers mark the way. A **ceramic orientation table** identifies surrounding peaks. Return to La Bérarde the same way.

 TAKE A BREAK

Squirrelled away roadside at the western end of La Bérarde, friendly hotel-*refuge*-restaurant **Le Champ de Pin** (04 76 79 54 09; www.lechampdepin.com; lunch & dinner May–late Sep;) is a delicious spot for refuelling post-hike on traditional *gratin de crozets au sarrasin* (buckwheat pasta with wild spinach, cheese and potatoes), *tartiflette* (oven-baked cheese, bacon and melted Reblochon cheese) and mixed charcuterie platters. Produce is strictly local and artisanal. Summer dining is alfresco beneath a mountain ash tree, and a wood-burning stove keeps the rustic interior warm and cosy.

20

LAC DES VACHES & COL DE LA VANOISE

Best for

ESCAPING THE CROWDS

DURATION	DIFFICULTY	DISTANCE	START/END
5-7hr return	Hard	15.2km	Les Fontanettes car park

TERRAIN	Forest trails, gravel roads & rocky mountain paths

A cinematic stone walkway across water, spectacular lakes and gargantuan glaciers are highlights of this challenging walk in Savoie's Massif de la Vanoise. Ensnared within France's oldest national park, the trail today (min/max altitude 1650/2516m) piggybacks part of the celebrated GR55.

GETTING HERE

The trail begins in the low-key mountain village of Pralognan-la-Vanoise on the western fringe of the Parc National de la Vanoise. Leave 1½ hours to drive from Chambéry (105km west) and an hour from Albertville (50km northwest) or Bourg St-Maurice (55km northeast). Approaching the village from the north along the D915, turn left at the roundabout before the village centre and head uphill for 2.5km, following signs for 'Les Fontanettes'.

STARTING POINT

Park in Les Fontanettes' car park, servicing a trio of ski lifts at 1650m. The trail starts by the yellow 'Parking des Fontanettes' waymarker opposite the Télésiège de l'Eidelweiss (chairlift).

01 Walk uphill along the gently inclined footpath through **pine forest and grassy ski piste**s, following signs for 'Refuge et Col de la Vanoise'. The first drag lift whisked winter skiers up the picturesque slopes here in 1937 and Pralognan-la-Vanoise has been an enchanting family ski resort ever since.

02 After 650m the forest path emerges onto a gravel road. Cross it and follow the footpath back into the forest, past the yellow 'Dou de l'Ecu' waymarker at 1770m. About 200m further, don't get confused when the path briefly crosses a mountain-bike track – simply continue uphill.

88/FRENCH ALPS & JURA

03 Emerging from the forest onto another gravel road, turn right and follow it briefly. At the yellow 'GR55' marker, follow 'Col de la Vanoise' signs back into the woods, arriving about 20 minutes later beneath a chairlift. Continue uphill for another five to **Refuge des Barmettes** at 2000m.

04 The trail continues up behind the *refuge*, winding right over a bridge to cross the crystal-clear **Torrent de la Glière**. Ahead, spellbinding views of the Massif de la Vanoise's mightiest peaks distract: the shark fin of **Aiguille de la Vanoise** (2797m) with its legendary north face and, to the left, the massif's highest peak **Grande Casse** (3855m).

05 The path curves gently uphill between **dry-stone walls**. These beautifully crafted walls trace part of the historic Salt Road across Plateau de la Glière. Underfoot is rocky now. To the right (east) rises the flat stoney crown of **Le Moriond** (2298m).

06 After passing the abandoned shepherds huts of **Chalets de la Glière** (2060m) the trail steepens.

Waterfalls crash down the mountainside ahead. Tall wooden poles sticking out of the path-side scrub every few metres were planted in the 1830s to guide early alpinists up to the Col de la Vanoise; many poles conveniently remain.

07 About 3.5km into the walk, the path steers closer to the banks of Torrent de la Glière. Cross the thundering glacial water using wooden footbridge **Pont de Canton** and continue up the rocky path towards Grande Casse and its glacier.

Route du Sel

The Col de la Vanoise has been a vital link between the high-altitude Maurienne and Tarentaise valleys since the Bronze Age.

The Romans used it to flit between Rome and Lyon, and in the 11th century the Dukes of Savoy travelled across it from Chambery to Turin.

In the 18th century mules laboured across the high mountain pass, carrying salt from the Royal Saltworks in nearby Moûtiers to Piedmont, Italy; they returned laden with spices and fabrics. Local Beaufort cheese, tanned leathers and mountain honey were likewise exchanged for potatoes, rice and corn on the strategic trade route.

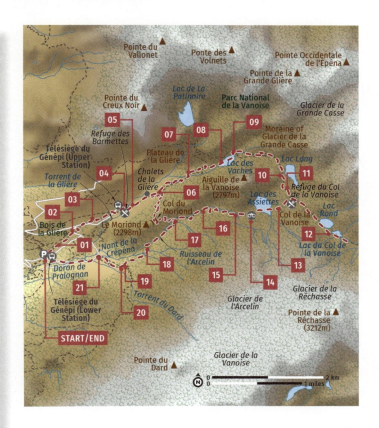

FRENCH ALPS & JURA/89

08 **Lac des Vaches** (Lake of Cows) is cradled in an amphitheatre at 2318m and is stunning. Giant stone slabs (pictured) form a spectacular **210m-long walkway** across the lake which, when shallow enough in August and September, doubles as boggy pasture for grazing Abondance cows.

09 From the lake, a rubble path zigzags steeply up the slate-grey moraine of the Glacier de la Grande Casse. Specks of glacier-white quartz in the grey dirt glitter in the sun, and **fuchsia-pink cornflowers and yellow star-shaped stonecrops** add colour to the desolate grey landscape.

10 Listen to the echoing voices of climbers dangling from the limestone crags of Aiguille de la Vanoise as you approach **Lac Long**, a lake right beneath the Glacier de la Grande Casse's icy tongue. You are now 6km into the walk.

11 The footpath flattens as it heads towards the grassy plain of Col de la Vanoise (2516m), 700m from Lac Long. Walkers on the long-distance GR55 trail bask on the sun-drenched terrace of **Refuge du Col de la Vanoise**, a historic mountain hut from 1902 completely rebuilt with solar panels and other ecological frills in 2014. **Views** of Grand Casse's western face are awe-inspiring.

12 Walk past the refuge on your right and follow the footpath for another kilometre across the flattish col and gently down through tufty alpine grass to bijou **Lac Rond** and, 200m further, **Lac du Col de la Vanoise**. Wedged between the mammoth peaks of Grand Caisse (left) and Pointe de la Réchasse (right), these two lakes are a sublime picnic spot.

13 Return to the refuge and bear left (southwest), past the helipad behind the modern building, to pick up the return trail to **Lac des Assiettes**, a 15-minute walk. Bear right at the fork and descend across rocks and boulders down to the lake bowl – as dry as a bone in summer.

14 Cross the flat-as-a-pancake bottom of the 'lake', admiring, on the right, huge views of Aiguille de la Vanoise's southern face. Scale the bank the other side to enjoy a new panorama of **Aiguille du Fruit** (3048m), **Petit Mont Blanc** (2680m) – named such after its Mont Blanc–like rounded dome coloured white with gypsum – and other peaks.

15 Follow the path gently downhill, enjoying **dramatic views** down the valley. Continue straight, crossing the summer-dry stream bed of the **Ruisseau de l'Arcelin**. Take it slow where the path scrambles across rocks.

16 The path now closely follows the course of the Arcelin. Marmot whistles warn of your descent past the rocky Aiguilles de l'Arcelin.

DABOOST/SHUTTERSTOCK ©

Parc National de la Vanoise

France's first national park, created in 1963, is a 529-sq-km protected zone packed with 100-plus peaks over 3000m in the Massif de la Vanoise. High-altitude glaciers, moraines and lichen-spattered rock rise above alpine meadows and spruce forests. Marmots, chamois and France's largest colony of *bouquetins* (alpine ibexes) – around 1800 – graze freely beneath larch trees and 125 bird species wheel overhead. Find information in situ at **Maison de la Vanoise** (04 79 08 71 49; www.pralognan.com; av de Chasseforêt, Pralognan-la-Vanoise; 9am-noon & 3-7pm late Dec-late Mar & late Jun-early Sep).

17 At the 11.8km mark the trail splits: right to **Col du Moriond** (30 minutes) and back to Refuge des Barmettes (one hour) along a family-friendly trail; or straight ahead via a more challenging descent only recommended on dry summer days. This walk tackles the latter.

18 The path descends sharply, crossing the hillside to arrive on the rocky right bank of the **Nant de la Crépéna**. After five minutes or so, follow the trail over the **wooden bridge** to the left bank of the dramatic rock-creviced stream. In late summer it can be completely dry.

19 Continue along the trail; yellow plaques emblazoned with a stubby arrow ensure you stay on track. A brief section between trees provides shade. Where the path splits, ignore the left-hand path signposted 'Col du Grand Marchais & Refuge de la Vallette' and continue downhill.

20 At the national park sign the path forks again; bear left and continue downhill, don't miss the dramatic view of the **Torrent du Dard waterfall** gushing out of the rocky mountainside high above on the left.

21 Arriving on a gravel road at the bottom of the **Cirque de l'Arcelin** (1720m), admire, to your right, the ice-blue river of Nant de la Crépéna thundering under a wooden-plank bridge. Don't cross it. Rather, head left along the gravel road for 15 minutes to the car park at Les Fontanettes.

TAKE A BREAK

An enchanting wood-decking terrace with mountain views and love hearts carved in its wooden balustrade lend **Refuge des Barmettes** (04 79 08 75 64; www.lesbarmettes-refuge.com; Pralognon-la-Vanoise; late Dec-Mar & Jun-Sep), atop the Génépi chairlift, instant sex appeal. Higher up, **Refuge du Col de la Vanoise** (04 79 08 25 23; www.refugecoldelavanoise.ffcam.fr; dm €25.50, mains €8-12; Mar-late Sep) serves salads, sweet and savoury crêpes, sandwiches to take away and irresistible blueberry tarts. Bookend stops at either address with shots of local *génépi*.

FRENCH ALPS & JURA/**91**

Also Try...

HUANG ZHENG/SHUTTERSTOCK ©

TOUR DU MONT BLANC

Hands-down the most revered multiday walk in the French Alps, the TMB takes you right around – literally – Europe's highest peak.

Beginning and ending in the Chamonix 'suburb' of Les Houches via drop-dead gorgeous trails in neighbouring Italy and Switzerland, the celebrated Tour du Mont Blanc is a 10-day loop encircling Mont Blanc. The classic 10-day, 170km-long, anticlockwise route involves 7km to 21km walking a day; many cut the trek into shorter multi-day chunks and it is also possible to mix-and-match walking with public transport. The trail never climbs higher than 3000m in altitude, meaning walkers don't require special equipment – anyone with a decent fitness level can walk it (pictured above). Find maps, route suggestions, accommodation lists, trail conditions, bus/train and cable-car timetables and other useful information at www.autourdumontblanc.com.

DURATION 10 days return
DIFFICULTY Moderate-hard
DISTANCE 170km

AIGUILLE DE LA GRANDE SASSIÈRE

Hanging out with the birds at a heady 3747m, this high-altitude summit in the Réserve Naturelle de la Grande Sassière is an epic invitation to stand on top of the world.

Unlike other mountain peaks of similar heights in the French Alps, Aiguille de la Grande Sassière can be summited without setting foot on its glacier – making a steep walk up to its panoramic summit (elevation gain 1510m) accessible to anyone with a decent fitness level. The weather (strictly sunny bluebird days only) and the time of year (late-June to August) is also crucial. The memorable trail climbs from the car park on the shore of Lac du Saut, 25 minutes' drive from the big-name ski resorts of Tignes and Val d'Isère, through grassy alpine pastures and barren rocks, to the icy edge of the Sassière glacier and beyond.

DURATION 6hr return
DIFFICULTY Hard
DISTANCE 14km

THE GR5

Walkers eager to 'do' the French Alps should consider this legendary long-distance trail.

This GR5 or 'Grande Traversée des Alpes Françaises' (Great French Alps Crossing) crosses the Alps en route from Thonon-les-Bains or St-Gingolph on Lake Geneva's southern shore to Nice or Menton on the Med. It tackles peaks and passes up to 3000m, wild valleys and glaciers in Haute-Savoie, Savoie, Chamonix, Parc National de la Vanoise and south to Haute-Provence and beyond. Leave 20 days to walk to Briançon – in one trek or chunks of approximately 20km a day.

DURATION 32-46 days one way
DIFFICULTY Hard
DISTANCE 650km

CIRQUE DU FER-À-CHEVAL

Accessed from Sixt-Fer-à-Cheval in the Grand Massif ski area, this circular walk plunges walkers into an amphitheatre of limestone cliffs spring-loaded with shimmering waterfalls.

This classic trail leads families to Le Bout de Monde – 'the end of the world'. Highlights include a Himalayan bridge across the river (pictured above) and snow fields well into early summer. June is the best month to admire the spectacular waterfalls crashing 500m down from the cliffs into the valley below.

DURATION 3hr return
DIFFICULTY Easy
DISTANCE 9km

CIRQUE DES ÉVETTES

Discovering one of France's most beautiful villages and the Alps' highest mountain-pass road are thrilling add-ons to this high-altitude loop in Parc National de la Vanoise.

A good one to tackle after Lac des Vaches & Col de la Vanoise (p88), this day walk (elevation 700m) begins near gorgeous Bonneval-sur-Arc (1850m) at the southern end of the world-famous Col de l'Iseran (2764m) road pass. It climbs from L'Écot up through gorges to the Reculaz waterfall and beyond to the glacial scape of Col des Évettes (2561m) with lake and *refuge*.

DURATION 6-7hr return
DIFFICULTY Hard
DISTANCE 9km

CENTRAL FRANCE

21 **Brantôme Circuit** A countryside amble around the river-laced town of Brantôme for all the family. p98

22 **Lac Chambon & Murol Circuit** Castle and lake combine to make a perfect family walk. p100

23 **Beynac Castle Loop** A fairy-tale castle and quiet woodlands make for a delightful walk. p102

24 **The Chemin de Halage** Walk to one of France's prettiest villages along a cliff-carved towpath. p104

25 **Pilgrimage Around Rocamadour** Follow in the footsteps of pilgrims walking to this cliffside village. p106

26 **Stevenson's Journey** A walk through literary history and rugged scenery. p108

27 **Climbing Puy de Dôme** Trek to the top of an ancient lava dome. p110

28 **Ascent to Puy de Sancy** Hiking to the top of this ancient stratovolcano reveals sublime views. p112

29 **Castles of the Dordogne** Towering castles, cliffside villages and beautiful oak woodlands. p114

CENTRAL FRANCE/95

Explore
CENTRAL FRANCE

Central France – the Dordogne, Lot and Auvergne regions – is the heart and soul of la belle France with lands of dense oak forests, ancient volcanoes and chains of cinder cones, winding rivers, emerald-green fields, fairy-tale châteaux and picture-perfect villages. Walking through this area offers the quintessential French experience.

BRANTÔME

Enchanting Brantôme's visual centrepiece is its impressive abbey sandwiched between a cliff face and a bend of the River Dronne. The town is a big tourist destination and has lots of places to stay and eat as well as good transport connections to other towns in the region.

SARLAT-LA-CANÉDA

The beautiful old-town heart of Sarlat-la-Canéda boasts some of the region's best-preserved medieval architecture and it makes an ideal base for walks 23 and 29. The start point for both of these walks is only around a 15-minute drive from Sarlat.

ROCAMADOUR

It's hard to resist a little gasp as Rocamadour first swings into view, its rooftops and shrines clamped dramatically to a plunging rock face of the Alzou Gorge. Most magical at sunset, the scene is topped by a dainty little 14th-century château on the overhanging clifftop above.

ST-CIRQ-LAPOPIE

Magical St-Cirq-Lapopie is the sort of place people take one look at and decide they'd like to stay forever. While you might not be in a situation to do this, if you do walk 24 then you'll at least have to spend a day here. As a small and very popular place it can be hard to get accommodation here in summer: book well in advance.

MUROL

Bisected by a gargling river and enclosed by forests, the stone village of Murol slows the pulse. There are a few two-star hotels and campgrounds near Lac Chambon, while Murol village has several B&Bs and *gîtes* (self-catering accommodation), which must be booked ahead.

LE PUY-EN-VELAY

With two volcanic pillars looming craggily above its rooftops, it would be impossible to mistake Le Puy-en-Velay for anywhere else in France. Topped with a 10th-century church and a vermillion statue of the Virgin Mary, these stone pinnacles tower hundreds of feet high, like two sacred rockets in the middle of blast-off.

There's a good choice of accommodation in all price ranges as well as *gîtes* and *chambres d'hôte* (B&Bs) in the surrounding countryside.

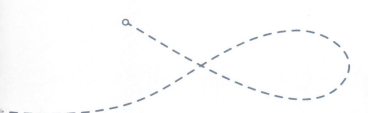

LE MONT-DORE

The Auvergne's most elegant mountain resort has a glint of 19th-century glamour among its fondue restaurants and gear-hire shops. Nestled in a narrow valley 42km southwest of Clermont-Ferrand, and 4km north of Puy de Sancy (1886m), the town originally rose to prominence as a spa resort. Today it's an ideal base for walkers taking on the nearby trails.

 WHEN TO GO

The Dordogne and Lot regions have a gentle climate that's rarely too hot and only truly cold for a few short weeks in midwinter. This means that you can hike in this area at pretty much anytime of the year. But winter and spring can see a lot of rainfall and many hotels and guesthouses close.

In summer the sheer popularity of the region can be an issue. Accommodation can be hard to come by and honeypot villages such as Brantôme and St-Cirq-Lapopie can be unpleasantly busy. May and June are great times to hike here, but the best period by far is September and early October. Time it right and you can get idyllic temperatures, blue skies and an autumnal colour show in the extensive chestnut and oak woodlands.

The Massif Central has a much more extreme climate and winters at altitude are cold indeed, with snowfall common. Avoid hiking here from late October to the end of April. Spring can be wet one year, perfect the next. The ideal period is May through to September.

 WHERE TO STAY

Central France offers a full range of places to stay from historic châteaux to farmhouse bed and breakfasts, camping grounds and many holiday-home rentals. Wherever you stay, it is usually essential to book ahead in July and August. From November to April much closes down, but what stays open is often great value.

 WHAT'S ON

La Ringueta (www.ringueta-sarlat.fr) Traditional sports and games of the region held in Sarlat over the Whit-Sunday weekend of even-numbered years.

Festival des Jeux du Théâtre (www.festival-theatre-sarlat.com; mid-Jul–early Aug) Held in Sarlat, this is one of the most important theatre festivals in France.

Semaine Mariale (early Sep) Held in Rocamadour, this week-long religious festival is dedicated to the Virgin and includes pilgrimages and a torchlit procession.

Rassemblement Européen de Montgolfières Major hot-air balloon festival held in Rocamadour on the third weekend in September.

 TRANSPORT

Bergerac, Limoges and Brive-la-Gaillarde have domestic and international flights. Bordeaux and Toulouse are also nearby hubs. Local train service in the region is limited. This, coupled with limited bus service keyed to school timetables, makes much of rural Central France a good place to hire a car.

21

BRANTÔME CIRCUIT

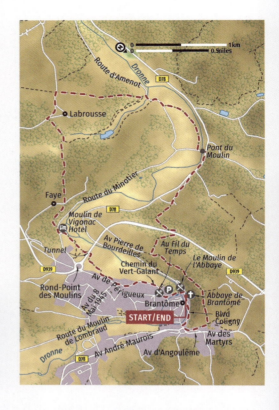

DURATION	DIFFICULTY	DISTANCE	START/END
3hr return	Easy	10km	Brantôme Abbey

TERRAIN	Road, walking trail

Built on a great bend of the River Dronne and overlooked by an enormous abbey, Brantôme is one of the most alluring towns in the Dordogne. This walk takes in the abbey as well as the patchwork of fields, woodlands and farming hamlets that surround the town.

With your back facing the **abbey** turn right and cross the **stone bridge** next to the Michelin-starred restaurant, **Le Moulin de l'Abbaye**, a much-photographed riverside delight. Cross through the park and right onto **chemin du Vert-Galant**. Just before the traffic lights, turn right down a track. After five minutes go through a tunnel under the D939 road. On the other side turn left and then immediately right. Walk past the **Moulin de Vigonac hotel**. Turn right by the stop sign and then left onto a walking trail through woodland.

Climb uphill to the village of **Faye** and then straight ahead on a forest trail. On reaching a road at the entrance to the village of **Labrousse**, turn right and go uphill.

Fifty metres after the last house, turn right and stroll across the fields into **oak woodlands**. Turn right along a quiet road and after 100m take the trail leading off left across **fields**. At another small road, turn left and cross the **metalled Pont du Moulin**. At the main road, turn right and after 200m you will see two roads turning off left. Take the **second road**. At the junction continue straight ahead down a track. At the fork go right and cross the D939 road via a **bridge**. Go left at the junction and walk for 15 minutes through a mix of woodland and farmland. At a meeting of junctions go right and then right again at the **T-junction** and re-enter Brantôme.

98/CENTRAL FRANCE

22

LAC CHAMBON & MUROL CIRCUIT

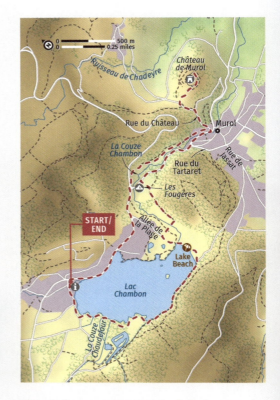

DURATION	DIFFICULTY	DISTANCE	START/END
2hr return	Easy	8km	Tourist office, Lac Chambon
TERRAIN	Level boardwalks and paved uphills			

Admire a hilly panorama from Château de Murol, then meander along tranquil lake shores. This family-friendly walk (min/max altitude 876/1050m) unites quaint streets, watery views and medieval ramparts that kids will love to clamber.

From the tourist office car park, turn left and stroll along Lac Chambon's north shore, heading east towards the village of Murol. To your right is the glass-still **crater lake** (altitude 876m). To the left, holiday homes and restaurants snooze by the water. At the second roundabout, follow tree-shaded rue de Levat along the north bank of the river. Continue for 15 minutes, past stone houses lining the babbling **Couze Chambon**.

Take a left uphill along rue du Château, weaving through beech forest to **Château de Murol**. A sweeping panorama of the Auvergne's volcano-sculpted terrain is the reward for the final ascent.

These 12th-century ramparts overlook the town from a basalt perch. Give your calf muscles a rest by staying awhile to tour the castle. **Château de Murol** (pictured) hosts glinting medieval weaponry and audiovisual displays to entrance the kids.

Descend from the castle, your head swirling with images of sparring knights. This time, at the foot of the hill take rue d'Estaing west through the village. Turn left into **Les Fougères** campground and continue south to the shore of Lac Chambon. Join the lakeside trail clockwise around Lac Chambon; **wooden boardwalks** guide your way. In winter, the shore is fringed with frost – watch your step on the slippery planks!

As you ramble the eastern shore, look across the water to see the **Massif de Sancy**, whose peaks are dusted with snow well into spring. Along Lac Chambon's pike-filled waters, signposts point back to the car park. A playground and summer kayak rental might prolong your stay.

23

BEYNAC CASTLE LOOP

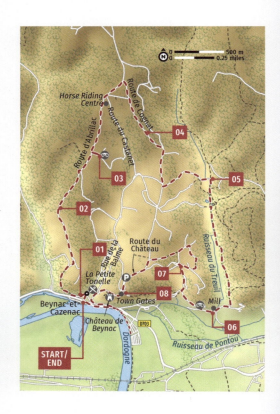

DURATION	DIFFICULTY	DISTANCE	START/END
3¼hr return	Easy	10km	Beynac
TERRAIN	Road, farm track, walking trail		

Fairy tales really do come true along the banks of slow-flowing rivers in Central France. Hoisted atop a beach-yellow cliff and with a honeycomb of wobbly medieval houses at its feet, the Château de Beynac is straight from a Hans Christian Anderson story. And this walk (suitable for families) will take you through dense woodlands where the big bad wolf once lived and down trails where knights in armour might once have searched for dragons to slay, before finally arriving at the old gates of this magical village and castle.

GETTING HERE

Beynac is 12km southwest of Sarlat; there is no public transport. Various parking lots cost €3.50 per day April to October, but are free out of season.

STARTING POINT

The walk begins from the riverfront at the bottom of the village. There are plenty of parking areas here, but in summer it's still hard to find a space.

01 Go up the main village street, **rue de la Balme**. Take the first narrow, **cobbled road** on the left. Go through the wooden barrier and into the woods.

02 When you reach a quiet road turn right. The road turns into a dirt track and loops left past a clutch of **stone houses**. Keep going straight.

03 After 35 minutes, you'll come to a road junction. Go left. Shortly afterwards, you'll see some walking signposts. The main route continues straight ahead, but turn right and walk 150m over the field to a fine **view over Beynac castle**. Return back to the main trail and carry on straight (northeast) past a horse-riding centre.

102/CENTRAL FRANCE

Château de Beynac

The 12th-century **Château de Beynac** (📞 05 53 29 50 40; www.chateau-beynac.com; Beynac-et-Cazenac; adult/child €9.50/7; ⏰ 10am-7pm) towers gloriously above the village (pictured).

The views from its battlements are a big draw and the interior retains a sparse, medieval feel with decor limited to carved fireplaces, wooden coffer-trunks and the odd tapestry.

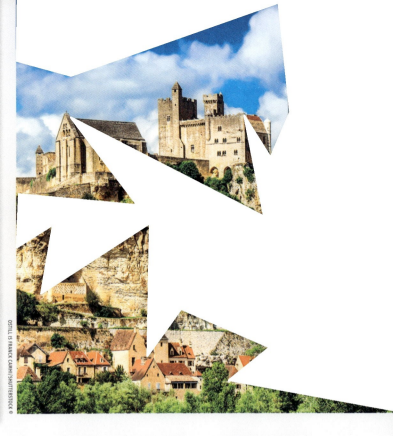

04 Immediately after is a road junction. Yellow walk arrows tell you to turn right and double back on yourself. Ignore these and instead carry on straight for another 200m to another junction. Go sharp right here and descend down a **quiet country lane**. You will soon pass a **row of houses**. At the road junction go right. After about 350m take the small country road veering off left. There's a yellow walk sign.

05 Turn right when you hit a bigger track and walk through some lovely **woodland**.

06 Go right when you hit the road again and pass a mill with **donkeys and peacocks** in a field beside it. A moment later the **Château de Beynac** makes a dramatic appearance on the cliffs ahead. Continue uphill.

07 At the junction, go right and then right again at the fork. As you reach the houses go left down a **grassy track**. When the road bends left and goes downhill, take the walking trail leading off to the right through **woodland**.

08 Go left on reaching the road and then right at the junction. A moment later the castle will reappear, this time towering above the village houses right in front of you. Walk past the **cemetery** and through the old town gates. Fork right and you'll come to the **castle entrance**. Allow a couple of hours for a visit. Afterwards drop steeply down through the pretty village until you get back to the river. Walk a short way along the river past the campsite for **postcard-worthy views**.

 TAKE A BREAK

La Petite Tonelle (📞 05 53 29 95 18; www.la-petite-tonnelle.fr; menus €20-45; ⏰ noon-2.30pm & 7-9.30pm Fri-Tue) serves an array of seasonal, local specialities (truffles, duck, lamb).

24

THE CHEMIN DE HALAGE

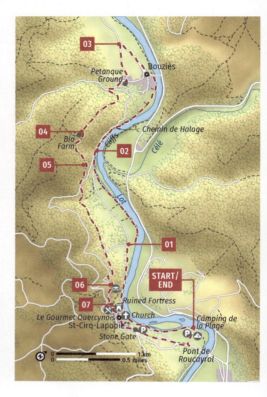

DURATION	DIFFICULTY	DISTANCE	START/END
4hr return	Easy	16km	Parking de la Plage

TERRAIN	Road, farm track, walking trail

Teetering at the crest of a sheer cliff, high above the River Lot, St-Cirq-Lapopie is a beautiful braid of terracotta-roofed houses and vertiginous streets that's rightly known as one of the most beautiful villages in France.

This walk gives you a variety of different views of the village, takes in a memorable boat towpath carved into a leering cliff face and rambles through extensive oak forests before finishing up back in the enchanted village of St-Cirq-Lapopie.

GETTING HERE
St-Cirq-Lapopie is 25km east of Cahors and 44km southwest of Figeac. There are irregular buses from Cahors and Figeac.

STARTING POINT
The walk begins from the Parking de la Plage, next to the Camping de la Plage and just east and downhill of St-Cirq-Lapopie. There are no facilities.

01 Follow the footpath along the River Lot in a downstream direction. The trail merges onto a country lane. The **views of St-Cirq-Lapopie** up ahead will put a wow in your step. After a good 40 minutes swerve right off the road and onto a **walking trail**, following signs for the **Chemin de Halage**. After 20 minutes the enjoyably easy riverside trail leads to the point where the sheer cliff face stands straight up against the river.

02 An amazing engineering feat, the **Chemin de Halage** (pictured) is a footpath carved into the side of the cliff face like a half-tunnel. After 300m pass an iron **train bridge** and a few minutes later enter the village of **Bouziès**. Continue along the river up to another iron bridge.

104/CENTRAL FRANCE

03 At the walk signs, turn left and head up to the main village road. Turn right and then at the fork go left and then left again. When you come to the **stone cross** bend left. Fifty metres later, in front of the **petanque ground**, turn right and then right again following the route to **Combe de Bouziès**. One hundred metres on, turn left sharply and, following yellow waymarkers, embark on a 20-minute haul uphill.

04 Just before the **bio farm**, take the footpath that leads off left. Pass through three gates.

05 After the final gate follow the footpath through **oak forest**. After 15 minutes cross a road and back onto the footpath, which continues its woodland descent.

06 On reaching a small **road**, follow it uphill and after five minutes take the walking trail that leads off left. A moment later, you will pass the first of the St-Cirq-Lapopie car parks. At the far end of the car park is a **viewpoint**.

07 Take the signed walkway next to the car park and a water tower. Follow this down to another set of car parks, turn left and drop down into **St-Cirq-Lapopie**. Climb up the crumbling **fortress walls** for aerial views. Go past the **church** and follow the road downhill right through the village before exiting through a stone gate. Keep going straight and start a slow drop to the river, and back to the car park.

 **TAKE A BREAK**

Le Gourmet Quercynois (📞 05 65 31 21 20; www.restaurant-legourmet quercynois.com; rue de la Peyrolerie; lunch/dinner from €14/23; 🕐 noon–1.30pm & 7-9pm mid-Feb–Dec) serves well-prepared local classics. The village of Bouziès has a few snack bars. There are also riverside picnic tables here.

CENTRAL FRANCE/105

25

PILGRIMAGE AROUND ROCAMADOUR

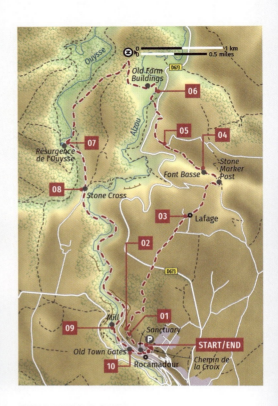

DURATION	DIFFICULTY	DISTANCE	START/END
3¾hr return	Moderate	12km	Le Château car park, Rocamadour

TERRAIN	Road, farm track, walking trail

This walk, up and along canyon ridges and across farmland, follows in the footsteps of medieval pilgrims bound for the cliff-side village of Rocamadour.

Today, Rocamadour sits precariously on the very edge of sheer cliff walls and is one of the biggest tourist draws in Central France, but by walking this circuit around the village you can escape the crowds and recreate the sense of awed wonder that must have swept over pilgrims when they first sighted the village.

GETTING HERE

Rocamadour-Padirac train station on the Figeac–Brive line is 5km northeast. By car, Rocamadour is 59km north of Cahors, 51km east of Sarlat.

STARTING POINT

The walk starts from the P2/Le Château car park, which is the uppermost car park.

01 Take the track heading south between dry-stone walls. Pass an old electrical transformer building and 50m later veer left off-trail onto a **narrow track** that goes downhill.

02 Go right at the fork and through a wire gate. Tiptoe along the lip of a **gorge** and into **woodland**. Go through another wire gate.

03 Twenty minutes from the start, cross a road and walk past vineyards towards **Lafage** village. Walk straight through, past a *chambre d'hôte*, and the tar road fades into a dirt road.

04 At the **walking signs**, go downhill towards Combe des Fontaines. Two hundred metres later turn left at the **old stone marker post**. Continue

106/CENTRAL FRANCE

straight ahead at the next stone marker post. Shortly after you'll pass a water source, **Font Basse**.

05 An hour from the start you'll reach a country lane. Follow the indistinct trail on the left through scrubby grass. It runs parallel to the road. The trail wends around the weathered canyon slope until it reaches a bigger road. Turn right and walk 30m before dropping left onto a minor walking track heading southwest.

06 Cross the normally dry **Alzou** riverbed and follow a farm track steeply uphill for 10 minutes. After the path levels out, go right at the fork and then left at the meeting of **farm** tracks.

07 A few minutes later, take the small trail that drops towards the river. The waters here form an enchanted natural pool known as the **Résurgence de l'Ouysse**.

08 Follow a tarmac road away from the river and then turn right a moment later where roads meet. You're now following red and white GR trail signs. At the trail junction on the crest of the hill go left past the **stone cross**. The road drops down to the canyon floor and crosses a **bridge**.

09 Forty-five minutes from the stone cross, turn right and walk down the tarmac road back into Rocamadour.

Pass an old, towered **mill** and take the small cobbled road going diagonally uphill past an **ivy-covered house**.

10 Stroll through the **old town gates**, then left up the steps to the **Sanctuary** (pictured p95). Walk through the tunnel and then follow the winding **Chemin de la Croix** (Stations of the Cross) up to the ramparts and back to the car.

 **TAKE A BREAK**

There are plenty of places to eat in Rocamadour, but none of them are very memorable. The Résurgence de l'Ouysse makes a delightful picnic spot.

26

STEVENSON'S JOURNEY

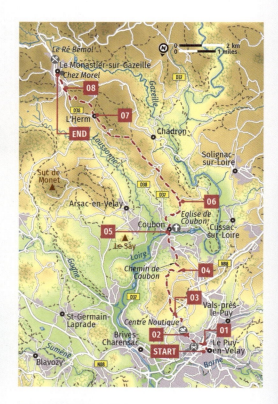

DURATION	DIFFICULTY	DISTANCE	START/END
7hr one way	Moderate	19km	Le Puy-en-Velay

TERRAIN	Road & meadows, hilly in places

Experience a journey infused with literary history. *Treasure Island* author Robert Louis Stevenson immortalised his 12-day solo hike in *Travels with a Donkey in the Cévennes* (1879) and this walk (min/max elevation 645/952m) links two way stations of his journey. Experience a glimpse of the Scottish writer's travels on this day walk or use it as a springboard for the full route.

GETTING HERE

Le Puy-en-Velay is linked to Clermont-Ferrand by SNCF bus and train (2½ hours). From Lyon or Paris, travel via St-Étienne. The hike is one way: prearrange onward transport, or a lift back to Le Puy, with La Malle Postale (www.lamallepostale.com).

STARTING POINT

Begin in Le Puy-en-Velay, the striking town of volcanic plumes and sacred chapels where Stevenson stayed ahead of his hike through the countryside, accompanied by his cantankerous donkey, Modestine.

01 From **place de la Mairie**, follow rue Chaussade east, then rue Crozatier south, turn left and cross the main road. Turn right along av Georges Clemenceau and, after about 180m, cross the junction and continue along rue Farigoule. Then, turn right and follow the av d'Ours Mons.

02 At the Centre Nautique, turn right and follow the GR430 as it cuts into meadows, before rejoining chemin de Bel Air. After crossing rte du Couderc, the route snakes into a field. Continue along chemin du Vallon, a sleepy tree-shaded road flanked on either side by farmland.

108/CENTRAL FRANCE

Chemin de Stevenson

For adventurous hikers, the full Chemin de Stevenson (Stevenson Trail; GR70) continues from Le Monastier-sur-Gazeille, first to the village of Goudet – see www.chemin-stevenson.org. The full route between Le Puy-en-Velay and Alès spans 272km of rugged hills, sweeping heathland and remote villages. Highlights of the full trek are the crater lake of Le Bouchet-St-Nicolas, attractive Pradelles and the lost-in-time village Le Pont-de-Montvert.

The author took 12 days to make this journey, but allow two full weeks to do this route justice. It is still possible to hire a donkey, just as Stevenson did, but most travellers go without an animal companion or tackle the route by mountain bike (be warned, it's a bumpy ride!).

Best for

EXPLORING HISTORY

PHILIPPE DESMAZES/AFP VIA GETTY IMAGES ©

03 Take the pedestrian crossing over the N88. When across, the path dips south. Follow it through the meadows for around 2km. A right turn leads you on to chemin de Lachamp, after which another right-hand bend directs you west.

04 Turn left at the T-junction at **chemin de Chaubon**, where the path leads downhill. Yrou'll see a spectacular unfurling of velvety green scenery.

05 After around 1.5km you'll cross the River Loire and stride into **Coubon**. This sleepy village has 10 centuries of history and a brick **church** with three crowning bells — you'll see it on the road to the right as you cross the bridge.

06 Leave Coubon by walking south along rte Dempeyre. Go right following rte de l'Olme, a narrow ribbon of pitted tarmac lined by trees. After 1.5km you'll walk through a cluster of houses where you'll turn left, taking you southeast.

07 After 4.5km, you'll reach pleasantly secluded **L'Herm**. GR430 signs guide you south and then east through a French pastoral fantasy with sweeping views of distant evergreens.

08 A final 2km leads to **Le Monastier-sur-Gazeille**.

Arriving here in 1878, Robert Louis Stevenson marvelled at the beauty of the setting, comparing it to his native Scottish high-lands. Look for the plaque at **Chez Morel** (now a pharmacy) commemorating his time in this quaint stone village.

 **TAKE A BREAK**

Le Ré Bémol (📞 04 71 03 87 16; 39 rue St-Jean, Le Monastier-sur-Gazeille; mains from €12) has gregarious staff, and regulars tuck in to tartines, meaty daily specials and regional wines. A few simple, clean guest rooms ensure there's only a few steps between dinner and bed, if you wish to linger in Le Monastier.

CENTRAL FRANCE/109

27

CLIMBING PUY DE DÔME

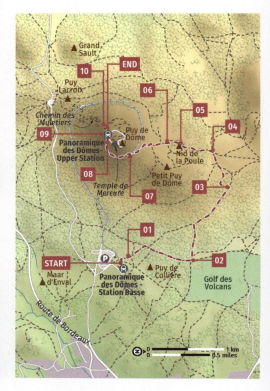

DURATION	DIFFICULTY	DISTANCE	START/END
2½–3½hr return	Moderate	4.9km	Panoramique des Dômes lower station

TERRAIN	Gravel, ungroomed meadows, occasional wooden steps

Trek to the top of Puy de Dôme, an ancient lava dome in the Auvergne. The Chemin des Chèvres (Chèvres Trail, min/max altitude 904/1465m) bestows mesmerising views from the peak's north face: a panorama of meadows, valleys and slumbering volcanoes.

GETTING HERE
The foot of Puy de Dôme is 9km west of Clermont-Ferrand. Car or taxi is easiest but, in July, August and during French school holidays, a twice-daily shuttle bus links the train station to Puy de Dôme. A scenic cog railway, the Panoramique des Dômes, rattles to the summit – though you're walking to the top, you can ride the rails back down!

STARTING POINT
At Panoramique des Dômes lower station visitor centre, you can get walking advice, buy snacks and (for convenience) purchase your return train ticket in advance.

01 Outside the **Panoramique des Dômes station base**, set out towards the mountain. Get directions from inside the station if you're unsure – signposting is scant at first, other than yellow markings on some trees. Where the trail divides, go right (signed 'Sommet Puy de Dôme').

02 After around 20 minutes of walking through silver birch trees, the path curves left and slightly uphill. Keep following the yellow dots as it rises up the flank of Puy de Dôme.

03 Around 45 minutes in, the path becomes more exposed, affording **views across the ashy peaks**. After a wooden hut and rough stone marker, the trail veers left through a stately birch grove.

04 Take the **wooden stairwell**, which appears through the forest as if by magic! Follow

110/CENTRAL FRANCE

signs for Circuit Boucle des Dômes, along a trail with brick-red soil.

05 Beyond the trees it gets blustery, but it's a painterly scene: in winter the charcoal-coloured path contrasts with snow; in summer you'll see wildflowers beneath a blazing blue sky.

06 Around 1¼ hours in, follow another set of wooden stairs. Take time to marvel at the volcanic peaks behind you. Higher up is a **lookout point**; on clear days you can see Clermont-Ferrand's twin-spired cathedral.

07 The path curves uphill, following the rail track. You're only a few minutes' walk from the summit.

08 When the train station is in view, take the right-hand path for a quick detour to the **Temple de Mercure**, a mysterious Gallo-Roman ruin.

09 Continue in the direction of the train station – you've made it! Time to gaze out at volcanic cones.

10 You can retrace your steps or tackle the alternative path – its name, **Chemin des Muletiers** (the Mule Track), is a good descriptor. But descending via the **Panoramique des Dômes train** is infinitely more relaxing. Sit on the right-hand side for views of the pine-furred panorama.

TAKE A BREAK

There's a canteen at the foot of Puy de Dôme and a restaurant up top, but the richest culinary rewards are in Clermont-Ferrand. The town has an abundance of restaurants serving rich *cuisine auvergnate*. In Clermont's old town **L'AOC** (04 73 19 12 12; www.restaurant-aoc-clermont.fr; 4 rue des Petits Gras; mains from €10/14; noon-2pm & 7.30-10pm Mon, Tue & Thu-Sat) chalks up a daily menu of prized produce.

CENTRAL FRANCE/111

28

ASCENT TO PUY DE SANCY

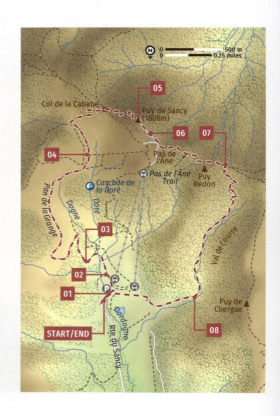

DURATION	DIFFICULTY	DISTANCE	START/END
3½hr return	Moderate	7km	Station de Mont-Dore car park
TERRAIN	Grassy uphills, wooden stairs			

From the peak of Puy de Sancy, gaze at saw-toothed mountains, glacier-scoured plains, and valleys where wild goats scamper. Journeying to the top of this ancient stratovolcano (min/max altitude 1329/1886m) reveals sublime views of the Auvergne. A popular trail wends clockwise around the mountain, darting up wooden stairs to dizzy heights before threading the scenic Val de Courre back down.

GETTING HERE

By public transport, reach Le Mont-Dore by daily direct SNCF buses from Clermont-Ferrand (€15.20, 1½ hours). Station de Mont-Dore is 3km south of Le Mont-Dore town – take a shuttle bus.

STARTING POINT

The walk begins from Station de Mont-Dore's car park, which fills early in high summer.

01 From the roundabout on rte du Sancy, take the left-hand road to the short tunnel beneath the ski slope. Follow the trail as it curves to the right, past a few piste-side businesses.

02 Follow the trail uphill. At the top of the ski lift, the path snakes to the left and you'll soon see a sign for **Pan de la Grange** (a blue run for boarders and skiers in winter). Look out for cyclists who hurtle down the mountain in summer!

03 Take a right-hand turn to follow the GR4E trail along **Col de la Cabane**. From the flanks of the mountain you might spy **Salers cattle**, prized for their gamey meat.

112/CENTRAL FRANCE

04 After half an hour of verdant trails you reach an altitude of 1775m, where **wooden steps** lead to the 1886m summit (pictured). Ignore the cable-car arrival platform – arriving on foot is far more gratifying!

05 It takes about 30 minutes to walk up all 864 wooden steps, and the reward is a **view** of four valleys, rolling hills and the Limagne and Cézallier plateaux. If you have binoculars, this is a prime vantage point to see **wildlife**. You could see chamois (goat-antelopes) scrambling between distant ridges or marmots popping their heads up.

06 With a spring in your step from the mind-blowing panorama, descend the wooden stairs. This time head northwest to embark on the **Pas de l'Âne trail**, just above the upper cable-car station (follow the GR30 signs).

07 Scramble the ridge to reach the **Puy Redon pass**, the only tough section of the route. A path leads right down a series of switchbacks along the **Val de Courre** (Courre Valley).

08 When the ground begins to level out, turn right towards the car park at the foot of the Sancy ski lifts. Head back to the roundabout or wait for a shuttle bus to whisk you back to Le Mont-Dore for a slap-up meal.

 **TAKE A BREAK**

Gorge yourself on *cuisine auvergnate* at **La Golmotte** (04 73 65 05 77; www.aubergelagolmotte.com; rte D996, Le Barbier; s/d incl breakfast €52/65; menus €20-40; noon-1.30pm Thu-Mon, 7-8.30pm Thu-Sat & Mon;), a rustic inn roughly 3km along the road from Le Mont-Dore to Lac de Guéry. All the regional favourites can be found here. And there are modest, good-value rooms to stay the night.

29

CASTLES OF THE DORDOGNE

DURATION	DIFFICULTY	DISTANCE	START/END
5½hr return	Moderate	18km	Castelnaud-la-Chapelle

TERRAIN	Road, farm track, footpath

This epic walk pieces together bits of many different shorter walks to create a long but exhilarating and scenically varied circular hike. It takes in some of the most famed tourist spots in the Dordogne and links them together with quiet riverside walks and ambles through oak and chestnut woodlands. There's one very short section along a busy road but otherwise it's country lanes and footpaths all the way. It's probably a bit long to be considered a family walk but otherwise it's a real classic.

GETTING HERE
Castelnaud-la-Chapelle is 15km south of Sarlat; there is no public transport. Various car parks cost €3.50.

STARTING POINT
The walk begins from the Parking Tournepique at the bottom of Castelnaud-la-Chapelle close to the bridge over the River Dordogne. In summer, though, you'll be lucky to actually get a parking space there.

01 From the car park, turn your back to the village (a hard thing to do to such a beautiful spot) and walk over the bridge spanning the **River Dordogne**. Go past a couple of buildings on your right and one on your left. Take the **farm track** that veers off the right-hand side of the road and wanders off over the fields.

You will pass a small **waterworks** building after 200m. The cliffs of La Roque-Gageac are visible ahead. Ignore any side trails and just keep going northeast.

02 As you draw closer to La Roque-Gageac, the River Dordogne will cosy up beside you on the right. When you reach the **campsite** entrance, turn right down to the river and follow the riverside footpath around the edge of the campsite to emerge on the D703 road. By the zebra crossing take the path going uphill to the left. There's a sign for the **Manoir de la Malartrie hotel**. There are stupendous **views** of the cliff-side village and the river from this path.

03 You'll come to a parking area and some walk signs. Don't drop down to the river but instead carry on straight ahead and climb up towards the upper part of the village. With its honeystone houses suckled up against a multicoloured cliff face in a manner more like an organic creature than a constructed village, it's hardly a surprise to learn that **La Roque-Gageac** is considered one of the loveliest villages in France. Halfway through the village, veer up the metalled steps leading up the cliff face to visit the **Troglodyte Fort** (📞 05 53 31 04 08).

04 Go through the **gateway** and take the narrow cliffside path on the left that runs east almost at the upper level of the village houses. Follow yellow waymarkers to the **Gageac quarter**. After five minutes turn left at the fork by the **ivy-covered building**. The path turns into a trail through leafy **oak and chestnut forest**. At the signed trail junction, turn right and head downhill. After a couple more minutes turn left on reaching the small road and go along the footpath leading back into the woodland.

05 A short but steep climb follows. Go straight over at the road. Eventually, the path levels out and runs through attractive mossy woodland. Turn right when you hit the dirt road,

Château de Castelnaud

The massive ramparts and metre-thick walls of the quintessential medieval fortress of **Castelnaud** (📞 05 53 31 30 00; www.castelnaud.com; adult/child €10.90/5.50; ⏰ 9am-8pm Jul & Aug, 10am-7pm Apr-Jun & Sep, shorter hours rest of year) rise through the trees above the hamlet (pictured). Climb narrow stairways to a superb series of rooms displaying a fine collection of ancient weaponry. There are fantastic views from the keep's upper terrace, encompassing the Dordogne bend and Castelnaud's arch-rival, the Château de Beynac (p102), 4km to the north.

Check the website for timetables of demonstrations and family activities. Evening mystery-game tours led by costumed actors are staged four days a week mid-July to August (pre-book online).

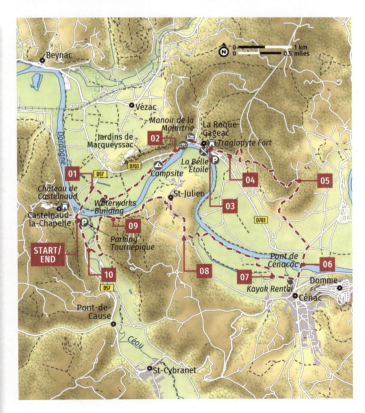

CENTRAL FRANCE/115

which turns into a surfaced road. There are a couple of signed walk trails leading off the road. Ignore all these and stick to the road as it makes a U-shaped bend and then heads downhill. Keep going straight ahead. After passing a couple of **farms** and big houses, you will see a distant village perched on a cliff ledge ahead (this is the village of **Domme**).

06 Turn right when you meet the main D46 road and follow it down to and over the **bridge** that crosses the River Dordogne. This is a busy road and the next few hundred metres constitutes the only slightly unpleasant part of this entire walk. Straight after the bridge, turn right onto a small road that goes past a stand-up paddleboard and **kayak rental** place. The turn-off is immediately past the Cénac town sign.

07 Follow the red and white GR trail markers past a waterworks. Turn right at the junction and continue along a **farm track** that bends down towards the river. A long, peaceful stroll down along the river now follows. Turn left away from the river when you come to the **green walk sign** with a scallop shell symbol (indicating that you are now on one of the medieval pilgrimage routes to Santiago de Compostela in northwest Spain).

08 The farm track traces a line along the base of a low cliff. At the point where it bends 90 degrees to the left, a **walk track** veers off right (signed with green, red and white markers). Take this and amble uphill through woodland. When you hit the road go right, then right again by the first houses and continue into pretty **St-Julien** village. As you enter the village there's a parking area on the left and a very sharp left turn. Take this turning and drop downhill. The surfaced road soon turns to a dirt road and dives into dense **deciduous woodland** full of birds.

09 After 10 minutes a tarmac road leads off the track to the left. Ignore this; it's a private road. Instead, continue along the woodland path with red and white GR markers. There are fleeting glimpses through the trees of the river just below. Go right at the trail junction a few minutes later. A long, leisurely walk through the **woods** now follows. In the autumn in particular, when the trees alight in red and oranges, it's an absolute delight of a walk. Castelnaud-la-Chapelle will appear ahead, but then the trail bends and the village will be behind you. When you reach the fields of the valley floor, turn right and follow the trail to a small tarmac road.

10 Cross a **bridge** over a small, clear and utterly still stream where the trees are reflected like a mirror and turn right. Just before the main road, a **cycle path** drops down to the right. Walk along this for a few minutes back into Castelnaud-la-Chapelle. Remember to allow time to explore this beautiful village and its huge castle before leaving.

 La Roque-Gageac

La Roque-Gageac's row of amber buildings, built into the cliff face along the River Dordogne, make it one of the most photographed villages in the central Dordogne Valley (pictured).

The village is a pleasure to explore (though in high summer it's often oppressively busy). The cliff that hangs above the village is incised with caves that once formed medieval defensive positions known as the **Troglodyte Fort**. The village is also a prime spot to hit the river waters in a kayak or on a river cruise. There are masses of summertime operators.

 TAKE A BREAK

If you set out on this walk early enough then you will have time to stop for a long lunch at **La Belle Étoile** (📞 05 53 29 51 44; www.belleetoile.fr; D703; menus €29-520; ⏱ 12.30-1.30pm Tue & Thu-Sun, 7.30-9pm Tue-Sun, closed Nov-Mar) in La Roque-Gageac. Sophisticated French food is served in a vine-shaded upper terrace with fine views across the Dordogne.

Also Try...

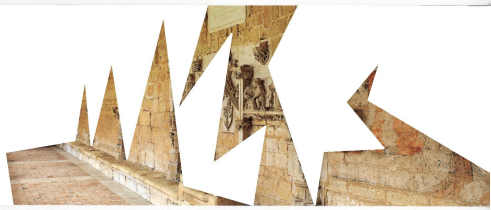

JULIAN KUMAR/GETTY IMAGES ©

MEANDERING AROUND CADOUIN ABBEY

Completely dominating the butter-coloured stone village of Cadouin (38km east of Bergerac), the Unesco-listed Cadouin Abbey, which houses cloth said to have been torn from the shroud that covered Christ (since proven to be a fake), has been drawing pilgrims since the 11th century. Today, the abbey continues to bring the faithful, but also attracts walkers who relish strolling the attractive woodlands surrounding the village.

This circular walk follows yellow waymarkers. Head east away from the abbey (pictured) and into chestnut woodland. You will pass the hamlets of Les Gavachoux and St-Blanchot. Cross through the Peyre forest and work your way towards and beyond the hamlet of Soulety before bending back around to Cadouin.

DURATION 2½hr return
DIFFICULTY Easy
DISTANCE 9.2km

VÉZÈRE PANORAMAS

There's a bit of everything on this walk: viewpoints, pauses in a dreamy riverside village and explorations of cliff-side cave dwellings that date back as far as 50,000 years ago.

The walk begins from the car park at La oque St-Christophe. With traces of human habitation dating back 50,000 years, the kilometre-long cliff here is dotted with around a hundred rock shelters raised some 80m off the ground. The site reached its pinnacle of habitation during the Middle Ages and guided tours bring some of the site alive. Leaving the past behind, the route crosses the River Vézère, climbs onto cliff ledges with great views and makes its way through woodland before descending down to the oh-so-pretty village of St-Léon-sur-Vézère. Crossing back over the river again, it's a countryside ramble back to the start point.

DURATION 5hr return
DIFFICULTY Medium
DISTANCE 17.5km

MARGOUILLAT PHOTO/SHUTTERSTOCK ©

MONBAZILLAC VINEYARDS

Famed countrywide for its sweet white wines, the small village of Monbazillac is built around the large château of the same name.

This short walk enables you to admire the architecture and stroll through the tapestry of vineyards. And remember, drink walking is considered acceptable! From the château, car park, follow yellow way-markers in a figure-eight pattern around the village via Le Tonibru, Les Croux, La Cattie and Péroudier. For the whole way, you'll walk on quiet country roads and farm tracks through a countryside ribbed with vines.

DURATION 2hr return
DIFFICULTY Easy
DISTANCE 6km

LAC PAVIN

Deep in the Auvergne countryside, the dark, forest-fringed and near perfectly circular Pavin lake is something of a place of legend.

Locals whisper that the lake (pictured) was created by the devil's tears. Scientists, somewhat less romantically, say it was created through volcanic actions. Whichever story is true, nobody can deny that this ethereal, 93m-deep lake is a magical hiking goal. The walk begins from the village of Besse-en-Chandesse and follows the red and white waymarkers of the GR30.

DURATION 3½hr return
DIFFICULTY Moderate
DISTANCE 13km

LE CÉZALLIER

This high, windy grassland plateau offers a very different kind of Auvergne walking experience than that of the volcanic craters dotting the landscape elsewhere in this region.

Walking here is about big horizons, flower meadows and cattle. An excellent half-day walk takes in the lakes d'En Haut and d'En Bas and the rounded summit of La Motte.

DURATION 4hr return
DIFFICULTY Moderate
DISTANCE 14km

CENTRAL FRANCE/**119**

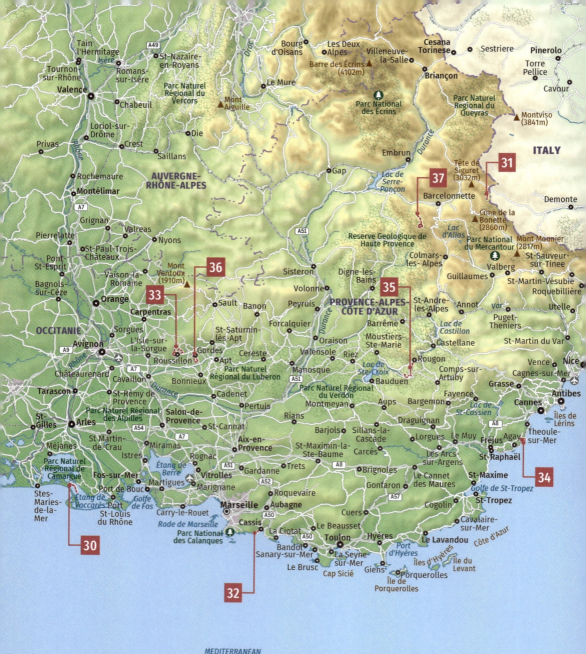

30 **Wetlands of the Camargue** Spot flamingoes in the vast wetlands of the Camargue. **p124**

31 **Lac du Lauzanier** Commune with marmots while walking to this stunning mountain lake. **p126**

32 **Port-Miou, Port-Pin & En-Vau** Discover the secret beaches of Les Calanques on this coastal walk. **p128**

33 **Roussillon Ramble** Wander past vineyards, pretty villages and bizarre rock formations. **p130**

34 **Cap Roux** Admire the coastal views from this Côte d'Azur vantage point. **p132**

35 **The Blanc-Martel Trail** Descend into the 'Grand Canyon' of Europe. **p134**

36 **Gordes Loops** Enjoy fields of lavender and Provence's most heavenly village. **p136**

37 **Les Eaux Tortes** Gasp at the glacial scenery surrounding this watery plateau. **p140**

Explore
PROVENCE & THE CÔTE D'AZUR

Fields of lavender, ancient olive groves, maquis-cloaked hills, snow-tipped mountains and France's deepest canyon. No wonder it sometimes feels as if Provence and the Côte d'Azur was purpose-built for walkers. And that's before we even mention the Mediterranean itself, a bright mirror of blue reflecting craggy cliffs and endless skies.

ARLES

Roman treasures, tree-shaded squares and plenty of culture make Arles a seductive stepping stone for walks in the watery world of the Camargue.

CASSIS

The charm of this fishing village, impeccably poised amongst the *calanques* (coves), has hardly been dented by its great popularity. Yes, you're more likely to rub shoulders with crisply dressed Marseillais than sun-creased fisherfolk, but Cassis is so beautiful – and so well stocked with good bistros, bars and boutiques – that really you couldn't ask for a more ideal base for walk number 32.

ROUSSILLON

Home to artists' and ceramicists' workshops, Roussillon is a red-tinged beauty of a village and

a lovely place to finish off the countryside ramble described in walk number 33.

CANNES

Glamorous Cannes sets camera flashes popping at its film festival in May, when stars pose on the red carpet in tuxes and couture gowns. But the glitz doesn't end there. Throughout the year, as you walk among the fashionable bars, designer shops and palaces of La Croisette, the wealth and glamour of this city cannot fail to impress. The city is an ideal base for walk 34.

MOUSTIERS STE-MARIE

Pushed up tight against giant rock stacks and cliffs, attractive Moustiers Ste-Marie is the standard base for those taking on the challenges of the Verdon Gorge. Despite its small size there are plenty of places to eat and sleep.

BARCELONNETTE

At the far northern edge of the Parc National du Mercantour, which covers a great swathe of the Alpes de Haute-Provence, the small ski and hiking resort of Barcelonnette is well endowed with places to stay and eat, and forms the prefect base for walks number 31 and 37.

GORDES

Gordes is stunning, a jumble of terracotta rooftops, church towers and winding lanes, and a classic image of rural Provence. There are good tourist facilities and lots of wonderful places to stay after an exhausting day completing walk 36.

WHEN TO GO

The climate in Provence and the Côte d'Azur is typical of the west Mediterranean, so you can

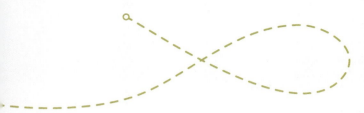

walk somewhere at any time of the year.

Winter (November to February) along the coast and in the Luberon region can be warm sunshine one week and torrential rain the next. Real cold (or snow) is rare though. By contrast, the northern mountains in winter are purely the domain of skiers.

Spring (March to early May) is by far the most unpredictable and often the wettest period of the year. Snow will keep mountain trails off-limits until at least early May.

Summer (June to September) is uniformly hot, dry and sunny. July and August are often too hot even for the high mountain routes. The heat can make many coastal walks very trying. June though can be a lovely time. The tourist crowds are yet to arrive, the days are long and the wildflowers blossom across both coastal and mountain slopes. For the lavender fields of the Luberon, the only option is July and August, when the entire countryside radiates a purple-blue colour.

Autumn (mid-September to October) is a superb time to walk almost anywhere here. The weather will still be settled, the sea is warm and the light beautiful and clear. As you get deeper into October, the autumn colours appear on the woodland trees and the mountain summits get a covering of fresh snow. It all looks magical at this time.

WHERE TO STAY

Provence and the Côte d'Azur have a huge and varied range of accommodation, from cosy rural cottages to swish pamper pads. It's wise to book well ahead everywhere in summer (online is easiest); prices are at their highest in July and August.

WHAT'S ON

Skiing (Dec-Apr) Provence and the Côte d'Azur's ski resorts are excellent: small, family-friendly, dotted with trees, sunny and easily accessible.

Pèlerinage des Gitans (24-25 May) Roma from Europe pour into remote seaside outpost Stes-Maries-de-la-Mer to honour their patron saint.

La Transhumance (Oct) Sheep and their shepherds descend from their summer pastures and crowd the roads of Haute-Provence, from the Verdon to Col d'Allos. The same happens in reverse in June.

Resources

Provence–Alpes–Côte d'Azur Tourisme (www.decouverte-paca.fr) The first port of call, with a wealth of info on what to do, where to go, where to stay and much more.

Tourisme Alpes Haute-Provence (www.tourism-alps-provence.com) Guide to the mountains.

Parc National du Mercantour (www.parc-mercantour.eu) Offical website of the Mercantour National Park.

Rando Alpes Haute Provence (www.rando-alpes-haute-provence.fr) Hundreds of route suggestions, pictures, maps and tips.

TRANSPORT

Public transport in Provence and the Côte d'Azur is generally good between bigger towns (especially along the coast), but limited to nonexistent in rural areas. A car gives maximum freedom, especially in rural parts, and is often the only way to reach trailheads. Cars can be hired in most larger towns and cities.

High-speed TGVs connect major cities; smaller towns are served by slower TER trains, sometimes supplemented by buses. Buses are useful for remote villages that aren't serviced by trains, but timetables revolve around school-term times; fewer services run on weekends and school holidays.

30

WETLANDS OF THE CAMARGUE

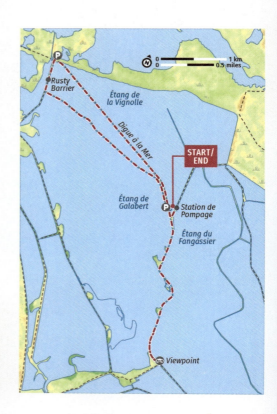

DURATION	DIFFICULTY	DISTANCE	START/END
3½hr return	Easy	12.5km	Parking Station de Pompage

TERRAIN	Walking trail, dirt road

Taking in empty horizons, blue lakes and pink flamingoes, this simple walk reveals the best of the wetland wilderness of the Camargue. It's a figure-of-eight-style walk, with the start point being the middle of the eight. This means that it's easy to just do one half of the walk if you wish. Combined with it being absolutely pancake flat and with a whole host of wildlife interest, it's an ideal family walk. Do, however, avoid very windy or hot days as there's no shelter at all. Finally, make sure you bring some binoculars.

The hardest part of this walk is getting to the start point. It's 15km west of Salin-de-Girud on a tiny dirt road that crosses the Étang du Fangassier and Étang de Galabert. There's an old water pump station here, a bird hide and a small parking area. To start, follow the wide trail signed **Phare de la Gacholle** (Gacholle Lighthouse).

The trail goes arrow straight between the two *étangs* (brackish lagoons). The one to your north (Étang du Fangassier) is a near-guaranteed place to see **flamingoes** (pictured). Approach them quietly. They're very timid and won't let you get too close. At the parking area, after 3km, turn left, pass a **rusty barrier** and then 100m later go left again following a very minor, **unsigned footpath**. It will return you to the start point.

Then, head south away from the car park, along a narrow dirt road again sandwiched between the same two *étangs*. After 40 minutes reach a **viewpoint** over a whole web of waterways. Retrace your steps back to the car.

124/PROVENCE & THE CÔTE D'AZUR

31

LAC DU LAUZANIER

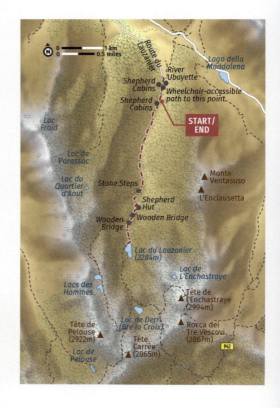

DURATION	DIFFICULTY	DISTANCE	START/END
3hr return	Easy	10.5km	Parking au Pont Rouge (Col de Larche)

TERRAIN	Walking trail, smooth track

This is mountain walking at its best. An idyllic valley filled with wildflowers and comical marmots leads to a spectacular lake surrounded by glacial mountain peaks. Not only is this walk (min/max altitude 1907/2284m) visually breathtaking, but it's also short and easy, making it a superb family walk.

Follow the wheelchair-accessible path south. You'll likely pass a multitude of very **tame marmots** playing around the grass verges (don't feed them). After around 500m the trail narrows and becomes distinctly less wheelchair accessible. It's then simply a case of following the gently rising path in a straight line pretty much all the way to the lake. Pass a couple of **shepherd cabins** surrounded by herds of sheep being watched over by guard dogs who are distinctly less friendly than the marmots (give the dogs a very wide berth and never allow a child to approach one).

The scenery is everything an alpine mountain valley is supposed to be and you half expect Heidi to come skipping down the trail towards you.

About an hour from the start and the trail starts gaining altitude as it climbs up **stone steps** and steep slopes. Come up onto a plateau with another shepherd hut and then cross two **wooden bridges** over the fledgling River Ubayette. Then it's one last haul up over another ridge and the glistening lake stands in front of you with a wall of 3km-high peaks reflected in its waters. Return by the same route.

126/PROVENCE & THE CÔTE D'AZUR

32

PORT-MIOU, PORT-PIN & EN-VAU

DURATION	DIFFICULTY	DISTANCE	START/END
4hr return	Moderate	10km	Parking de la Presqu'île

TERRAIN	Footpath, dirt road

With their light-shifting geometry, rich plant and animal life, and idyllic hidden coves, Les Calanques are the adventure playground of the Marseillais, and a wonderful walking – and beach-hopping – destination for everyone. Just remember to bring your swimming things! Note that, in summer, the trail is sometimes closed because of the high risk of forest fire.

GETTING HERE
The walk begins at the parking at the far southwestern edge of Cassis. From the town, follow road signs to Calanque.

STARTING POINT
Parking costs €8 for the day (the nearby streets are metered at the same rate). Don't leave anything of value in the car.

01 Walk back up **av Notre Dame**. Immediately after a **cube-shaped house** turn left down a footpath. Go left when you hit the road and drop down towards the fjord-like *calanque*.

02 Walk along the west bank of the **Calanque de Port-Miou** (pictured). When you near the end of the *calanque* you will be offered a choice of an upper path and a lower one. Take the upper path, which leads to a dirt road.

03 Near the top of the hill, where the road bends right, a footpath veers off to the left (straight ahead). Take this trail and then, a few metres later at the fork, take the upper right-hand track. You will come to a **trail junction**. The main trail, signed with red and white trail markers, goes right. Instead, take the smaller path that continues straight ahead and onto the **Presqu'île de Cacau** headland.

128/PROVENCE & THE CÔTE D'AZUR

Best for COASTAL VIEWS

04 Work your way down to the end of the sunburnt headland. The **coastal views** are marvellous. Return back to the main trail.

05 Drop down onto the beach at the head of the **Calanque de Port-Pin**. With its jewel-blue waters, this is everything a Mediterranean beach is supposed to be.

06 From the far end of the beach, there's a choice of two trails. Take the one heading southwest along the headland. It's signed for the **Sentier Panoramique** and follows blue waymarkers.

07 The trail bends around the end of the headland and starts to climb more steeply. At one point, you will pass an **old refuge** (mountain hut). After a fair bit of huffing and puffing, you'll find yourself at a spectacular **vantage point**.

08 Continuing along the cliff-top path you'll come to another **viewpoint**. Just beyond this is a junction. Go right. At a major signed meeting of junctions go left towards the **Calanque d'En-Vau**. The descent to the beach is very steep and can be slippery. The **beach** here, squashed between sheer cliff faces, is one of the region's finest.

09 Return back to the signed trail junction. This time take the path signed for Cassis. It drops back to the beach at the Calanque de Port-Pin. Take the wider trail cutting straight over the headland to the Calanque de Port-Miou and back to the parking.

TAKE A BREAK

It's a pleasure to discover that none of the beaches have been marred by bars or restaurants. Bring a picnic.

PROVENCE & THE CÔTE D'AZUR

33
ROUSSILLON RAMBLE

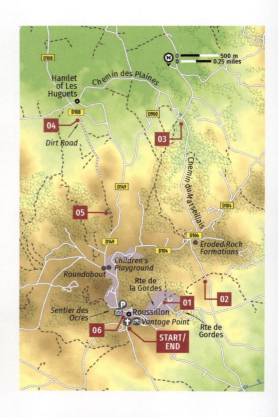

DURATION	DIFFICULTY	DISTANCE	START/END
3½hr return	Moderate	11km	Parking St-Michel, Roussillon
TERRAIN	Road, farm track, footpath			

Roussillon is one of the prettiest villages in France. The houses, all of which are painted faded blushing red, look out over countryside ribbed in vineyards and dotted with strangely contorted cliffs. This family-friendly route reveals it all.

GETTING HERE
The walk starts from the Parking St-Michel, which is by the roundabout at the end of the D227, a few hundred metres north of Roussillon centre.

STARTING POINT
You have to pay for all the car parks all around Roussillon. There are no walker facilities here except a toilet block.

01 Follow the road up the hill and into the village centre. Turn right and then right again down **rue des Bourgades**. At the edge of the village go left down **rte de la Gordes**. You will come to a junction known as **Ribas**. There are some hiking route signposts. Turn left down a small road that quickly becomes a walking track that descends through **pretty oak woodlands**. There are red and white trail markers.

02 When you reach a road at the **Cabiscol junction**, head left (direction Pie Conil). After a few minutes' uphill climb, you'll pass some weird **eroded rock formations**. A moment later, on reaching the road junction with the D104, turn right. Eighty metres later leave the road for a track on the left signed Goult. Pass some houses and then walk gently downhill
along a farm track hemmed by vineyards, patches of woodland and a few lavender fields. The red and white waymarkers are now largely replaced with yellow ones.

130/PROVENCE & THE CÔTE D'AZUR

Sentier des Ocres

This hike doesn't come to an end when you stroll back into Roussillon. Oh no, in fact one of the highlights of the walk awaits.

The **Sentier des Ocres** (Ochre Trail; adult/child €3/free; 9.30am-6.30pm May-Sep, 10am-5pm Mar & Oct, 11am-3.30pm Feb, Nov & Dec;) consists of two circular trails, taking 30 or 50 minutes to complete, which twist through mini-desert landscapes on the edge of the village (pictured).

03 At the bottom of the hill you'll come to a large, peach-pink stone house on a junction signed as **la Petite Verrerie**. Go left and pass a farm and vineyard, where you can buy a tipple for your picnic. At the road junction take a right (going straight ahead). A **beautiful vista** of vineyards and hazy hills spreads out before you. At the next junction continue straight into the hamlet of **Les Huguets**, a delightful place of cream-pink stone houses.

04 At the junction with the D108 turn left, then, 120m later, just before the road bends, a small dirt road leads off north (straight ahead). It's signed Les Mas des Iris and Le Jas. Head up this following the yellow waymarkers. You'll pass a peaceful succession of **vineyards** and patches of **woodland**. The path starts to climb quite steeply. On a hot day this can be the hardest part of the whole walk but, fortunately, **oak trees** provide some shade. After a five-minute climb, things level out and oak turns to pine.

05 Reaching a **trail fork** there's a house entry on the left and a gateway on the right. Go through the gateway and at the point where the track bends right, take the discreet turn-off marked in faded yellow paint on a boulder. Follow this route through pine woods. Turn right at the road junction and left at the roundabout (next to a **children's playground**). Continue straight and arrive back in the old part of Roussillon.

06 Before leaving, take the time to explore the village. Walk up to the oh-so-pretty **village hall** and carry on up to the **church** from where there's a superb **vantage point**.

 TAKE A BREAK

There are lots of touristy restaurants in the village. Market day is Thursday morning. Time your visit for this and stock up on picnic treats.

34

CAP ROUX

DURATION	DIFFICULTY	DISTANCE	START/END
4½hr return	Moderate	11km	Pointe de l'Observatoire/ Pointe du Cap Roux
TERRAIN	Footpath, dirt road		

The Massif de l'Esterel is a great pile of sunset-tinged boulders and rock pinnacles hugging the shores of the Mediterranean. The walk (min/max altitude 0/454m) described here is one of the classics of the massif, and even though Cap Roux offers Oscar-winning views across the Côte d'Azur and down onto the millionaire villas of Cannes, the Massif de l'Esterel is a world apart from the Hollywood glam of the Côte d'Azur. Indeed, you're far more likely to stumble into a wild boar in the mountain woodlands than a Hollywood starlet.

In summer the trail is sometimes closed because of the high risk of forest fire.

GETTING HERE

The walk begins from the small parking area by the Pointe de l'Observatoire/Pointe du Cap Roux on the main Corniche de l'Estérel road (D5559). From central Cannes it's 22km. From St-Raphaël it's 18km. While buses do pass by the start point, it's much easier to have your own vehicle.

STARTING POINT

At the start point, there are a couple of walking and fire risk information panels. Don't leave anything of value in your vehicle.

01 Turn left out of the parking area and walk 50m down the road. Just after the **railway bridge**, there's a turn-off right leading uphill. Follow this dirt road up through herb-scented scrub. Ignore the yellow waymarked turn-off after 15 minutes and carry on uphill. You will pass some **information panels** on the massif's plant life.

132/PROVENCE & THE CÔTE D'AZUR

Best for

ESCAPING THE CROWDS

02 Where the dirt road bends sharp right in front of a huge rocky outcrop, take the **pebble track** on the right. There are yellow paint slashes. Thirty minutes from the dirt road you will come to the **Col du St-Pilon** (281m), a low pass. Turn right.

03 Bending around to the cooler northern side of the massif, the woodland becomes denser and damper. At the fork go left. Turn right at the big trail junction next to a **natural water source**. The trail crosses two big **rockfall zones** but otherwise remains in deep forest. You then come to a third, larger, rockfall area. The path zigzags up the side of it.

04 Two hours from the start, emerge from the forest. At a pass a couple of minutes later, turn right and after 100m reach the summit of **Cap Roux** (454m). On a clear day the entire coastline will be visible (pictured). Looking the other way, the southern Alps will shimmer in the haze.

05 Return to the main trail and go right. After 15 minutes reach the **Col du Cap Roux** (404m) at the base of two sugarloaf fingers of rock. Go left, then left again and over a huge rockfall. Twenty minutes later, at another junction, turn sharp right and go downhill into a **forest**. After a long descent you will come to a wide trail junction. Go right here. At the point where the trail starts rising again, there's a small turn-off left with steps and a yellow cross painted on the rock. Turn down here and then left 200m later back onto the dirt road you walked up earlier. A moment later, you'll reach the car park.

06 Walk 100m across the low headland by the car park for **sea views**. You can also drop down to a small cove **beach**.

TAKE A BREAK

There's nowhere to buy food and drink on the trail. Bring a picnic and a *lot* of water.

PROVENCE & THE CÔTE D'AZUR/133

35

THE BLANC-MARTEL TRAIL

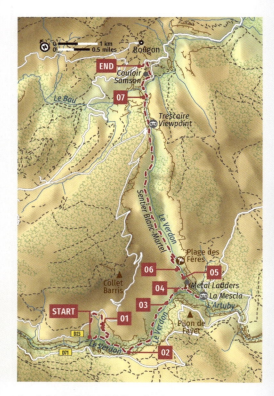

DURATION	DIFFICULTY	DISTANCE	START/END
6hr one way	Moderate	13km	Chalet de la Maline/ Auberge Point Sublime
TERRAIN	Footpath, steep cliff-face ladders		

The Blanc-Martel trail along Europe's 'Grand Canyon' is one of the iconic walks of France. It's a long and tiring walk, but with cliff-face bolted ladders to descend and long, dark tunnels to negotiate, there's always something of interest. And that's before we even mention the natural beauty of the glowing blue river waters and soaring rainbow-tinged canyon walls. The trail is very clearly waymarked all the way along. Bring a torch for the tunnels.

GETTING HERE

The walk begins from the Chalet de la Maline, 8km from La Palud-sur-Verdon, and ends at the Auberge Point Sublime on the edge of the hamlet of Rougon. A **navette** (📞 04 92 77 32 02) runs from La Palud-sur-Verdon to the Chalet de la Maline and another from the Auberge Point Sublime back to La Palud-sur-Verdon. Or you can leave a car at the end point and get a taxi to the start point, but taxi numbers are limited, so book at least a week in advance.

STARTING POINT

There are walk information panels and toilets at the Chalet de la Maline. Food and drinks with a view are also served here.

01 Follow the GR4 sign down past the **Chalet de la Maline** along a clear trail through mixed woodland. After 40 minutes you'll reach a trail junction. Go left. Five minutes later you'll reach the banks of the **River Verdon** and the bottom of the gorge.

02 A long, easy amble follows. Sometimes you'll be walking very close to the river and at other times the path rises upward and away from the waters.

03 After 1½ hours things will start to get a little harder. Handrails will help ease you up a steeper bit of rocky terrain and then you cross a landslip area via a set of steps with an **excitingly airy view** down to the river below.

04 Fifteen minutes later you'll pass by a big cave, the **Baume aux Bœufs**, where the bones of prehistoric cattle were found. The path continues to climb sharply up the gorge walls until, a few minutes later, you reach a junction. Go left for the main trail, but we highly recommend taking the 15-minute (one-way) detour down to **La Mescla** (pictured). It's a small, low headland above the meeting points of the Verdon and the Artuby rivers, and the mingling of **luminous turquoise waters** here is simply magical. Return back to the main trail.

05 After a few minutes of steep climbing you'll come to the **Brèche d'Imbert** (710m), a small gap in the rock face. Immediately beyond this is the most infamous section of the entire trail. **Metal ladders** fall almost completely vertically all the way back down to the river far below. There are handrails to help you down, but even so, it's a little hair-raising.

06 It's now a three-hour walk along the gorge floor. You'll pass the **Plage des Fères**, where most people are tempted to swim.

07 Some five hours from the start you'll reach a series of tunnels known as the **Couloir Samson**. The second is around 1km long and you'll need a torch to navigate it. You come out into the bright light of day close to the **Auberge Point Sublime**.

 **TAKE A BREAK**

There's nowhere to get food or drink in the gorge, so bring a picnic and plenty of water – however, a cool beer awaits at Auberge Point Sublime!

36
GORDES LOOPS

Best for PRETTY VILLAGES

DURATION	DIFFICULTY	DISTANCE	START/END
6hr return	Moderate	20.5km	Parking Gendarmerie, Gordes

TERRAIN	Road, farm track, walking trail

Arguably the scenic queen of the Luberon's hilltop villages, the tiered village of Gordes seems to teeter improbably on the edge of the sheer rock faces of the Vaucluse plateau from which it rises. And that same plateau is blanketed in fields of lavender and broadleaf woodlands, and scarred with small gorges. All of which are encountered on this walk, which also takes in a famed abbey, sterling views of Gordes and an interesting historical site.

Although the walking itself is easy, this is a very long walk. The good news though is that because the route makes a very neat figure-of-eight shape, with the start and end point being the middle of the eight, it's easy, and in many ways advisable, to split the walk into two shorter days.

GETTING HERE
ZOU! Bus line 17 (€2.60, four daily July to September, one daily Monday to Friday October to June) stops in Gordes on its way from Apt to Cavaillon. It also stops in Roussillon along the way. The walk begins from the car park in front of the gendarmerie at the bottom of the old part of the village.

STARTING POINT
There are no facilities for walkers at the start point (unless of course you happen to need a police officer!). All parking in Gordes is metered.

01 Leaving the car park, walk a few metres down the D15 away from the old village. Pass an old **water source** on the right and straight afterward go right, uphill along a **small track**. Hitting the D177 road go right, then 150m later, at a dead-end sign, turn left down a little country

136/PROVENCE & THE CÔTE D'AZUR

road. There are now both red and white GR trail markers and yellow waymarkers. Fifty metres later go right at the **walking signs** and follow the trail that runs between two old dry-stone walls.

02 The path rolls lovingly between the **dry-stone walls** with **olive groves** and patches of woodland on either side. After 15 minutes turn right and then immediately left when you hit the wider path. A few minutes further on, you'll meet the D177. Turn left and follow the road around the sharp bend.

03 After 200m leave the road for a **footpath** on the left that drops downhill through woodland to the large **Abbaye Notre-Dame de Sénanque**, which is surrounded by lavender fields (pictured p121). From this quiet, elevated position it looks an absolute treat. Allow at least an hour (not included in walk times stated here) to explore the abbey, but be careful not to trip over one of the selfie-seeking tourists standing among the lavender fields.

04 Return to the sharp bend in the D177 road via the same footpath. Follow the sign and yellow waymarkers south in the direction of **Les Dilais** on a narrow forest trail. The path wends along the lip of the **Gorges de la Sénanque**, although for the most part you can't see down into the gorge because of all the trees.

05 After 20 minutes turn right by a **grey house gate** and a walking sign marked Senancole (1.2km). The path sweeps steeply (in places very steeply) down along the gorge. The trail heads back up the gorge a short way, crosses a rock face and reaches a junction. Heading straight on will take you back to the abbey.

Abbaye Notre-Dame de Sénanque

Surrounded by fields of lavender, the Cistercian **Abbey Notre-Dame de Sénanque** (📞 04 90 72 18 24; www.senanque.fr; off D177; guided/unguided tour €8/9.50; ⏰ 10-11.30am & 1-5.30pm Mon-Sat, 1.30-5.30pm Sun) is one of the most photographed sites in Provence.

Founded in 1148, the abbey is still home to a small monastic community, members of which conduct guided tours (in French) throughout the year. You can also take an unguided tour. Reservations are essential, as are conservative dress and reverential silence.

The abbey is closed on religious holidays.

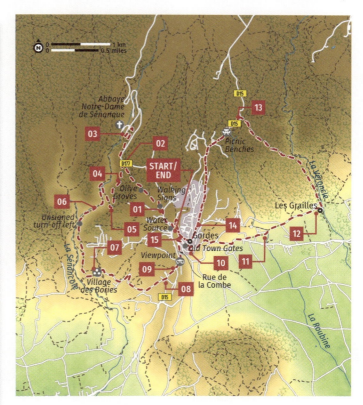

PROVENCE & THE CÔTE D'AZUR/137

Instead, spin around and head south down the **gorge**. Ignore the yellow crosses saying you've gone the wrong way.

06 After 100m of very steep and slippery descent (take great care here), you'll bump down onto the floor of the gorge by a meeting of trails. Go left (south) down the gorge on a clear trail next to a normally dry **riverbed** (be careful of flash floods after heavy rain). Compared to the dry, scrubby woodlands up on the gorge slopes, what you're now walking through seems more like the Amazon jungle!

07 After 15 minutes go straight on towards the Village des Bories at the signed junction. A few minutes later there's a discreet, unsigned turn-off left. Take this and 20 minutes later roll into the **Village des Bories**, a series of beehive-shaped stone huts (pictured) used by shepherds for hundreds of years.

08 Leave the site via the car parks and follow the signed route along a road to Les Grangiers. It's now just a relaxing walk along country lanes. At the next junction with walking signposts go left. When you reach the busy road (D15), take the small road on the left next to some large **cypress trees**. Thirty metres later continue straight ahead and then straight over the main road again.

FABIO MICHELE CAPELLI/SHUTTERSTOCK ©

09 Next up is a walk highlight, an epic **viewpoint** of Gordes framed between trees. Follow the path down to the base of the village and then head up into the old quarter via a wide cobbled road, which passes through the **old town gates** and emerges just behind the **château**. You can now either call it a day and return to your car or continue with the second, marginally shorter, part of the walk.

10 From where you stand behind the château head downhill towards the signed **belvédère**, which has wonderful views over the farming plains of Provence. Drop down a stone stairway to the right then follow red and white trail markers left (southeast). At the bottom of the hill follow the sign for Le Touron. You'll pass an old **water source** (not drinkable) and reach the busy D2 road. Go left along the road for 75m then turn left and almost instantly right onto a **grassy trail** in front of a big stone house.

11 A clear, flat trail runs for 10 minutes through farming countryside and past big houses. Cross the quiet D102 and carry straight on. Do the same at the next junction.

12 You'll come to the hamlet of **Les Grailles**. Go left by the walking trail junction and follow a stony path uphill along the lip of Les Grailles. After

138/PROVENCE & THE CÔTE D'AZUR

 Village des Bories

Beehive-shaped *bories* (stone huts) bespeckle Provence and the **Village des Bories** (☎ 04 90 72 03 48; adult/child €6/4; ⏲ 9am-sunset) is an entire village of them can be explored. Constructed of slivered limestone, *bories* were built during the Bronze Age, inhabited by shepherds until 1839, then abandoned until their restoration in the 1970s.

10 minutes, ignore the trail sign saying to go right and instead carry on straight ahead (north) along the edge of the gorge. A long upward slog awaits, during which you'll gain 250m in height in just 45 minutes. There's no shade so be prepared to get hot!

13 Finally, after a long, sun-exposed climb, you'll come to the D15 road. Turn left and walk along the road verge. You'll pass some **picnic benches** after a few minutes. A short while later the road bends right. A small road goes off to the left of this bend (there are some **road bollards** next to it). Head down this road, which runs between dry-stone walls and houses.

14 At the road junction continue straight ahead on a smaller track. It's now downhill all the way and there are **stunning views** eastward over a patchwork of vines, lavender, oak and honey-stone houses. The track becomes a footpath, but the views don't change. Pass by the **cemetery** at the edge of Gordes.

15 Go through a small car park and follow rue St-Pons to the château in the heart of the village. After exploring the old village follow **rue de la Combe** for five minutes from the front of the château downhill and back to your car.

 TAKE A BREAK

There's nowhere to get food and drink out on the trail so bring a picnic and plenty of water.

At the end of your walk treat yourself at **Le Mas** (☎ 04 90 04 03 57; www.lemasrestaurantgordes.com; chemin de St-Blaise les Imberts; menu lunch/dinner €27/49; ⏲ 12.30-2pm & 7.30-9.30pm Jul-Sep, 7.30-9.30pm Thu, 12.30-2pm & 7.30-9.30pm Fri-Mon Oct-Jun). Heavy on Provençal flavours, it's one of the region's culinary highlights. Expect lots of stuffed aubergines, slow-roasted tomatoes, and lashings of olive oil and *herbes de Provence*. It's 3.5km south of Gordes off the D2.

PROVENCE & THE CÔTE D'AZUR/**139**

37

LES EAUX TORTES

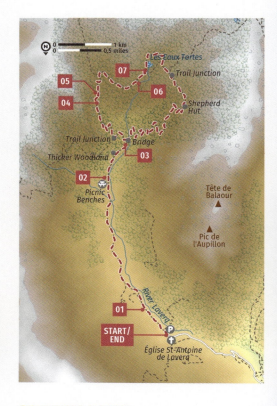

DURATION	DIFFICULTY	DISTANCE	START/END
5½hr return	Hard	17.5km	Abbaye de Laverq
TERRAIN	Mountain trail		

Les Eaux Tortes is a water-logged plateau of meandering streams set at the foot of a huge cirque of 3km-high glacier-coated mountain peaks. En route to the plateau, this popular trail (min/max altitude 1640/2400m) carries you through rich scenic variety: woodlands, sheep pastures and a soul-satisfying mountain valley.

GETTING HERE

The Église St-Antoine de Laverq is a long way from anywhere. From Barcelonnette take the D900 west for 14km to Le Martinet. Head south on a minor mountain road past the hamlets of St-Barthélémy and Les Clarionds. The road deteriorates into a bumpy track for the last 2.5km to the abbey. There's no public transport to the start point.

STARTING POINT

There are walk information panels andj, in summer, shepherds set up shop selling cheese and other mountain delights. At the time of research a big new mountain lodge was under construction and it's likely that food and drink will be available here when completed.

01 From the abbey, follow the dirt road south. There are red and white waymarkers. After 20 minutes pass the parking de Plan Bas. Continue in the same direction, ignoring any turn-offs. The route climbs gently upwards alongside the **River Laverq** through open woodland and sheep pastures.

02 After an hour you'll pass some **picnic benches** on the edge of a deeper bit of forest. Straight after these, the path starts to climb a little more vigorously into thicker **woodland**.

140/PROVENCE & THE CÔTE D'AZUR

Shepherd Dogs

Mountain pastures in the Alps and the Pyrenees are often grazed by sheep, but the mountains of France are also home to a fast-growing wolf population, and there's nothing the big bad wolf likes to eat more than a tasty lamb. To protect the flock, shepherds use huge, snowy-white Pyrenean mountain dogs (known as a *patou* in French).

From afar they might look friendly, but don't try and stroke one. These dogs don't do petting. They do biting. Give them a very wide berth and if one approaches back slowly away while talking calmly to it and holding a bag or other object between you and it. Never throw stones at them or run away (they will give chase).

STUART BUTLER/LONELY PLANET ©

03 Two hours from the start you'll reach a trail junction in a small forest clearing with two cabins. Go left and gently wend your way uphill through a quiet forest. Ten minutes from the cabins, go right (south) at the **trail junction**. You're now following yellow waymarkers.

04 After a long and increasingly hard climb, the forest starts to fade away. Shortly afterward the trail picks its way through a rockfall area opposite a **waterfall**. With loose rock and little streams of water flooding over the path, it can be slippery and hard going.

05 The reward for the hard work comes as you clamber up onto a simply gorgeous **mountain pasture** framed by huge mountain peaks to the south. There's a **shepherd cabin** off to your right and sheep are often grazing the pastures.

06 Cross another stream and rise up onto another, rockier pasture. The path bends away from the cirque and makes a great looping turn past a **small lake**. The **views** of the snow peaks to the south and the stark, table-top peaks to the north will keep you transfixed.

07 Three hours after you set out, you'll reach the green plateau of **Eaux Tortes**. Turn left and circumnavigate the plateau in 20 minutes. When your loop is almost complete you'll come to a **trail junction** and signposts. Go right. For a while the trail remains up on a high ridge with **beautiful views** all the way. After passing another **shepherd hut** you'll start dropping down quickly through forest. One hour later cross a **bridge** and you'll be back at the forest clearing with the cabins (stop 03). Retrace your steps back to the car.

TAKE A BREAK

Tuck into a picnic in one of the mountain meadows.

Also Try...

VALLÉE DES MERVEILLES

Wedged between the Vésubie and Roya valleys, this narrow, remote canyon is famous for its amazing Bronze Age petroglyphs – ancient pictures carved into rock. In total, the valley contains more than 36,000 prehistoric carvings of figures, symbols and animals, thought to have been etched by members of a Ligurian cult between 1800 and 1500 BCE.

And the good news is that most can only be seen on foot. Access is restricted without a guide, which you can arrange through the Parc National du Mercantour visitor centres. There are many different walk routes, but the trail from the Lac des Merveilles to the Refuge des Merveilles is a favourite (pictured).

DURATION 7½hr return
DIFFICULTY Difficult
DISTANCE 19km

SENTIER IMBUT

There's more to the Gorges du Verdon than the Blanc-Martel trail. There's also the Sentier Imbut, and most people consider it the most beautiful of all the routes. The fact that it's a loop walk that starts and ends from the same point is also a bonus and, at five hours, it's shorter than the Blanc-Martel trail. So why doesn't everyone just do this walk?

Good question. Did we mention that removing yourself from the gorge involves a heart-in-the-mouth vertical climb straight up the gorge walls on a series of iron ladders? Even those without a fear of heights get halfway up the ladders and suddenly realise that they do in fact have a fear of heights. But by then it's too late. The climb is so steep and potentially dangerous that it's actually illegal to descend back down the ladders.

DURATION 5hr return
DIFFICULTY Difficult
DISTANCE 19km

JUERGEN WACKENHUT/SHUTTERSTOCK ©

CIRCUIT DE LA ROCHE TROUÉE

In a remote corner of the Parc National du Mercantour, this wild walk is a great one for wildlife-watchers and those with a geological bent.

The upper levels of this route bend around a giant, rocky, cirque that looks like something from the American Midwest rather than the southern Alps. The sheer needles of rock are a favourite with ibex and you can normally catch sight of a few defying gravity as they scramble from ridge to ridge. This quiet walk is well marked and not too steep but the trail is very rocky.

DURATION 4hr return
DIFFICULTY Moderate
DISTANCE 10km

SENTIER DU LITTORAL

Take a dramatic cape-to-cape walk along an unexpectedly peaceful part of the Côte d'Azur.

Starting in Roquebrune-Cap-Martin and running through to Cap d'Ail you can, with the exception of a 4km stretch through Monaco, walk this entire coastal path without seeing a car. What you will see instead are rugged coastal cliffs and some dreamy beaches that may well tempt you to forget about walking any further (pictured)!

DURATION 4hr return
DIFFICULTY Easy
DISTANCE 13km

LAC D'ALLOS

You couldn't ask for a more rewarding family mountain walk than this short and simple stroll to what's touted as the largest high-altitude lake in Europe.

The walk begins from parking du Laus, from where it's just a short scramble (100m elevation gain) to the lake and its surrounding marmot-filled meadows. Add an hour or so to your walk and you can circumnavigate the lake, admiring the way the surrounding mountains are reflected in the still waters.

DURATION 1½hr return
DIFFICULTY Easy
DISTANCE 4km

LANGUEDOC-ROUSSILLON

38 **Gorges d'Héric** A gorgeous gorge walk through the mountains – plus natural pools to cool off in. p148

39 **Cirque de Mourèze** A fairy-tale circuit of strange rock formations, with a fine ridge walk offering views over Lac du Salagou. p150

40 **Roc des Hourtous** Get a bird's-eye view on the Gorges du Tarn, and take a punt on a river barge. p152

41 **Pic St-Loup** Views of vineyards unfurl from one of the region's most distinctive peaks. p154

42 **Cirque de Navacelles** Follow a circuit round a huge river basin and visit a medieval mill along the way. p156

43 **Mont Aigoual** Tackle this taxing trek for some of the finest views in the Cévennes (and a historic observatory). p158

Explore LANGUEDOC-ROUSSILLON

Curling round the Mediterranean coast from Provence to the Pyrenees, this sun-toasted region often plays second fiddle to the glitzy glamour of the Côte d'Azur to the east. But for walkers, in many ways it's a more varied and rewarding region: a land of salt flats, dusty plains, high limestone mountains and forested hills. The hiking is equally varied – but avoid the scorching summer unless you want your boot soles to burn to a crisp...

MONTPELLIER

Graceful, elegant and easy-going, Montpellier offers shaded backstreets, peaceful public gardens and one of the best art museums in southwest France, the fantastic **Musée Fabre** (04 67 14 83 00; www.museefabre.fr; 39 bd de Bonne Nouvelle; adult/child €8/5.50; 10am-6pm Tue-Sun).

It's also a beach town, with several kilometres of sandy coastline. It's a transport hub, with fast TGV links to the rest of France, and has a huge range of excellent restaurants, bars and accommodation options. It's an ideal place to base yourself for walks in the Hérault *département*.

NÎMES

Nîmes is a dynamic and lively southern city, with handsome, palm-lined streets and an old town ripe for exploring. Two millennia ago, it was also one of the most important cities of Roman Gaul and several Roman buildings can still be visited. There are plenty of hotels to choose from and no shortage of good restaurants, especially in the old town. It's easy to reach by train and is a good gateway for travel to the Cévennes.

PERPIGNAN

Framed against the snow-topped Pyrenees, Perpignan is a sultry, sun-baked town with a distinctly Spanish flavour. Palm-shaded squares and winding lanes characterise the attractive old town, dotted with good regional restaurants and lively backstreet bars. It's easily reached by train or car, and is a good launch pad for hikes in the Haut-Languedoc and the lower Pyrenees.

WHEN TO GO

The summer in Languedoc-Roussillon seriously simmers, with scorching temperatures, so it's far from ideal for comfortable hiking. Spring and autumn are much better times for walking, with cooler temperatures and fewer crowds. Snow falls on the mountains and higher hills in winter, so hiking at elevation is only for the experienced.

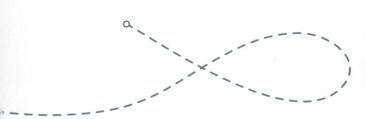

WHERE TO STAY

Accommodation options are ample and varied in this region. Unsurprisingly, the larger cities, particularly Montpellier, Nîmes and Carcassonne, offer the largest choices, from boutique hotels and five-star establishments to budget ventures and chain hotels. Book well ahead in summer, both inland and along the coast.

Having your own wheels opens up the region's rural landscape and the choice is even greater, with charming rural retreats and bijou bed and breakfasts.

WHAT'S ON

Carnaval de Limoux (www.limoux.fr; ⏲ Jan-Mar) One of the region's biggest carnivals runs over several weekends.

Les Grands Jeux de Nîmes (www.arenes-nimes.com; ⏲ Apr) Nîmes' amphitheatre hosts this Roman-themed extravaganza, complete with staged gladiatorial battles and a triumphal street parade.

Montpellier Danse (www.montpellierdanse.com; ⏲ Jul) Dance, both classical and contemporary, is celebrated in Montpellier.

Embrasement de la Cité (www.carcassonne.org; ⏲ Jul) Bastille Day culminates with a knockout fireworks display over Carcassonne's medieval city.

Joutes Nautiques (www.tourisme-sete.com/joute-nautiques-fete-tradition.html; ⏲ Aug) Water jousting tournaments take place on Sète's canals, where rival teams attempt to knock each other out of their boats using long poles. Bonkers and brilliant.

TRANSPORT

The main airports in Languedoc-Roussillon are in Montpellier, Nîmes and Perpignan, which are served by a number of regional low-cost carriers from many French and European cities, including easyJet, Volotea, Air France, Transavia and KLM.

Getting here by train is straightforward: frequent, fast services run across the Spanish and Italian borders, and from Paris, which has onward connections to the UK, Germany, the Netherlands and other northern European countries.

Montpellier is a hub, with fast TGV trains all over France. The TGV Midi-Méditerranée links Paris' Gare de Lyon with Montpellier's two stations (central St-Roch and the new Sud de France station outside town) in just over three hours.

Local buses can be tricky to navigate, as there are multiple companies and timetables often revolve around school term times. Having a car makes exploring rural areas much easier.

38

GORGES D'HÉRIC

DURATION	DIFFICULTY	DISTANCE	START/END
3hr return	Easy	9km return	Gorges d'Héric car park

TERRAIN	Paved

You don't always have to bust a gut to enjoy big views. This lovely canyon trail is easy-going, paved all the way (so suitable for wheelchairs and pushchairs), involves a gentle climb (min/max altitude 785m/1100m) and even has a cute seasonal cafe at the end – and the mountain views are absolutely majestic.

The route begins at the gorge car park, just outside the village of Mons (arrive early in high season, as this is a popular walk and the car park's often full up by 9am). From here, the tarmac trail winds up straight into the gorges, and, before too long, you'll find yourself framed on either side by seriously high mountains, with **thickets of chestnuts** and green oak carpeting the lower slopes. Signed panels provide information on local nature and wildlife.

The path ascends gradually, following the right bank of the river. As you walk, you'll pass plenty of **natural plunge pools** filled with crystal-clear mountain water (pictured): they're perfect for cooling off in on a hot day, but take care climbing down as the rocks can be slippery and it's easy to twist an ankle.

The mountains get ever higher as you climb further into the **Massif du Caroux**. These mountains are home to some of the Haut-Languedoc's classic climbing routes, so keep your eyes peeled for rock-bunnies picking their way up the sheer cliffs.

After about 1½ hours, the trail climbs around a sharp bend and eventually arrives at the tiny hamlet of **Héric**, little more than a cluster of stone farmhouses and slate-roofed barns. In summer, there's a little cafe here where you can refresh yourself with a drink and a snack before retracing your steps back down the valley.

148/ LANGUEDOC-ROUSSILLON

39

CIRQUE DE MOURÈZE

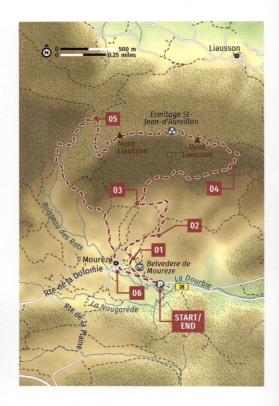

DURATION	DIFFICULTY	DISTANCE	START/END
3-4hr return	Moderate	7.5km	Mourèze village car park
TERRAIN	Rocky paths, forest trails			

This hike (min/max altitude 200m/535m) explores a strange amphitheatre of limestone peaks, then climbs onto a rocky ridge for wonderful views of the Lac du Salagou and the surrounding Languedoc landscape.

GETTING HERE
The walk is directly accessed from the village of Mourèze. There are regular buses from Montpellier (Line 663 or 685, 45 minutes; six daily Monday to Saturday, three on Sunday). See www.herault-transport.fr for timetables.

STARTING POINT
The village car park is on the edge of Mourèze and clearly signposted. There is also limited parking available along the roadside if the car park is full.

01 From the car park, follow trail signs for the cirque (bring extra water and a hat, as the cirque acts like a cauldron on hot summer days). You'll climb up a short staircase and then enter the amphitheatre proper. **Dolomite peaks** appear immediately, carved out into all kinds of weird shapes by aeons of erosion. Before long you'll pass a viewpoint, the **Belvédère des Courtinals**, which offers a panoramic view of the cirque, and the rooftops of Mourèze beyond. Many of the rocks are said to resemble things – see if you can spot the Sphinx, the Camel and the Grand Manitou.

02 There are several trails to follow through the cirque. They're well signed, but it's quite easy to miss the markers, so keep your eyes open. The trail dips and dives between the **rock pillars** and **towers**; it's not too tough, but can be dusty and slippery underfoot. You'll pass thickets of **garrigue**, the hardy, fragrant shrubs that are about the only things that can grow in the Languedoc's dry

150/ LANGUEDOC-ROUSSILLON

Lac du Salagou

Created in 1968 by damming the Salagou River, this reservoir is popular for hiking, horse riding and summer picnics.

Covering 750 hectares, it's known for its crimson-orange rock and strangely shaped islands, making it look rather like a lake might on Mars. It's 48km northwest of Montpellier.

landscape: rosemary, heather, juniper and arbutus. During the Middle Ages the cirque was used by local shepherds as a natural pen for their sheep flocks, which kept the vegetation in check.

03 After a while you'll see signs for the **Circuit des Charbonniers**, which is the next route to follow. It meanders gradually up to the edge of the cirque, then climbs sharply up into a forest of stubby green oaks that provide some very welcome shade.

04 The uphill, winding section through the trees is steep and tough work – about 300m of ascent – so take your time, and as many breathers as you need.

After about 20 to 30 minutes of climbing, you'll emerge on a rocky ridge called the **Mont Liausson**. It affords an impressive outlook south over the cirque, and also north across the Lac du Salagou. There are also the ruins of a medieval hermitage of **St-Jean-d'Aureillan**, but these are off-limits. The ridge is a perfect place for a picnic lunch, if you've brought one: there are plenty of shaded spots to choose from. When you've fuelled up, follow the path west along the ridge, then downhill: this section is rocky and rubbly, so watch your step.

05 You'll reach a junction – the **Col de Portes** – turn left, following it south back into the cirque. You'll pass rock formations before eventually rejoining the Sentier des Courtinals.

06 From here, it's easy walking to **Mourèze** (pictured), where there are several cafes. The **medieval church** is also worth a look before heading off.

 **TAKE A BREAK**

For lunch, **L'Art de la Flamme** (04 67 96 08 11; www.art-de-la-flamme.fr) on the edge of Mourèze is a decent spot (vegetarians aren't well catered for unfortunately).

LANGUEDOC-ROUSSILLON/**151**

40

ROC DES HOURTOUS

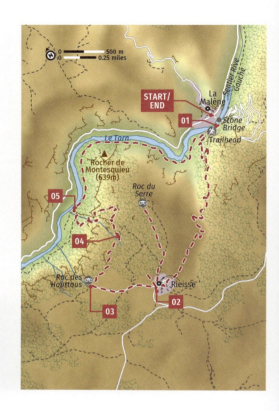

DURATION	DIFFICULTY	DISTANCE	START/END
4hr return	Moderate	9.5km	La Malène

TERRAIN	Rocky paths, steep woodland trail

The Parc National des Cévennes offers hundreds of superb walks. This one (min/max altitude 560m/915m) takes in a panoramic view over the Tarn valley and the moonscape of the Causse Méjean.

GETTING HERE
Your own wheels are the best way to explore the gorges. In July and August there are daily shuttle buses between Florac, Ste-Énimie and Le Rozier, but none of these go to La Malène.

STARTING POINT
There is a large public car park along the banks of the river in La Malène, but there's no village shop.

01 From the car park, cross the **bridge** over the river (pictured) and turn right. Soon, you'll see a trailhead ascending up the steep hillside to your left. Take it, and follow it as it switchbacks steeply up the cliff. There are a couple of excellent viewpoints along the way, offering super views over the valley, the clattering river and the rooftops of La Malène.

02 It's initially steep-going as you climb, but eventually the trail starts to level off as you reach the top of the cliff. After about an hour of climbing, you'll eventually come to the pretty little hamlet of **Rieisse**, with its stone farm buildings, chicken coops and the occasional puttering tractor.

If you wish, there's a detour trail from the village that leads north to the top of the **Roc du Serre**, where there's an orientation table that helps interpret the view. It's about 50 minutes there and back if you choose to take it.

152/ LANGUEDOC-ROUSSILLON

On the River

Right up until the early 20th century, the Tarn was still used to carry goods and passengers between the surrounding valleys. Historically, boatmen would have used flat-bottomed barges known as *barques*, but nowadays canoes and kayaks are a much more common sight on the river.

If you'd prefer to experience the river the traditional way, **Les Bateliers de la Malène** (04 66 48 51 10; www.gorges dutarn.com; per 4 people €92; 9am-noon & 1.30-5pm Apr-Oct) will punt you down an 8km stretch of the gorge from La Malène in an authentic old-fashioned barge, then drive you back. The journey time is one hour, depending on river conditions.

03 Continue west from Rieisse. As you leave the village, look out for a cross and signs to the **Roc des Hourtous**, which you'll reach after about 20 minutes of walking.

There's a cafe and car park at the Roc where you can stop for refreshments if you wish, with a grassy picnic area and tables looking directly out over the valley. Continue northeast along the rocky ridge line along the cliff edge, skirting through the trees. There are several **viewpoints** along the way where you can look out over the chasm, and stare down to the river several hundred metres below.

04 After about 800m, signs lead down off the ridge – they're easy to miss, so stay alert. From here, the trail descends very sharply on the steep cliff face beneath the Roc des Hourtous. The trail is very rocky and slippery at times, but is at least fairly easy to follow – walking poles might come in handy. Just be grateful you're climbing down rather than climbing up…

05 Eventually, you'll reach the end of the downhill path and emerge onto the south bank of the **Tarn**. Follow the path as it leads right (east), looping round the base of the **Rocher de Montesquieu** before returning to the start point at La Malène.

 TAKE A BREAK

There are several places to eat in La Malène, but the 13th-century, turreted **Manoir de Montesquiou** (04 66 48 51 12; www.manoir-montesquiou.com; d €82-152, 4-person apt €160; menus from €18; Apr-Oct; P ❄ 🛜) is the pick. The attractive restaurant has a plane-tree-shaded terrace overlooking the river and La Malène's old stone bridge, and serves excellent, locally inspired dishes.

LANGUEDOC-ROUSSILLON /153

41

PIC ST-LOUP

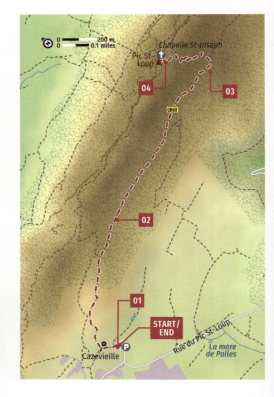

DURATION	DIFFICULTY	DISTANCE	START/END
2hr return	Moderate	5.5km	Pic St-Loup car park
TERRAIN	Rocky paths		

Another of the Languedoc classics, this uphill hike (min/max altitude 220m/658m) ascends to the summit of one of the region's most distinctive peaks – the shark-fin-shaped Pic St-Loup, topped by a medieval church.

GETTING HERE
The village of Cazevieille is a 25km drive from Montpellier. Public transport is a pain: the nearest bus runs as far as Les Matelles, 9km from the village.

STARTING POINT
The car park for Pic St-Loup is signposted from Cazevieille.

01 From the car park, follow the signposted trail uphill, passing a small stone shelter and bearing right up the stony path. Dead ahead, you'll see the distinctive pyramidal profile of **Pic St-Loup**, one of the most famous geological features in the Languedoc – not least because it graces countless local wine labels. The path climbs gradually through fragrant **garrigue** and stands of holm oak, boxwood and juniper – the only trees hardy enough to survive in this dry, sunbaked environment. The ecosystem is delicate, so stick to the trail to avoid erosion.

02 The path continues on a gentle incline for about 1.5km. The mountain remains ever in view. It was formed some 190 million years ago during the Jurassic period, when the entire landscape around was covered by sea, and tectonic movements shifted the seabed, forming the chain of mountains stretching from Provence to the Pyrenees. Around 65 million years ago, the waters receded and the peak of St-Loup was, for many millennia, a 1000m-high island. Forty-five million years ago the seas retreated further, and a long process of erosion pared the summit down to its current height

154/ LANGUEDOC-ROUSSILLON

The Legend of Pic St-Loup

The Chapelle St-Joseph is involved in the medieval legend that gave the peak its name. Three brothers (Loup, Guiral and Clair) all fell in love with the same girl before going off on a holy crusade. When they returned, they were distraught to discover that their beloved had died. Heartbroken, they resolved to become hermits, and each chose a solitary summit on which they would build a fire in her memory every year. Loup (Wolf) also built the chapel on the mountaintop. He was the last of the three brothers to die; in their honour, local villagers named their peaks after them – Mont St-Guiral, Mont St-Clair and Pic St-Loup.

of 658m, carving out its sheer sides in the process. It's been a protected site since 1978.

03 You'll reach a junction: ignore the path descending to the right, and continue through a tunnel of holm oaks. Not too far along you'll reach another junction, known as the **Crossroads of the Croisette**. Turn left (uphill). Here's where the trail gets steep: it winds through a series of switchbacks, ascending fairly sharply up the hillside. At times the path is narrow and rubbly, and a bit unstable underfoot – after periods of rain, it can be slippery. It's a stiff climb to the summit, 300m or so further up.

04 It's easy to know when you've reached the top – it's marked by the medieval **Chapelle St-Joseph**, which was restored in 1995 but is probably built on a much older sacred site. The summit has also clearly been a holy place for many centuries: the surrounding area is covered with many tumuli and ancient remains. Nearby, a striking iron cross reaches skyward, and a **belvédère** opens out onto a stunning view over the surrounding valley (pictured). The ridge of **Col de Fambétou** lies dead ahead; on a clear day you can make out the summits of **Mont Lozère** and **Mont Aigoual** in the Cévennes to the northeast and, way off to the east, is the snow-dusted hump of **Mont Ventoux**, Provence's queen of mountains. The valley below is filled with vineyards; wine was first grown here by the Phoenicians, and has been a vital part of the economy ever since. When you've enjoyed the views and had a picnic, retrace your steps back to the car park, about 2.7km downhill.

 TAKE A BREAK

Cazevieille is tiny, so there's not much choice for sustenance – most people pack a picnic and eat it at the summit beside the Chapelle St-Joseph (real connoisseurs might even pack a bottle of local Pic St-Loup wine).

LANGUEDOC-ROUSSILLON /155

42

CIRQUE DE NAVACELLES

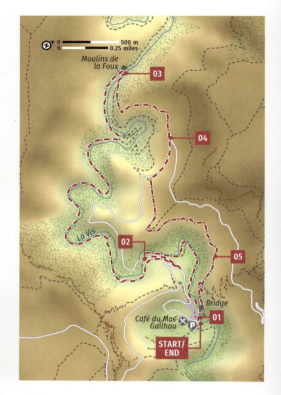

DURATION	DIFFICULTY	DISTANCE	START/END
3½hr return	Moderate	10km	Cirque de Navacelles car park
TERRAIN	Well-signed stone paths		

This amazing natural amphitheatre looks like a crater from an ancient meteorite strike. In fact, it's the result of nothing more devastating than aeons of natural erosion.

GETTING HERE

The cirque is a 77km drive from Montpellier, between the villages of St-Maurice-Navacelles and Blandas (if you're using sat nav, don't get confused with the other Navacelles, which is miles away in the foothills of the Cévennes). Buses (Line 108) run from Montpellier to the nearby village of Le Vigan, from where there are shuttle buses in summer.

STARTING POINT

There are a couple of car parks down in the village, but they fill up quickly in summer – arrive early to be sure of a spot.

01 From the car park on the riverbank, follow the river until you get to the handsome **arched stone bridge** that crosses the Vis, but don't take it; for the first section of the walk you'll be tracing the right riverbank. It's a pleasant walk through **woods**, with the clattering **Vis** a constant presence on your right.

02 The trail loops back on itself and eventually you'll reach a junction with the road (D130E). Turn left and walk uphill on the road for about 400m; where the road branches, you'll see a trail on your right heading away from the road to the southeast. Take it, and follow it downhill as it meanders back down towards the river. The trail becomes **increasingly wooded** as you continue; some sections can be slippery after rain, and a few points near the river occasionally get flooded (signs will indicate if this is the case). Follow the path all the way to the Moulins de la Foux.

156/ LANGUEDOC-ROUSSILLON

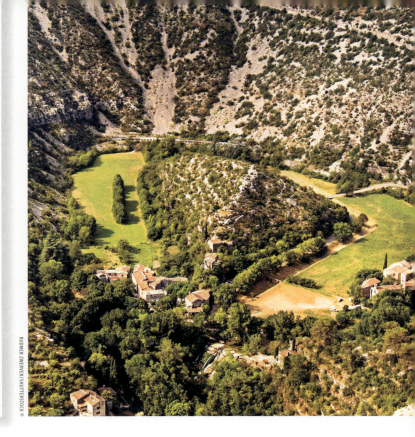

 ## The Source of the Vis

Even though local folk tales say that the Vis is bottomless, several cave-diving expeditions have tried to find the source.

The deepest dives were made in 2006 by divers from the European Karst Plain Project, who penetrated 2.3km at a depth of 104m, an epic dive that lasted six hours and 19 minutes.

A subsequent dive the following year managed a further 600m, reaching as far as the village of Vissec on the Causse du Larzac – but so far, the true source remains a mystery.

03 The **medieval mill** marks the rough halfway point of the walk, so it's a good place for a picnic. It's perched beside a rushing, roaring cascade (the word *foux* comes from the Occitan word *fos* meaning spring). Thanks to the force of water, there's been a mill here since the late 11th century; the present buildings were built in 1629 – although one was swept away by a massive flood in 1741 – and continued working until 1907. The mills were carefully restored in 2000. You can walk inside, and at times gaze down through the stone floor into the foaming tumult below. During very dry periods and very hot summers, the river occasionally peters out to a trickle, and sometimes disappears altogether – so to see it in full flow, it's best to come in spring or early summer, after there's been a day or two of rain.

04 Cross over the bridge next to the mill and follow the trail on your left as it climbs up. After a while you'll reach a junction with the D713. Follow it downhill for a while, then take the trail left.

05 Before long you'll find yourself quite a distance above the valley floor, with steep scree slopes tumbling down to your right – a bit daunting if you're wary of heights, but offering **impressive views**. The path continues like this all the way to a series of zigzagging switchbacks that lead back down the hillside and into the village. Cross the bridge and you'll be back where you began.

 ## TAKE A BREAK

The **Café du Mas Guilhou** (06 47 62 77 23; www.masguilhou.fr) is a convivial place for lunch, serving salads, tartines and sharing platters. It also offers B&B rooms and *gîte*-style bunks if you feel like staying overnight.

LANGUEDOC-ROUSSILLON /157

43

MONT AIGOUAL

DURATION	DIFFICULTY	DISTANCE	START/END
8hr return	Hard	24km	Valleraugue

TERRAIN	Mountain paths, forest trails

This epic walk is also known as the Sentier des 4000 Marches (Trail of 4000 Steps) – which gives you a hint that there might be some climbing involved. The reward? One of the finest mountain views in the South of France – but boy, you have to earn it (min/max altitude 350m/1565m).

This is the classic walk of the Cévennes, a loop route via the summit of Mont Aigoual. But there's no getting around it: it's a tough, full-day proposition, with just over 1400m of ascent and mixed terrain, so definitely for hardened hikers only. Make sure you pack plenty of food and water, a waterproof jacket and proper high-ankle boots.

GETTING HERE

Valleraugue is about 60km south of Florac, or 72km north of Montpellier, an easy 1½-hour drive. There is a daily bus between Montpellier and Le Vigan (Line 608), and another which travels onwards to Valleraugue (Line 108), but you'll probably have to overnight in Valleraugue as you'll need an early-morning start to ensure adequate time to complete the walk. See www.herault-transport.fr for full timetables.

STARTING POINT

Check in at the Maison du Pays (which also doubles as Valleraugue's tourist office) for the latest weather forecast and route tips.

01 Despite its name, there actually aren't that many steps on this route – and no one's quite sure how it got its moniker. There's a bit of tricky trail-finding along the way, so a good map will come in very handy: *IGN Top 25 2641ET Mont Aigoual/le Vigan/Parc national des Cévennes* is the one you want, at 1:25,000 scale.

Leaving from the Maison du Pays, turn left and walk along the rue de Luxemburg. At the bridge turn right and cross the river. Continue uphill on the chemin du Mas Mouret. After about 130m, turn right onto the chemin du Stade and walk (alongside a football pitch) for 60m until you reach a fork in the road, go left (uphill) onto the narrow, tree-lined chemin du Magnel until you reach an impressive **belvédère** where you can stop and enjoy the view before starting on the walk proper.

02 From here, the path begins to climb. It's a reasonably sharp ascent, passing through groves of **chestnut trees** planted by villagers in previous centuries, when they relied on the trees to provide food and flour. Gradually the **views** open up as you ascend towards l'Estivel.

03 After about 3km of climbing, you'll reach the **Estivel plateau**, a good place for a breather. Ignore any side trails on the right and continue climbing. There's some hard graft involved here, as this is where you'll be making the majority of the day's ascent, but you just have to push on and tick off the metres. It's another 4km to the top, but it'll take a while because of the gradient. You'll pass through some beech groves and eventually reach the crossroads at **l'Hort de Dieu** and the distinctive menhir known as the **Font de Trépalou**.

04 From here, make a left detour to stand on the **absolute summit** of the mountain at 1567m. It's impossible to miss thanks to the castle-like observatory built at the top, which is well worth a visit. Even if you don't go inside,

The Transhumance

The Cévennes is one of only a handful of places in France where the age-old spectacle known as the transhumance can be seen.

Every spring, local shepherds lead their flocks on foot up from their lowland farms to the higher mountain pastures, where they'll spend the rest of the summer, before returning them again in autumn.

It's a colourful spectacle, with the animals decorated with coloured ribbons and bells, and the shepherds dressed in their traditional finery – and a throwback to a way of life that's sustained the Cévennes for many centuries.

LANGUEDOC-ROUSSILLON /159

there's a **majestic vista** from the viewpoint, encompassing the whole Cévennes and, on the very clearest days, an unbroken panorama that sweeps from the Alps to the Mediterranean and the Pyrenees. It's an incredible spot, and one that makes the hard slog uphill from Valleraugue suddenly seem worth every step.

Opened in 1894, the **Mont Aigoual Observatory** (📞 04 67 42 59 83; www.aigoual.fr; ⏱10am-7pm Jul & Aug, 10am-1pm & 2-6pm May, Jun & Sep) is the last remaining mountain-based meteorological station in France (pictured). Inside, you can learn the science behind weather forecasting and cloud formation. There's also an orientation table from where you can take in the wrap-around views of the central Cévennes.

05 After the observatory, return to the menhir and take the trail signed for Aire-de-Côte/Sentier des Botanistes. This is also a section of the GR6, GR66 and GR7 long-distance trails, and follows a ledge with **big views** over the southern valleys, and big drops off to the right: watch your step.

06 This is where the trail map will come in handy, as there are several side trails involved here. Continue around a couple of hairpin bends, and after the second one look out for a track that leads quite steeply down into the forest. Take the next path on the right, which again tumbles down a steep slope for about 50m, then takes another turn at a stone cairn down onto a shale

Travels with a Donkey

Famously, the author Robert Louis Stevenson trekked across the Cévennes in 1878 with his recalcitrant donkey Modestine, a journey recounted in his classic travelogue, *Travels with a Donkey in the Cévennes*. His route now provides the backbone of the GR70 long-distance trail, which runs for 272km from Le Puy-en-Velay to Alès (slightly longer than Stevenson's original route).

It's the Cévennes' most famous walk, and one of the best long-distance routes in France, travelling from the forests of the Cévennes across the Mont Lozère massif into the farmland and valleys of Gévaudan and Velay. To do the full route takes around two weeks, or you can just tackle one of the individual sections.

slope. Look out for a gap in the rocks, and follow a fence until it reaches the ridgeline, dips through patches of pine forest and eventually rejoins the main GR6/GR7/GR66 trail.

07 Continue on the trail until you reach **Aire-de-Côte** at 1085m, another natural point of rest. From here, you'll be following the tarmac D100 road southeast.

08 After about 1.5km, a trail appears on your right, heading southwest away from the road, signposted for Col du Pas. Take it and walk for about 1km.

09 When you reach **Col du Pas** – a popular target for cyclists – you'll see another trail signed for Valleraugue. From here, the path descends quite steeply into the Vallée des Salles, switchbacking downhill into the little rural hamlet of **Berthezène**.

10 Cross over a **bridge** spanning the River Clarou, and follow the D10 road all the way back to your starting point in Valleraugue. A tough, long day on the mountain for sure – but congratulations are due: you've just climbed up and down to the rooftop of the Cévennes.

 **TAKE A BREAK**

Valleraugue has a small convenience store for supplies, or stop at the simple **Café du Jardin** (04 67 27 37 23; www.cafedujardin-valleraugue.fr) on rue du Luxembourg for a pre-hike coffee hit or a post-hike fuel stop.

Also Try...

JEROME PARIS/SHUTTERSTOCK ©

THE CANAL DU MIDI

You don't necessarily need a *péniche* (narrowboat) to enjoy the delights of the Canal du Midi: its towpaths provide plenty of walking potential too (with the benefit of also being pancake-flat).

Pretty much any section is worth a wander, but an easy one is the short walk from the hilltop town of Béziers to the famous stepladder of locks known as the **Écluses de Fonséranes** (www.beziers-in-mediterranee.com/en/the-9-locks-of-fonseranes; rue des Écluses; parking incl audioguide €7; 3D cinema & shop 10am-7pm mid-Mar–Oct), southwest of town (pictured). The eight locks and nine gates were built to negotiate a drop of 21.5m from the canal down to the level of the River Orb.

DURATION 3hr return
DIFFICULTY Easy
DISTANCE 4km

SIGNAL ST-PIERRE

An impressive walk along an old drovers' route leads up to another of the Cévennes' signature viewpoints, the signal point of St-Pierre at 695m.

It's a glorious place, elevated from the surrounding forest and offering a 360-degree view over the treetops: on clear days you should be able to see the Mediterranean away to the south, and the humps of the Massif Central off to the north.

The first section of the route traces the GR70, also known as the Chemin de Stevenson – the route followed by Robert Louis Stevenson and his donkey Modestine in 1878.

DURATION 3½hr return
DIFFICULTY Moderate
DISTANCE 9km

TRABANTOS/SHUTTERSTOCK ©

CARCASSONNE: LA BASTIDE TO THE CITÉ

While Carcassonne's dramatic medieval fortress unsurprisingly gets most of the attention, there's actually another side to the town: a square *bastide* (fortified town) dating from the 13th century, with its distinctive grid of straight streets.

The walk between the two is easy and very rewarding, and en route you get to cross the pedestrianised Pont-Vieux, one of the few surviving medieval bridges in France, prized for its graceful arches and compact dimensions (pictured).

DURATION 2hr return
DIFFICULTY Easy
DISTANCE 4km

SOMMET DE FINIELS

The highest point in the Cévennes is Mont Lozère at 1699m – or to be specific, the Sommet de Finiels.

Unlike the much tougher route to Mont Aigoual, there's a surprisingly easy way to reach the top: you can get a head start by parking at the Chalet du Mont Lozère at 1416m, with just 283m of climbing left to reach the summit. There's an orientation table at the top, and a view that takes in the Monts du Cantal, the Grands Causses and the distant Alps.

DURATION 3hr return
DIFFICULTY Moderate
DISTANCE 9km

MONT CANIGOU

At 2784m, this snow-capped peak is sacred to Catalan people.

The route to the top is best attempted in summer, when the weather is at its most settled. The easiest way to ascend is to get a lift by 4WD to the ski station of Les Courtalets, from where it's a two-to-2½-hour hike, followed by a 1½-to-two-hour return. Even in summer it's a proper mountain walk: wear appropriate gear, and consider employing the services of a local guide for maximum safety.

DURATION 4hr return
DIFFICULTY Moderate-hard
DISTANCE 8km

LANGUEDOC-ROUSSILLON /163

THE PYRENEES

44 **Plateau de Bellevue** Is this the best family mountain walk in France? **p168**

45 **Refuge des Oulettes de Gaube** Stare in awe at the mighty north face of the Vignemale. **p170**

46 **Lac d'Ayous Circuit** The centrepiece of this stunning walk is the distinctive Pic du Midi d'Ossau. **p172**

47 **Brèche de Roland** March over glaciers and snowfields to this legendary pass. **p174**

48 **Cirque de Troumouse** Relish this wide and wild cinematic landscape. **p176**

49 **Lac Vert** Dip your toes into Lac Vert, a hypnotic, emerald-green haze. **p178**

50 **Lac d'Oo & Lac Saussat** Compare lakes on this classic Pyrenean outing. **p180**

51 **Pic du Tarbésou & the Blue & Black Lakes** An exhilarating ridge walk past a triplet of mesmerising, multicoloured lakes. **p182**

52 **Marcadau Valley & the Cardinquère Lakes** The very best of the Pyrenees in one stunning, lake-studded walk. **p184**

53 **Col & Pic de Madamète** A long and challenging hike showcasing lakes, high passes and lofty peaks. **p188**

THE PYRENEES/165

Explore
THE PYRENEES

The Pyrenees are something special. Sure, they might lack the height of the Alps, but the mirror-glass lakes, the picture-postcard flower meadows, the candy-green fields in the valleys, the neat stone villages and the extensive mossy forests all combine to make these snow-dusted mountains among the most beautiful in Europe.

EAUX-BONNES

During the 19th century, the pretty village of Eaux-Bonnes (literally, Good Waters) flourished as a spa resort thanks to its geothermal hot springs. People still come here to take to the waters, but today hiking and skiing are the mainstay of the local economy. It's an ideal base for walk 46.

CAUTERETS

The delightful mountain town of Cauterets is full of fin-de-siècle character, with a stately spa and grand 19th-century residences dotted round town. Today it's a busy mountain resort serving both nearby hiking trails and ski slopes. From campsites to swanky hotels, there are plenty of places to stay and, in summer, there are minibus transfers to some of the most popular walking trailheads. Use it as a base for walks 45 and 52.

LUZ-ST-SAUVEUR

Topped by a tumbledown old castle and hemmed in on all sides by mighty peaks, attractive Luz-St-Sauveur is a mountain resort par-excellence. With hiking shops, lots of restaurants and supermarkets and a whole host of different accommodation options, this is an ideal base for walks 44, 47, 48 and 53.

BAGNÈRES-DE-LUCHON

Bagnères-de-Luchon (or simply Luchon) is a trim little town of gracious 19th-century buildings, expanded to accommodate the *curistes* who came to take the waters at its splendid spa. It's now one of the Pyrenees' most popular walking and ski areas. In summer minibus transfers are available to some of the most popular trailheads. Base yourself here for walks 49 and 50.

WHEN TO GO

We'll get straight to the point. If you can, go in late September and early October. This is when the leaves of the beech trees that blanket the mountain slopes turn a flaming red and orange, and a dusting of new snow on the summits hints to the coming winter yet the weather remains stable, sunny, and just the right kind of warm.

Autumn might be the best period, but summer is naturally the most popular time to walk here. Days are long and

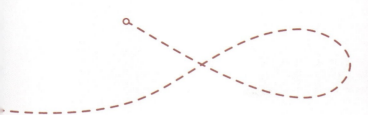

the weather is very settled. However, it can be too hot and afternoon thunderstorms are common.

Spring (April and May) can be hit and miss. Some years can be wonderful but others can be very wet (or snowy up high) and unsettled. Many of the higher passes remain blocked by snow.

Winter is generally a bad time to walk in the Pyrenees thanks to short days and periods of unsettled, stormy weather. The snow line is often down as low as 1000m, making most walking routes impassable. That said, in recent years winters have been surprisingly dry and settled and snowfall fairly rare until after Christmas. Increasingly, skiing is giving way to walking.

 WHERE TO STAY

You'll find a great variety of lodging on offer in the Pyrenees, including pretty farmhouse B&Bs with mountain views and campsites near hiking spots.

There is a superb series of *refuges* (mountain lodges) deep in the mountains throughout the Pyrenees, where accommodation is generally dorm style. From May to October many of these are staffed and meals can be provided for guests and often non-guests. Although basic, they have a great atmosphere and are good places to meet up with other walkers and exchange info on the trails.

Reserve all accommodation way ahead in the summer. Outside the ski areas, rural lodging generally closes down from about November to March.

👍 WHAT'S ON

Le Transhumance de Lourdios (🕐 Jun) Follow the livestock and shepherds during their annual migration to the high mountain pastures. The Vallée d'Aspe has the best known transhumance.

Foire au Fromage (cheese fair; 🕐 Oct) Annual fair held in Laruns in the Vallée d'Ossau that celebrates the valley's famed cheese.

Ski season (🕐 Dec-Apr) The ski resorts of the Pyrenees are much more low key and local than those of the Alps.

 TRANSPORT

The most convenient airport for the Pyrenees is Pau, but international flights are limited. Biarritz and Toulouse are much busier.

Buses between towns and villages in the Pyrenees are limited and to most walking trail heads they're virtually non-existent (though some tourist offices lay on summer-only minibus transfer services to the most popular walking areas). To properly explore you'll need wheels.

THE PYRENEES/167

4.4

PLATEAU DE BELLEVUE

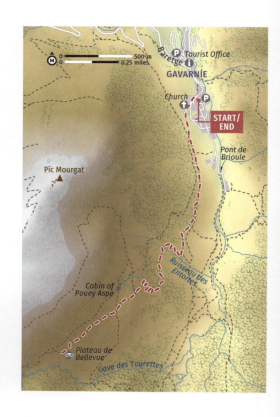

DURATION	DIFFICULTY	DISTANCE	START/END
2hr return	Easy	5.5km	Main car park, Gavarnie
TERRAIN	Mountain trail		

Is this the best family mountain walk in France? Walk (min/max altitude 1365/1700m) to this stunning viewpoint overlooking the famed Cirque de Gavarnie on a warm day in October, when the sky is blue, the leaves on the beech trees are golden and the mountain summits are fluffed with the white of the first winter snows, and you'll probably agree that it is.

From the main car park in Gavarnie, take the cobbled road up past the **church** and **cemetery**. Pass some walking signs and continue along a clear track that rises gently and enters a **deciduous forest**. You'll be able to see the main trail to the **Cirque de Gavarnie** below you, and if it's a nice day then chances are it will be packed with day-tripping tourists. By contrast, you'll likely be alone and tranquil.

The views of the cirque will get better as you climb. The path starts getting steeper and weaves in great curves up the slope. After a little under an hour, you'll clear the tree line and emerge onto the plateau. The small **cabin of Pouey Aspé** is off to the right.

Continue onwards for another 15 minutes until you come to the edge of the **Plateau de Bellevue**, a walk signpost and a great pile of rocks. You now have a grandstand view of the **Cirque de Gavarnie**. The peak to the extreme left is the **Casque du Marbauré** (3325m), **le Casque** (3006m) is more centre, and **Taillon** (3144m) is the biggie on the far right.

From here you can descend into the cirque, but it's a steep, long walk that's not suitable for families. Return instead by the way you came.

45

REFUGE DES OULETTES DE GAUBE

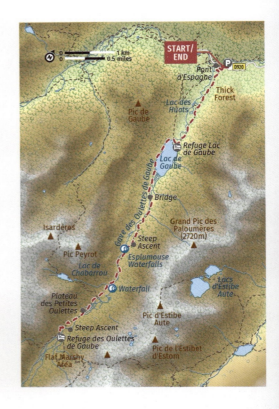

DURATION	DIFFICULTY	DISTANCE	START/END
5hr return	Moderate	15km	Parking du Pont d'Espagne
TERRAIN	Mountain trail		

This spectacular walk to the glaciers and soaring cliffs of the Vignemale (3298m), the highest point of the French Pyrenees, offers wild forests, sublime lakes, quiet mountain meadows and a face-to-face encounter with some of the mightiest of Pyrenean peaks. Although quite a long walk (min/max altitude 1460/2151m), and one that takes you deep into the high mountains, this is actually a pretty simple hike along a well-signed trail that can even be accomplished by children.

From the park gates head left along a path signed for the GR10 and Lac de Gaube. A couple of hundred metres later, veer left and clamber up through **mixed forest**. After an hour, you'll trip over a rise and arrive on the glimmering blue shores of the large **Lac de Gaube** (pictured). Many families make this the goal of their walk before returning back to the car (1¾ hours return).

Continue around the western shore of the lake on a clear, flat path and then carry on onward and upward. After 2½ hours pass the **Esplumouse waterfalls** on your left. There are great views back down the valley. A short time later, the path levels out at the **Plateau des Petites Oulettes** and the views of the Vignemale fill the horizon ahead.

After another half-hour, during which you climb quite sharply, you will come to the **Refuge des Oulettes de Gaube**. In front of you is a large, waterlogged plateau, at the end of which is the sheer, vertical wall of the mighty north face of the **Vignemale** (3298m) and its **huge glacier**. Return by the same route.

170/THE PYRENEES

46

LAC D'AYOUS CIRCUIT

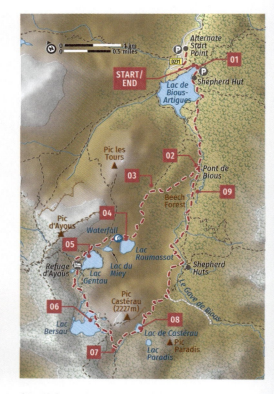

DURATION	DIFFICULTY	DISTANCE	START/END
5½hr return	Moderate	14km	Parking Lac de Bious-Artigues
TERRAIN	Mountain trail, very clearly signed			

This walk (min/max altitude 1419/2103m) is forever throwing something of interest towards you: pastures filled with docile-eyed cows and sheep, soaring fang-like pillars of rock, mossy forests, streams filled with fat trout, not to mention a dazzling multitude of lakes. But as the scenery immediately around you changes one thing remains constant: the towering presence of the Pic du Midi d'Ossau (2884m) just across the valley.

GETTING HERE
The nearest village is Gabas. There's very little public transport.

STARTING POINT
The walk begins from the Lac de Bious-Artigues, which is a steep 4.5km uphill drive along the D231 from Gabas. The upper car park is small and fills up fast. Unless you get here early, chances are you will end up parked in the lower car park, which is a very steep, energy-sapping 20- to 30-minute walk to the start point of this hike.

01 From the upper car park follow the signed path past a **snack shop**, along the eastern bank of the reservoir and uphill through mixed woodlands.

02 After a sweaty half-hour, the trail levels out at a metal farm gate. Go through this and 100m later the woodlands peel back to reveal a vast pasture shot through by a **fast-flowing stream**. Right at the start of this pasture, the trail forks at a clear **signpost**. Go right (southwest) and uphill back into woodlands.

03 The next half-hour involves zigzagging uphill through **beech forest** to a small **flower meadow** with **views** over to the Pic du Midi d'Ossau.

172/THE PYRENEES

Best for

WILDLIFE

04 The next scenic highlight is the **Lac Roumassot**, the first of a multitude of lakes you'll pass. The trail works its way past the lake and then uphill again, flirting with a small **waterfall** as it does so.

05 Pass more small lakes and pools, then climb up and over another ridge to the spectacular **Lac Gentau** (pictured p165). On a still day, its blue waters beautifully reflect the Pic du Midi d'Ossau. On a bluff just above the lake is the **Refuge d'Ayous**.

06 The trail works its way uphill through a rocky, desolate landscape. You will soon reach a couple of different lakes. The biggest is the final lake, **Lac Bersau.**

07 As you leave Lac Bersau the trail forks. The obvious path carries on straight ahead (south-southwest). Do not take this one. Instead, veer sharp left (east) and downhill. Instantly, the horizon opens out into a **memorable view** of a grand expanse of high peaks, while just to your left is the bizarre thumb-shaped rocky outcrop of the **Pic Castérau** (2227m; pictured).

08 The path tumbles in a series of sharp bends down to the **Lac de Castèrau** and then starts a long, leg-aching descent to the valley floor.

09 Soon enough, you hit the valley floor, where there are often **free-ranging cows and sheep**. In spring the grasslands sparkle with **wildflowers**. You will come to a rough cement road (authorised vehicles only). Follow this for 20 minutes until you reach the metal gate that first welcomed you to this upland paradise.

Retrace your steps back downhill to the car.

 **TAKE A BREAK**

The **Marche au Crêpes** snack bar is a little shack, right next to where the walk starts, selling crêpes, galettes and a few other snacks.

THE PYRENEES/173

47

BRÈCHE DE ROLAND

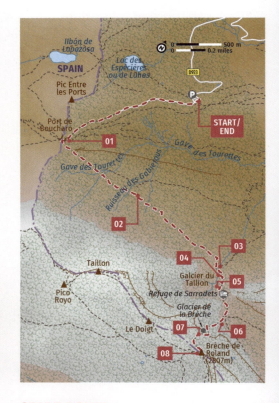

DURATION	DIFFICULTY	DISTANCE	START/END
5hr return	Moderate	13km	Col de Tentes

TERRAIN	Well-marked mountain trail plus a glacier crossing

If you want to get up into the frosty realms of the high mountains fast then this is the walk for you. On this trail (min/max altitude 2200/2807m), you'll scramble across scree slopes, tip-toe across the foot of a glacier and then, at the walk's culminating point, stand in the dramatic rock gateway of the Brèche de Roland. But there is a catch...deep snow renders this walk inaccessible for much of the year. You should only attempt this route in fine, settled weather between late July and early October. During these months, this is a very popular walk.

GETTING HERE

The village of Gavarnie is an obvious base. The Col des Tentes is a spectacular 25-minute drive southwest of Gavarnie along the D923.

START POINT

The walk begins from the car park at the Col des Tentes. There are no facilities here, but there are grand views.

01 Take the track heading southwest towards the **Port de Boucharo** (at the France–Spain border). A couple of different walk trails meet here. Our route veers sharp left (east) and climbs upward.

02 For the next hour the trail leads gently upwards along the steep northern flank of **Le Taillon** (3144m).

03 The first real challenge is crossing a **multifingered stream**. The waters flow fast and it's very slippery. There's no set crossing point. Just watch where other people are crossing (pictured).

174/THE PYRENEES

04 The trail climbs steeply for 15 minutes before popping up onto flatter ground at the foot of the **Galcier du Tallion**. Pick your way around the edge of the glacier. In July this might involve walking on the last of the winter snow. Always stick to the obvious trail.

05 Next stop is the **Col de Sarradets** (2589m) and the **Refuge de Sarradets**. From here there's an incredible view of **Cirque de Gavarnie**. The **Grande Cascade** (Large Waterfall) is directly in front of you. For those walking with children, this is a good place to call it a day. Simply retrace your steps to make a walk of 3½ to four hours.

06 For those carrying on to the Brèche de Roland, the way ahead is obvious if a little daunting. The trail climbs very steeply upwards along a **ridge of scree**. If you're here early (or late) in the season and the ridge is covered in snow with no obvious path through it, do not ascend any further.

07 Cresting a ridge, the Brèche de Roland is now just above you, but between you and it lies the **Glacier de la Brèche**; a giant ice ramp that leads to the rock gateway. The trail over the ice and snow is normally obvious but still requires a lot of care and attention.

08 Ten minutes later, you'll find yourself standing in the shadow of the **Brèche de Roland** (2807m). The views south into Spain and north over France are astounding. The Spanish side is a desert-like wilderness of empty rock scarred and wrinkled by ice. By contrast, the views over the French side lead the eye over distant fertile mountain pastures. Retrace your steps the way you came.

 **TAKE A BREAK**

The **Refuge de Sarradets** serves full evening meals for people staying, and drinks and snacks at lunchtime for those just passing through.

THE PYRENEES/**175**

48

CIRQUE DE TROUMOUSE

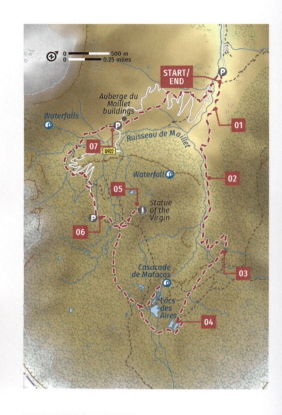

DURATION	DIFFICULTY	DISTANCE	START/END
4½hr return	Moderate	12.5km	Parking de la Chapelle d'Héas
TERRAIN	Mountain trail		

From first-time hiker to hardened mountain yeti, there's something for everyone on this fabulous circular walk (min/max altitude 1517/2135m) around the base of the Cirque de Troumouse. The cinematic landscape here is wide and wild: a huge rolling pasture dotted with small pools stands at the foot of a wall of grey-brown rock and snow-dusted peaks.

GETTING HERE

The walk begins from the hamlet of Héas. To get there from the attractive town of Luz-St-Sauveur, drive south along the D921 to Gèdre, then take the minor D922 to Héas. It's 20km from Luz-St-Sauveur and 8.5km from Gèdre. When you're in Héas, park at the large car park on the right just beyond the church. There's no public transport.

STARTING POINT

There are no facilities at the start point except some walk information signs.

01 From the car park, head uphill on the clear **stone track** signed for the Cirque de Troumouse. At the junction 50m from the start continue straight.

02 After 30 minutes, the trail flattens a little and you enter a **pasture** with views to the mountains ahead and a **waterfall** to your west. At the head of the pasture, the trail starts climbing, first slowly and then in steep zigzags. This is the part of the walk where you earn your ticket to the cirque! Allow at least 45 minutes for this climb.

03 At the **signed junction** continue straight ahead (south) towards the wall of mountains. A few minutes later, the path levels up and you start to enter the **cirque**.

176/THE PYRENEES

Family Version

For a shorter, more family-friendly version of this walk (3½-hour return without stops) follow stages 01 to 04 and then simply turn around and return by the way you came.

This part of the walk is possible with young children without too many dramas – though be sure to take a whole load of snacks and leave a full day to complete.

STUART BUTLER/LONELY PLANET ©

04 The floor of the cirque is a wide grassy basin pocked with small hills and dotted with **pools and lakes**. The path makes a slow semicircle as it traverses the floor of the cirque (pictured). The **views** just seem to get better and better with a solid line of 3000m-plus peaks forming one giant wall. There are numerous short side trails leading off the main path to **pools**, **drop-offs** and **viewpoints**.

05 The trail works over a low ridge and bends slightly northwest away from the mountain wall. You will come to a junction. Head straight on (north) to a table-shaped rise topped with a **statue of the Virgin**. From here, you can admire staggering **mountain views**.

06 Return back to the main trail, cross the bridge and head towards a small car park. Descend on a trail that crosses the road multiple times.

07 The trail leaves the road and heads towards a dramatic series of **waterfalls**, before bending back around and arriving in a lower car park. Drop down to the lower of two buildings here, cross a cattle grid and go immediately left before the stone bridge on a faint trail that follows the course of some electricity pylons. As you walk, the trail becomes clearer. A long, tiring and very steep descent now follows, during which you cross the road a couple of times. After a muscle-burning, knee-jarring hour, you will arrive back at your car.

 **TAKE A BREAK**

Bring a picnic and enjoy it in the quieter eastern side of the cirque.

THE Pyrenees/177

49

LAC VERT

DURATION	DIFFICULTY	DISTANCE	START/END
5½hr return	Moderate	12.5km	Parking Vallée du Lis
TERRAIN	Mountain trail		

You don't have to spend long walking in the Pyrenees to realise that lakes are an essential element of any walk here. All of them are beautiful, but perhaps none more so than Lac Vert (Green Lake). High above the floor of the Lis Valley and reached via a trail (min/max altitude 1135/2010m) that wends through forests and up and down ridges, Lac Vert is a hypnotic emerald-green haze backed by dark mountain slopes and surrounded by lush meadows.

GETTING HERE

From Luchon take the road (D125 and D46) towards Superbagnères, but veer off onto the D46a that leads into the Vallée du Lis (Lis Valley) before dead-ending at the large car park near the electrical plant. It's 11.5km from Luchon.

START POINT

There's a large car park, but several classic walking routes start from here; in summer, the car park fills up early and you may have to find a parking space somewhere back along the road. Facilities include walk information panels and a restaurant.

01 From the parking area, cross the bridge over the **River Lis** and, around 100m later, leave the road for a signed grassy track on the left. The trail rises steeply southeast through thick beech forests and then pine. It's hard going but at least it's shaded!

02 After a little under an hour, the path levels out and you emerge onto a summer livestock pasture with a **shepherds' cabin** (1390m). At the trail junction, take the left fork (straight ahead). You'll quickly be back into forest and the climb resumes. Along the way you'll pass a couple of impressive **waterfalls** that make good spots to rest and cool off.

178/THE PYRENEES

Family Walk

For a great family outing (2½ hours; min/max altitude 1132/1390m) take a walk up to the shepherds' cabin mentioned in stop 02.

From here, turn right and descend to the Gouffre d'Enfer (a lake and dam) and then loop down to the valley floor and the dramatic Cascade d'Enfer (Enfer Waterfall).

03 Around 1½ hours from the start, you come to a second cabin (**Cabane de la Coume**; 1715m) and the trail forks again with Lac Vert signed in both directions. Take the left fork.

04 As you continue to climb steeply, the trees get smaller and then finally die away completely, and you will find yourself walking over grassy pastures with mountains starting to fill in the view ahead. The path zigzags upward and bends to the right (south). With a final heave, you'll come face to face with the small **Lac des Grauès**.

05 The going is easier as the clear trail undulates over a couple of ridges before bringing you to the shores of the large, surreal **Lac Vert** (2001m). Walk along the northern shore of this almost figure-eight-shaped lake and watch how the waters change colour with the movement of sunlight and cloud.

06 The path rises and falls along the lake and then starts a long descent. **Metal chains** are bolted to the rocky slope to ease you down a steep section (in fine weather you don't really need the help of the chains). Eventually a smaller, darker lake springs into view.

This is the **Lac Noir** (Black Lake); shortly after, you pass the **Cabane de Prat-Long** where the path forks again. Turn sharp right (east) and start a tiring, long drop through forest to the junction at the Cabane de la Coume. From here, simply retrace your steps back down to your car.

TAKE A BREAK

The delightful **Ô Berges du Lys** (☎09 71 21 28 47; ⏰10am-6pm Apr-Oct) at the end of the Vallée du Lis serves delicious sizzling steaks, duck and burgers all cooked up on a *plancha* (griddle). The vibe is more funky cool than traditional mountain hut.

THE PYRENEES/**179**

50

LAC D'OO & LAC SAUSSAT

DURATION	DIFFICULTY	DISTANCE	START/END
4¾hr return	Moderate	13km	Granges d'Astau

TERRAIN	Mountain trail

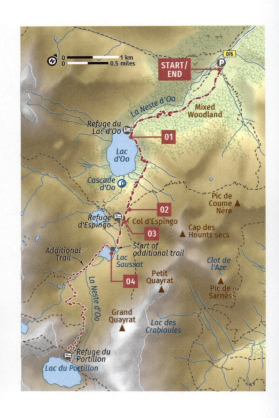

Lac d'Oo is a huge, startling coloured sheet of water bookended by spectacular cliffs and crashing waterfalls, while the higher-altitude Lac Saussat is smaller, wilder and more intimate. The walk (min/max altitude 1139/1967m) to either of them is a non-stop succession of changing scenery and there's something in this valley suitable for all types of walker. It's no surprise then that this is one of the more popular walks in the Pyrenees. Go early or try and avoid high summer if you want a hint of peace.

GETTING HERE

The nearest town – and an ideal base for this walk – is Bagnères-de-Luchon (normally just Luchon). A *navette* (shuttle-bus service) runs from outside the tourist office in Luchon to the Granges d'Astau twice a day (adult/child return €11/5) throughout July and August. Otherwise, it's a 14km drive southwest from Luchon along the D76.

START POINT

There's a large car park at Granges d'Astau, with walk information panels and places to buy snacks.

01 The route up to Lac d'Oo is very clear. Simply follow the signed track away from the parking area and start climbing through **mixed woodland**. After a while, the wide track shrinks to a smaller footpath, but it remains

 ## Additional Trail

For a more challenging walk (8½ hours return), you can continue onwards from the Lac Saussat to the **Refuge du Portillon** (2570m), which sits on the often frozen shores of the lake of the same name. The vista from the *refuge* out across the lake to the wall of mountains piled up around the lake is one of the best views in the Pyrenees.

Other than the distance this isn't an especially hard walk in fine summer weather, but we would suggest overnighting at the *refuge* in order to fully appreciate the high-mountain ambience.

---

obvious. The climb is generally very gentle. An hour after setting out, you will arrive on the shores of the large **Lac d'Oo** (pictured). It's a marvellous spot; light woodland lines its banks, and at the far southern end a wall of rock rises up more dramatically, down which plunges a 275m-high **waterfall**. Lac d'Oo is a good goal for families with younger children.

02 The trail, which has red and white GR waymarkers, makes its way along the eastern side of Lac d'Oo and, towards the far end of the lake, begins to climb more steadily. Both the trees and the crowds start to slowly thin out as you gain altitude. Pass a small waterfall and a little while later veer right at the trail fork.

03 After a further 1½ hours you will climb breathlessly up onto the **Col d'Espingo** (1967m). From here, there are **views** to the south of a solid wall of 3000m-plus mountain peaks. Just beyond the pass is the **Refuge d'Espingo**, just off the trail to the right, and the pretty **Lac d'Espingo**.

04 Many people call it a day at the *refuge*, but it's worth carrying on another 10 minutes to the slightly lower (1940m) **Lac Saussat**. Much quieter than either Lac d'Oo or Lac d'Espingo and with the mountains reflected brilliantly in its lime-green waters, this is an ideal place to idle a while before returning to your car via the same route (leave two hours for this).

 ### TAKE A BREAK

At both Lac d'Oo and Lac d'Espingo there are mountain *refuges* that serve snacks, drinks and even full meals. Many people also just picnic on the shores of one of the lakes.

51

PIC DU TARBÉSOU & THE BLUE & BLACK LAKES

DURATION	DIFFICULTY	DISTANCE	START/END
4½hr return	Moderate	12.5km	Parking Pla de Mounégou

TERRAIN	Well-marked mountain trail

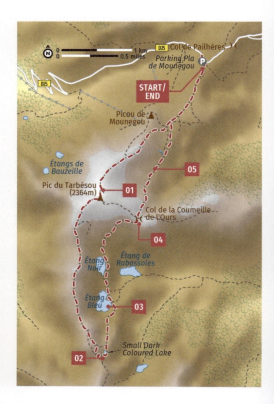

With a bracing summit ascent, a grandstand view of a huge swathe of the Pyrenees and an exhilarating ridge walk past a triplet of mesmerising, multicoloured lakes, this walk (min/max altitude 1920/2364m) packs a lot of punch. The scenic rewards will keep even the most hardened mountain walker content, but it's also a good bet for adventurous families.

GETTING HERE
The best base is the village of Ascou, which is 12km west of the trail head at Parking Pla de Mounégou.

STARTING POINT
The start point is from the Pla de Mounégou car park, a few hundred metres west and down slope of the Col de Pailhères. There are picnic tables and information panels.

01 Take the clear, wide trail heading south-southwest away from the parking area. After 15 minutes, a small foot trail veers off left (southwest) signed in yellow for the Pic du Tarbésou, all the time climbing steadily up the left-hand side of the mountain. After a while, you'll come to a subtle trail junction. Follow the yellow waymarkers right (southwest) and upwards.

A short while later the trail rises triumphantly onto the summit of the **Pic du Tarbésou** (2364m). The summit offers a grandstand view of the main Pyrenean range to the south and foothills to the north. But the real surprise is reserved for when you walk to the southern edge of the summit for your first view over a triple crown of **multicoloured lakes**: the **Étang de Rabassoles** and the appropriately named **Étang Bleu** (Blue) and **Étang Noir** (Black).

182/THE PYRENEES

02 The yellow waymarked trail drops down in a southwest direction very steeply towards the obvious **ridge**. The trail creeps along the ridge with stunning views whichever way you care to glance. From the top of the last crest, drop southeast. After a few minutes the path forks.

The main route stays high and bends around a ridge to a **small dark-coloured lake** that up until now has remained hidden from view. From a small pass just to the south of this lake, a minor trail breaks away left (north) off the main route and descends to the lake.

03 Walk along the eastern shore of this small lake. You will now be following red and white GR trail markers. You will soon arrive on the eastern side of the turquoise-blue **Étang Bleu**. From the northern end of the lake, take the trail with the red and white GR waymarkers and not the wider, more obvious trail heading eastwards. The trail climbs up another ridge to the **Étang Noir** and passes along the eastern shore.

04 There's now a gruelling half-hour climb up to the **Col de la Coumeille de l'Ours**, from where you get a lingering last glance back at the lakes (pictured).

05 It's then just a gentle half-hour amble along the plateau back to the car. About halfway through this stage, you'll meet up with the dirt road that you walked along at the very start.

 **TAKE A BREAK**

There are no cafes or restaurants along this trail. The meadows surrounding the Étang Bleu call out for a picnic stop.

THE PYRENEES/183

52

MARCADAU VALLEY & THE CARDINQUÈRE LAKES

DURATION	DIFFICULTY	DISTANCE	START/END
6½hr retun	Hard	18.5km	Pont d'Espagne

TERRAIN	Mountain trail

From the thunderous waterfall at the Pont d'Espagne, to autumnal red beech forests, highland pastures and sharp mountain spires speckled in snow, this long walk is one of the classics of the Pyrenees. With a high pass to cross, luminous lakes to linger by, gushy rivers and fields of flowers that could make a florist blush in envy, this is a walk (min/max altitude 1460/2429m) that just keeps on giving.

GETTING HERE

Cauterets is the closest base to this walk. There's a bus from the town to the Pont d'Espagne car park six times daily from July to early September and four times daily at other times. The cost is €7.50 return.

STARTING POINT

The walk starts from the huge Pont d'Espagne car park (€7 per day parking fee). It's 8km from Cauterets along the steep and twisting D920. There's a park information office and walk information panels.

01 Kick into gear by walking to the famed **Pont d'Espagne** (Spanish Bridge; pictured), an impressive 19th-century bridge that's totally overshadowed by the incredible wedding-cake waterfalls that crash and smash behind it.

02 From the bridge follow the signs for the chalet, **Refuge du Clot**, a few minutes' walk away. Just afterwards, the track forks. You can go either way but we start by taking the newer route and will return by the older and more interesting route. Take the left fork (south) over the bridge and walk along a driveable track through mixed forest. After around 40 minutes, the forests surrender to an open plateau where the river meanders in looping lines and cattle graze.

03 An hour from the start you reach another signed junction. Ignore the sign pointing right for the Circuit des Lacs (we will return down this route at the end of the day) and head left (southeast), following the trail to Refuge Wallon.

The trail marches through forest and across riverside meadows. After a further hour, it bursts out into a pasture dotted with trees and giant granite boulders. At this point, the mountains really start to make their presence known. To the south is the **Grand Pic d'Arratille** (2900m) and slightly to the southwest is the **Grand Pic de Peterneille** (2764m). Turn right (west) at the trail junction and in a couple of minutes you'll be at the **Refuge Wallon** (1865m).

This is a real hikers' crossroads of the central Pyrenees and numerous day and multiday trails fan out from here. The *refuge* reopened in summer 2021 after a full refurbishment. If you're a family with smaller children, this is probably a good place to have a picnic and dip your toes in the river before returning by the same way that you came.

04 Leaving the idyllic valley around the *refuge*, take the small trail northwest that passes behind the small stone **Chapelle du Marcadau**. Twenty minutes after leaving the *refuge* and chapel, the trail shimmies out of the forest and onto a barren grass plateau known as the **Pédet-Malh**.

At a signed trail junction take the right (north) fork. The trail zigzags steadily uphill into ever

The Pyrenean Brown Bear

In 2004 the last native brown bear left in France was shot by a boar-hunter, supposedly in self-defence. The demise of the female bear, known as Cannelle to conservationists, marked the extinction of a species that a century ago was still a relatively common sight in the Pyrenees.

The species has since been reintroduced using bears imported from Slovenia. They have bred successfully, and it's thought that by 2020 there were around 60 brown bears roaming across the mountains. However, not everyone is celebrating the return of the bears. Some local shepherds and farmers see the bears as dangerous predators that pose an unwelcome threat to their flocks and livelihoods.

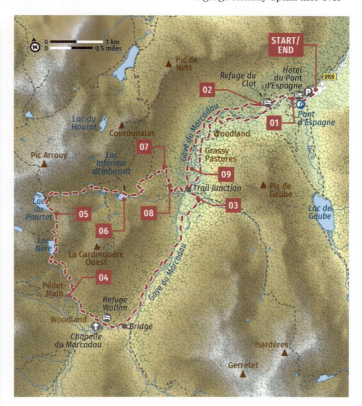

more barren territory. Ahead, a sheet of steep rock rears up with a small stream and waterfall running down the side of it. Follow this stream up to the nick in the rock face to arrive at the **Lac Nère** (2307m), a green-tinged lake settled into a small mountain bowl.

05 The trail climbs for a further 20 minutes up over scree slopes to the **Lac du Pourtet** (2420m). Don't forget to look behind you and take in the **stellar view** of the mountains filling in the southern end of the Marcadau Valley. Snug in a glacial cirque, and surrounded by jagged, rocky spires, the Lac du Pourtet is a large, icy-blue lake that beautifully offsets the forbidding high mountain terrain that surrounds it. It can be cold and windy here even in high summer.

The route picks its way around the eastern side of the lake and in places is narrow and with a sheer drop to the waters below. An abrupt right (east) turn at the far end of the lake rewards with a view of the trail cartwheeling down to a **chain of jewel-blue lakes** far below. It's one of the best viewpoints on the walk.

06 The next hour of walking, during which you will lose some 400m of height, is simply delightful. The path is easy to follow, and not too steep (pictured). As it drops, it passes lake after glorious lake. These are the **Embarrat Lakes** and there are at least four of them, plus some minor pools and marshes. The first lake is surrounded by the detritus of rockfalls and avalanches, but then, with each lake passed, the landscape gets greener and more lush.

07 Dragging yourself away from the lakes, you enter a different habitat. Just beyond the far end of the final lake, the **Lac Inférieur d'Embarrat**, the trail turns sharp left (north) and moves away from the river. Trees start to make a return to the scene and there are views across folds of mountains and down into the Marcadau Valley that you walked up earlier in the day. Soon you reach an **avalanche area**. Pick your way gingerly over the rocks.

As you near the end of the rockfall area, look for an indistinct fork in the trail that turns sharply back on itself and drops downhill to the right. Take this. Do not carry on straight ahead. It's easy to overlook this junction.

08 The trail now drops steeply through increasingly **thick and varied woodland** for the next 50 minutes. The last half-hour, in particular, is especially steep. You'll be glad you're heading downhill here and not up! Eventually, you arrive on the valley floor and a trail junction and signpost. You're now back by the river (**Gave du Marcadau**) that you followed on the way to the Refuge Wallon. However, instead of crossing over the river and following this same trail back to the car, we are going to take the old path back to the Refuge du Clot by staying on the left (west) side of the river.

09 For the next 45 minutes, the path undulates along the edge of **boggy pastures** – sometimes it runs close to the river; sometimes it moves further away. Sheep and cows graze here and the clanging of cow bells is a musical accompaniment to the final stages of your walk.

When you reach the Refuge du Clot, simply follow the path back downhill past the Pont d'Espagne to the car park.

☕ TAKE A BREAK

The meadows around the Refuge Wallon make for a delightful picnic spot. The *refuge* itself also sells basic meals and snacks to non-guests.

53

COL & PIC DE MADAMÈTE

DURATION	DIFFICULTY	DISTANCE	START/END
7½hr return	Hard	18km	Pont de la Gaubie
TERRAIN	Clear mountain trail; snow can block pass until late June			

Sitting north of the main ridge of Pyrenean peaks, the Réserve Naturelle de Néouvielle contains some epic mountain scenery. This circular hike to the Col (pass) and Pic de Madamète (2657m) combines silky blue lakes, bucolic meadows, glacial tarns, soaring mountains and a dramatic crossing of a high pass followed by a scramble to a lofty summit, making for a spectacular day out.

But beauty comes with a sting. This is a very long and demanding hike (min/max altitude 1538/2657m). Walking at a solid pace and without stopping, it will take you at least seven hours. But because you will want to stop and admire the lakes and viewpoints and dawdle through the meadows, then really you should set aside 10 or 11 hours.

GETTING HERE

The nearest town is the small ski resort of Barèges. However, only a few minutes' drive further downhill is Luz-St-Sauveur, an attractive and bustling little town with lots of places to stay and eat. From either of these towns take the D918 uphill towards the Col du Tourmalet. At the télésiege de Caoubère (10km from Luz-St-Sauveur and 3km from Barèges), there's a small turn-off to the south. Drive 1.5km down this to the Pont de la Gaubie.

STARTING POINT

There are only a very limited number of parking places (six or seven) at the Pont de la Gaubie. Unless you're here very early, you will need to park in the huge car park at the télésiege de Caoubère and walk from there (add a total of 25 minutes to your overall walk time).

01 The first half of the trail to the Col de Madamète follows the GR10 long-distance trail. Signage is exceptionally clear and easy. Just follow the obvious trail with the red and white waymarkers painted at frequent intervals on rocks and trees. After about eight minutes, there's an unmarked junction. Turn right (south). Twenty minutes later, at another fork in the trail, take the left-hand trail. You will be returning much later in the day via the other trail.

02 Fifty minutes from the start of the walk, during which you have been ambling over pastures with many cows and sheep, you arrive at a dreamy little **meadow** with a clear **stream**. At the end of this meadow take the left-hand trail fork and cross over the stream. The trail dips back into woodland and continues on its gentle, but steady, uphill climb.

03 Around two hours from the start of the walk, you'll reach a small meadow with a **marshy lake**. Follow a ridge line above the lake and gawp at the big mountains that are increasingly ganging up at the head of the valley.

04 After a further half-hour, the **Lac de Coueyla-Gran** appears. It's a wonderful spot to rest for a while and admire the reflections of the mountains in its still, cold waters.

05 Things toughen up when you leave the lakeside. The trail veers back on itself slightly and then sets a high course for the head of the valley. After a sharp 30-minute climb up a rocky slope, you reach the **Lac de Madamète**, a pretty, green-blue lake filled with fat trout. Behind the lake, you can clearly see the Col and Pic de Madamète. A sign indicates that it's an (optimistic) 45 minutes to the pass.

Snow & Trail Breaks

Snow can be an issue on the Col de Madamète and – even more so – on the summit of the Pic de Madamète and the ridge that follows between late October and late June. If the route is blocked by snow, you will need to retrace your steps back the way you came.

If possible, we suggest breaking this trek into a leisurely two-day affair. There's a simple six-bed, unmanned *refuge* at the **Lac de Coueyla-Gran** (a new, large and modern *refuge* is also under construction here).

Many families walk to the Lac de Coueyla-Gran for a picnic and then return the way they came (leave 4½ hours without stops).

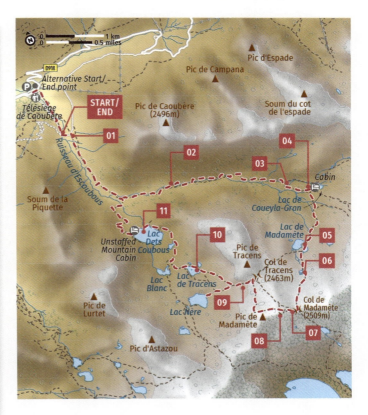

THE PYRENEES/189

06 The trail climbs again and passes a whole flurry of **little lakes**. You're now in the high mountains and the scenery is very different from the gentle green valleys and pastures that you started the morning in. With each successive lake, the landscape becomes more barren and broken and the higher lakes often remain covered in ice until early summer (pictured p188).

07 After a final, brisk 10-minute haul, you'll stand atop the **Col de Madamète** (2509m). The views from this lofty vantage point will make you catch your breath. Looking back the way you came, the numerous lakes you sauntered past lie scattered like glowing jewels over the stark landscape. But the real treat is the view south. The land drops steeply away from the pass to a series of large lakes (Aumar, Aubert, Orédon and Cap de Long) and around them massive mountain hulks and glaciers, including, just to the southwest, the eternal snow-covered **Pic de Néouvielle** (3091m).

08 For an even better view (pictured), scramble for 25 minutes up the zigzag trail to the 2657m-high summit of **Pic de Madamète** (the rounded peak immediately to your right – west – when standing on the pass looking south). The summit and the ridge you'll be following afterwards are often snowbound until much later in the season than the Col de Madamète. If you're in any doubt, do not continue – instead return to the car the way you came (leave three hours). If the snow has cleared, then drop down from

190/THE PYRENEES

the summit to the obvious ridge to the northwest and then onto the **Col de Tracens** (2463m).

09 Beyond the Col de Tracens, a torn-up landscape of **giant boulders** cast aside by ancient glaciers awaits. The trail-finding can be a little complicated but just keep heading northwest. The 20-minute (return) detour to the **Lac Nère** is recommended.

10 Around 45 minutes after leaving the summit, the trail, which by now is becoming much clearer and easier to follow, passes by the **Lac de Tracens**, where grass and stunted trees return. This is followed a few minutes later by the beautiful **Lac Blanc**.

11 Continue downwards and across a marshy plateau. Finally, the last, and largest, lake of the day, **Lac Dets Coubous**, looms into sight. There's a small cabin here and the northern end of the lake has been dammed, but it's still an attractive parting shot.

You may now think that you're home and dry, but there remains one final challenge. A leg-searingly steep descent zigzags downwards to the trail junction you passed much earlier in the day. From here, it's a simple but exhausting half-hour walk back to the car, retracing the route you took at the start of the day.

 TAKE A BREAK

There's nowhere to get food on the trail, but each and every lake makes for a perfect picnic spot.

THE PYRENEES/**191**

Also Try...

CIRQUE DE GAVARNIE

The family-friendly walk into the belly of the stunning Cirque de Gavarnie is easily the single most famous day walk in the Pyrenees. And for good reason: when you reach the end of the path, you will stare in awe at this bowl-shaped wall of glacier-covered rock. From the valley floor to the summit peaks is a vertical 1.5km and down the sheer sides crashes the highest waterfall in France. It's like being in nature's very own Colosseum.

But on a walk like this, you can't expect to walk alone and, in high summer, thousands of people trudge the trail every day. If you can, come out of season. The walk begins from Gavarnie village and is just a gentle uphill stroll along a clear, smooth trail (the first part is wheelchair accessible) to the Hôtellerie du Cirque (pictured).

DURATION 3½hr return
DIFFICULTY Easy
DISTANCE 11km

THE GR10

Long-distance walks don't come much more epic than the GR10, or the Grand Traversée des Pyrénées.

Starting wth your boots in the Atlantic Ocean in Hendaye, this near two-month-long traverse of the mountains ends when you rush headlong into the Mediterranean in Banyuls. During this marathon hike, you will climb and descend some 48,000m, but the reward for this effort is a straight-line sweep through the very best of the Pyrenees (and you'll have legs of steel afterwards). And, when you've done it one way, you could spin around and walk the GR11, which also traverses the Pyrenees but this time on the Spanish side of the border.

DURATION 52 days one way
DIFFICULTY Hard
DISTANCE 866km

THE NÉOUVIELLE LAKE CIRCUIT

Slightly north of the main Pyrenean range, the Néouvielle region is a lake-plastered paradise of soft grasslands and rocky summits. This enjoyably challenging three-day circuit showcases the absolute best of the region.

Day one sees you walking from the Lac d'Orédon to the Refuge de la Glère via a high pass crossing. Day two swings through wild countryside to the Cabane d'Aygues-Cluses and on day three you skip your way back to the start point via another high pass and a handful of lakes.

DURATION 3 days return
DIFFICULTY Difficult
DISTANCE 45km

PIC DES TROIS SEIGNEURS

Walkers familiar with the wild peaks of the Ariège region tend to talk about this fabulous circular hike in excited tones of wonder. From the achievable summit of the Pic des Trois Seigneurs (2199m), a huge view opens out that takes in most of the great mountains of the eastern part of the Pyrenees.

This diverse walk begins from the parking Port de Lers and swings through lakes, meadows, rivers and rocky passes on its way to and from the summit (pictured).

DURATION 5hr return
DIFFICULTY Moderate
DISTANCE 10km

PUIG CARLIT

This exciting but challenging ascent of Puig Carlit (2921m) is the classic walk of the far-eastern part of the Pyrenees. You have to be prepared for a very steep final ascent, with snow likely even in high summer. But along the way, you'll get to enjoy a sprinkling of jewel lakes surrounded by summer flowers.

The walk begins from the parking Barrage des Bouillouses at the end of the D60 road and the route is well marked.

DURATION 6hr return
DIFFICULTY Difficult
DISTANCE 15km

CORSICA

54   **Cascade des Anglais** Charming family walk to a pretty series of waterfalls. **p198**

55   **Capu Pertusato & Bonifacio** Appreciate Bonifacio's precarious cliff-side position on this coastal walk. **p200**

56   **Sentier des Douaniers** Stunning sandy beaches and extraordinary water colours on the Cap Corse peninsula. **p202**

57   **Vallée du Tavignano** Walk through narrow valley walls crowned with jagged rock spires. **p204**

58   **Capo Rosso** Are you brave enough to take in the view from Capo Rosso? **p206**

59   **Lac de Nino** Dawdle on the shores of this idyllic mountain lake. **p208**

60   **Lac de Melo & Lac de Capitello** Be awed by the beauty of these high-altitude mountain lakes. **p210**

CORSICA/195

Explore
CORSICA

Jutting from the Mediterranean like a rock fortress, Corsica has astounding geographical diversity. Set out on a walking trail here and, within an hour, the landscape can see-saw spectacularly from glittering bays and fabulous beaches to sawtooth mountain ridges and dense forests. All of which makes Corsica a wonderfully rewarding place for hikers.

BONIFACIO

Protected by vast smooth walls, the southern town of Bonifacio stretches along a narrow, top-heavy promontory, undercut by creamy-white limestone cliffs hollowed out by centuries of ceaseless waves. The old city, though, is what truly lingers in the mind, a ravishingly romantic web of alleyways lined by ramshackle medieval houses and chapels with faded pastel plasterwork.

There's a huge array of tourist accommodation in and around Bonifacio as well as an equal number of restaurants and bars. All this makes it the perfect base for walk 55.

MACINAGGIO

A port since Roman times, Macinaggio, high up along the barren but beautiful Cap

Corse peninsula, today centres on a pleasure marina used by summer excursion boats. To explore the coastline north of town, you've got no option but to strike out on foot, which is exactly what we do on walk 56. Macinaggio has places to stay and eat for when you return back to town.

PIANA

Teetering above the Golfe de Porto, the village of Piana makes a useful launching pad for hiking Capo Rosso. It's also ideal for exploring Les Calanques (Calanche) de Piana.

CORTE

Blessed with a stunning natural setting, circled by jagged peaks at the confluence of several rivers, the mountain stronghold of Corte is as forbidding as it is spectacular. Home to Corsica's

only university, its strong youthful energy is boosted in summer when hikers, bikers and climbers flock in to explore the nearby valleys.

It's the perfect base for walks 54, 57, 59 and 60.

☀ WHEN TO GO

Corsica is the quintessential Mediterranean island and has about the most forgiving climate in France. Between May and the end of October you can near-enough guarantee endless long sunny days, and even in winter there are enough crisp, clear days to make the island's coastal trails inviting.

Winter (November to February), though, is a very mixed affair. Some years can be an endless succession of storms interspersed with a few sunny

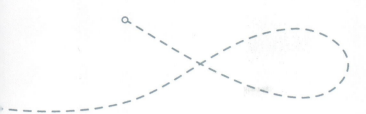

periods, but in other years the settled periods vastly outnumber the wet spells. In fine weather, all the coastal routes can be walked. Mountain routes though are often blanketed in snow.

Spring (March to early May) is by far the most unpredictable season and is often the wettest period of the calendar. Snow can also remain a problem on higher routes.

It hardly needs saying that summer (June to September) is uniformly hot and sunny. Often too hot even for the high mountain routes. The heat can make many coastal walks very trying indeed, but there's invariably a beach to cool off at somewhere along the way.

This leaves autumn (mid-September to October), with still largely settled, sunny weather, warm coastal waters, beautiful clear light, and perhaps the first frosts and light snow dustings on the mountain summits, as far and away the best time of year to walk almost anywhere in Corsica.

Corsica's tourism is heavily seasonal. Most hotels, restaurants and even sights open only from Easter to October, so winter visitors will need patience.

WHERE TO STAY

From seaside hotels with sweeping Mediterranean views to mountain retreats that invite you to cosy up by the fireside, Corsican accommodation is generally comfortable and of high quality. Budget travellers will find campgrounds island-wide, and simple *refuges* (huts) along the high mountain trails.

WHAT'S ON

Semaine Sainte (Mar & Apr) Elaborate religious processions march through the streets of Bonifacio, Corte and other towns.

Cavall'in Festa (early Jun) The mountain town of Corte celebrates the humble horse with processions, dressage shows and other events.

Corsica Raid (https://en.corsicaraid.com; early Jun) Held in locations throughout Corsica, this event mixes canyoning, trail-running, kayaking and mountain biking.

TRANSPORT

By far the best way to get around Corsica is by car, and many trailheads can only be reached by a private vehicle. Public transport only connects the larger towns and cities, from which local explorations can continue on foot or by bike or scooter (both readily available for hire).

Corsica's only train line, the Chemin de Fer de la Corse (www.cf-corse.corsica), is an attractive if limited option, running across the stunning mountainous interior between Bastia and Ajaccio, with a branch route to Calvi and L'Île-Rousse. The bus network is more comprehensive but often there's only one bus per day, and none on Sunday.

Corsica Bus & Train (www.corsicabus.org) is a one-stop website displaying up-to-date bus and train timetables, island-wide.

Resources

Visit Corsica (www.visit-corsica.com) Tourist-board website that includes hiking suggestions.

Corte Tourisme (www.corte-tourisme.com) Covering Corte and surrounding mountain regions.

Bonifacio Tourisme (www.bonifacio.fr) Gives the lowdown on this cliff-side town.

Bastia Tourisme (www.bastia-tourisme.com) Information on Bastia and Cap Corse.

Ouest Corsica (www.ouest corsica.com) Covering the jagged, mountainous west of the island.

54

CASCADE DES ANGLAIS

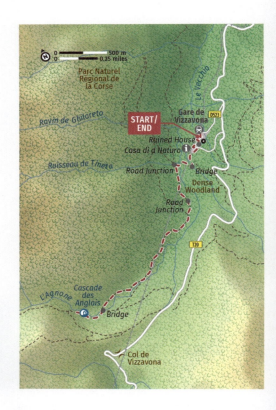

DURATION	DIFFICULTY	DISTANCE	START/END
1½hr return	Easy	6.5km	Gare de Vizzavona

TERRAIN	Road, walking trail

While many of the mountain walks in Corsica are a bit tough for children, this charming walk through thick beech forest to a pretty series of cascades and rapids is the ideal Corsican mountain hike for families. It's true that in high summer it gets busy, but the shade, cool freshwater and sense of peace that comes with being in the forest make it worthwhile. If you can, walk this route (min/max altitude 915/1100m) in October, when the leaves on the beech trees are the colour of the setting sun.

From the tiny train station, walk uphill along the road signed for the cascades, pass a huge, **ruined house** and then the **Casa di a Natura** (park information office). Follow red and white GR trail signs along a track lined by a dry-stone wall and into a beech forest.

Cross a bridge over the **River Agnone** and turn right immediately afterwards; then shortly after that cross another bridge and start marching uphill to a wide, dirt road. Turn left here and follow the road through the forest.

When you get to a road junction go straight over and then, a few minutes later, veer left off the **dirt road** by the signpost. After 50 minutes, the path moves slightly away from the river before returning and crossing a **bridge** at the bottom part of the **Cascades des Anglais** (pictured).

Continue up the trail, which clambers around rocks among the forest, passing numerous magical **waterfalls** and **pools of rapids**. When you reach the top of the last of the waterfalls, turn around and retrace your steps back to where you started.

55

CAPU PERTUSATO & BONIFACIO

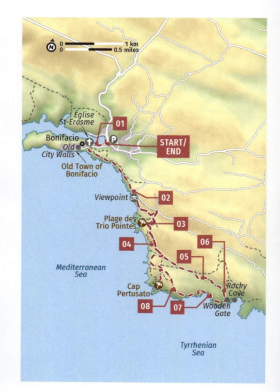

DURATION	DIFFICULTY	DISTANCE	START/END
3hr return	Easy	9.5km	Port de Bonifacio

TERRAIN	Road, walking trail

From the tourist hustle of Bonifacio, you only have to walk a short way to discover a world of secret beaches, breezy headlands and woodlands full of birdsong. This ideal family walk also takes in an exciting cliff walk and the chance to snap that clichéd photo of Bonifacio perched atop the cliffs. Don't forget your swimming things!

GETTING HERE
The walk starts from the main port in Bonifacio. From the old town, simply walk or drive down the hill to where the boats to the Île Lavezzi depart.

STARTING POINT
There are large car parks just behind the port and the whole area is awash in bars and restaurants, but there's nothing walker-specific here.

01 Walk along the eastern side of the port and take a left to the **Église St-Erasme**. To the left of this, a wide set of steps rises up. Emerging at the top of these steps you will find yourself facing the **old city walls**. Cross the road and go up the cobbled road. Turn left and start off along high cliffs.

02 It's now an easy walk along a footpath that scrapes along the edge of chalky white cliffs. After around 15 minutes, you will reach a **viewpoint** that offers that classic postcard view of Bonifacio hanging on its cliffside perch (pictured).

03 The trail moves away from the cliff edge and meets a road. Turn right, drop downhill, pass a ruined building and go past a parking area.

04 Continue along the dirt road past a **military control tower**. Drop downhill and at the junction, veer left (east) down a track.

200/CORSICA

Best for

PRETTY VILLAGE

05 After 15 minutes look for a discreet path on the left marked with **rock cairns**. The turn-off is about 25m before an entrance to a private property.

06 The trail wends through a brushy forest and passes through a gateway. Go right when you reach a junction with another trail. A moment or so later, you will reach a small, **rocky cove**. Turn sharp right and go through a **wooden gate**.

07 The trail now heads westwards along low **ruddy-coloured cliffs** with the **clear, blue sea** just below. A few minutes later, you will come to the most thrilling part of the walk: a **narrow ledge** etched into the cliff face underneath a big overhang of rock. It's only around a hundred metres – and is perfectly safe – but it will still keep you on your toes!

08 Afterwards, the path goes back into woodland and climbs. It takes about 20 minutes to reach the **Pertusato lighthouse**. Follow the wider path back northwards until you see a trail veering off left signed 'Plage'. Take this and drop down to a spectacular **desert-like beach** of chalky-white sand, with cliffs and rock stacks eroded into bizarre shapes.

Return to the junction, turn left and, a couple of minutes later, you'll be back on familiar ground. Retrace your route back along the cliffs to Bonifacio.

TAKE A BREAK

Surprisingly, there's nowhere to get refreshments when you leave Bonifacio. In summer, you will need a lot of water. Back in town treat yourself to a meal at **Kissing Pigs** (04 95 73 56 09; www.facebook.com/kissingpigs; 15 quai Banda del Ferro; mains €11-23.50, menus €21-23; 11.30am-3pm Thu-Tue, 6.30-11pm Thu-Sat, Mon & Tue), which serves wonderfully rich Corsican dishes.

56

SENTIER DES DOUANIERS

DURATION	DIFFICULTY	DISTANCE	START/END
3½hr return	Easy	12.5km	Parking Port de Macinaggio

TERRAIN	Footpath

The Sentier des Douaniers (Customs Trail) is a glimpse back in time to how much of the Mediterranean coastline must have looked before the arrival of mass tourism. This superb family walk, along a clear footpath, enjoys stunning sandy beaches, extraordinary blue seas and a wild, wooded hinterland. Although you can do the walk in half a day, we would recommend bringing your swimming things and a picnic and making a day of it.

GETTING HERE
The small town of Macinaggio, close to the end of the Cap Corse peninsula, is 37km and an hour's drive north of Bastia along the D80. There are one or two buses per day (€8, one hour, no Sunday service).

STARTING POINT
There are a couple of car parks close to the port in Macinaggio. This walk starts from the most northerly one.

01 Head north past the pleasure boat marina and then onto **Macinaggio beach**, a long, broad sandy expanse. Head towards the low headland at the far end of the beach.

02 A clearly signed trail leads off the beach and onto the headland. Straight away go right at the **trail junction**. Follow the path to the tip of the headland and past the **old cannon**. At the next junction go right, continuing around cliffs.

03 Follow a dirt road to **Plage de Tamarone** (pictured), a gorgeous stretch of sand backed by fields.

202/CORSICA

To the End of Corsica

You can continue onwards from Cala Francese (stop 06) to the small town of Barcaggio and its magnificent beach, which is about another 1¾ hours.

You can then either walk all the way back again (total 6¾ hours) or catch a summertime water taxi (📞 06 14 78 14 16).

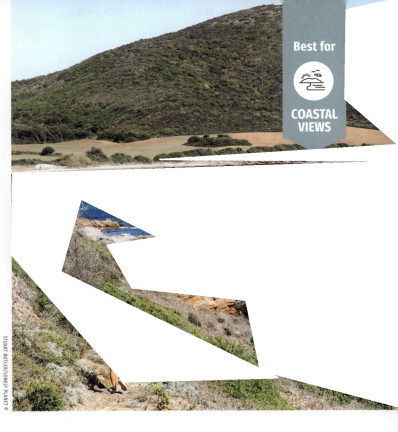

Best for

COASTAL VIEWS

04 Make sandy footprints all the way up to the northern end of the beach. At the trail junction go right and follow the trail around the headland. At one point you'll climb up quite steeply but from the top of the headland there are wonderful **coastal views**.

05 Stroll through tough, sun-blasted scrub until coming to a third beach, **Plage des Îles**. As the name suggests, just off the northern end of the beach are three small, **rocky islands**. Continue up to and around the headland to the north. You'll come to a turn-off to the left for the Chapel Santa Maria. Ignore this and continue on down to the next beach, which has a semi-restored **Genoese tower** built on a tiny rock outcrop.

06 Over another headland and a big decision awaits. Two gorgeous **silver-sand beaches** – Cala Francese and Cala Genovese (pictured p195) – are separated by a swathe of greenery and massaged by glowing turquoise waters. But at which one will you choose to take a break?

07 To return retrace your steps back past the Genoese tower and its beach and then, instead of following the headland around, cut down past the dour **Chapel Santa Maria** and take the inland path heading straight south. The path runs through pretty Mediterranean scrub that smells of the sun and emerges onto Plage de Tamarone. At the southern end of this, again take the inland trail rather than the headland trail. There are two turn-offs on the left. Ignore the first but take the second one, which quickly drops you back to **Macinaggio beach**.

 **TAKE A BREAK**

On Plage de Tamarone there's a little **wooden beach shack** selling drinks and snacks in summer only. Otherwise bring a picnic and plenty of water.

CORSICA/203

57

VALLÉE DU TAVIGNANO

DURATION	DIFFICULTY	DISTANCE	START/END
5½hr return	Easy	13km	Corte

TERRAIN	Rough paved trail

The mountains of Corsica are shot through with vertically inclined narrow valleys and gorges through which rivers crash and smash. This compelling walk (min/max altitude 450/760m), which follows the course of an old mule path, slinks along the sheer northern side of the valley and rewards with views of the river surrounded by thick forests and the ever narrower valley walls crowned with jagged rock spires on either side.

GETTING HERE
The walk begins from Corte town, which makes it a good one for those reliant on public transport. From the town centre, walk or drive to the small (pay) car park at the end of rue St-Joseph.

STARTING POINT
Just past the car park there are a number of different walking route signposts. Look for the one that reads Passerelle Russulinu.

01 From the car park, head down the footpath and through a gate. You're now at the start of the **Mare a Mare** long-distance hiking trail, which is very well marked with orange paint splodges.

02 The trail climbs up gently through heathland and passes a **small white shrine** (although because of its positioning in relation to the trail you might not notice it until you return back along the trail at the end of the day).

03 Gradually the trail descends towards the river and the trees – a real mixed bag of high mountain pines and lower altitude

Family Walk

This is a very simple walk with little elevation gain and no possibility of getting lost. However, if you walk all the way to the bridge at the Passerelle Russulinu, it does make for quite a long day. Because of this, even though the views get better the further along the valley you walk, many people don't get this far and turn around when they've seen enough.

This makes it quite a good family walk (though be careful near cliff ledges and avoid hot days when the valley can turn into a furnace), as you can just walk as far as the little ones' legs will carry them.

Mediterranean oak and chestnut – start to close in. After around 1¼ hours, the trail reaches a small side stream that you will need to hop across to a stone **shepherds' cabin**. There's also a water source here.

04 Thirty minutes on from the shepherds' cabin, the trail forks. Turn right and go uphill, still following the orange waymarkers. A few minutes later, the trees clear to reveal the first of a number of **impressive viewpoints**. Looking further up the valley, you will see a giant grey wall of tortured and torn rock (pictured) and, looking the other way, you'll be able to spy Corte in the valley floor.

05 The valley walls now close in tight around you, the cliffs fall steeply away and the river becomes much fuller, crashing over the boulders. You will pass another couple of **viewpoints** with sheer drop-offs.

06 Cross another small stream and, rounding a corner a moment later, you will come to a **bridge** spanning the **Tavignano River**. There's also another water source here. This is the **Passerelle Russulinu**. Although the Mare a Mare route continues over the bridge and along the river (eventually coming to the source of the river at the Lac de Nino), this is where we turn around and retrace our steps back to Corte.

TAKE A BREAK

While there are many restaurants, cafes and bars in Corte, there's nowhere to find food along this trail. In summer the valley can get uncomfortably hot so bring plenty of water.

CORSICA/205

58

CAPO ROSSO

DURATION	DIFFICULTY	DISTANCE	START/END
3½hr return	Moderate	9.5km	Parking Capo Rosso
TERRAIN	Walking trail		

Standing next to the 16th-century Genoese Tower on the tip of Capo Rosso (Capu Rossu), a vertical-edged lump of rock protruding deep into the Mediterranean, you'll feel like a gull soaring on the breezes. This short coastal walk to the most westerly point of Corsica offers one of the most extraordinary views on the entire island – if you're brave enough to peer over the cliff edge, that is!

GETTING HERE

The best base for the walk is the small town of Piana. Despite its diminutive size, there are plenty of tourist facilities. From Piana take the D824 for 6km in a westerly direction towards the Plage d'Arone. At the point at which the road makes a sharp bend to the left, there is a small car park. The walk starts here.

STARTING POINT

There's a walk information sign and a snack bar.

01 Follow the clear footpath northwest out of the car park and then go left a moment later at the **dry-stone wall.** Start descending. A short while later, you will pass a **ruined hut**, with **sea views** opening out to the south.

02 Go left at the junction among stumpy, weathered trees and giant heathers but, before you do, pause to take in the **view** down cascading cliffs.

03 When you reach the level plateau, take the right fork signed for **Capo Rosso Torra di Turghju**. The trail continues to dip down towards sea level, before coming to a **stone house**. Head right here.

206/CORSICA

Genoese Towers

Looking like squat lighthouses, the Genoese towers that dot the Corsican coast in some ways serve a similar purpose, except they weren't warning approaching ships of danger but, instead, they were warning frightened Corsican coastal communities that ships were approaching. Pirate ships!

In the 1500s, Corsica was controlled by the Genoese, but Turkish corsairs sailed the western Mediterranean in ships rowed by captured Christian slaves, and the coastal villages of Corsica were a favourite hunting ground. In order to help protect them, the Genoese built around a hundred defensive towers, and many of them remain standing today.

04 At the **walk signposts** 50m later, go straight on and start to climb. At first, it's a gentle climb but it quickly becomes much steeper. The trail then mellows again as it nudges ever closer to what, from this angle, appears to be a sheer-sided, rust-orange cliff face that you somehow will have to negotiate.

05 The answer to how you get up this cliff reveals itself a few moments later: a hidden **rock stairway** carved discreetly into the cliff face. The climb is relatively short but with the sun likely pounding down onto your back, you do have to work for it a bit. When the steps stop, the trail continues upward over an exposed red-rock slope. It can be a little tricky to make out the proper path. Keep an eye out for **rock cairns**.

06 Two hours after you set out, you will find yourself standing triumphantly on the summit (pictured) next to the **Tour de Turghiu**, a Genoese tower. But of course we know you didn't walk all the way out here to look at an old building. Go on then, walk towards the edge of the cliff and peer over. Now that is a view! You might only be at an altitude of 331m but the sheer violence with which the rock sheers away below you gives the impression that you're actually standing atop a mountain. The sea is a deep, glittering blue and rugged cliffs stretch off northwards up the coast. It really is one of the **best viewpoints** on the island. To return simply retrace your steps (leave 1½ hours for this).

TAKE A BREAK

There's a small seasonal (April to October) **snack bar** in the car park with a breezy terrace and sensational sea views. Otherwise, picnic with a view next to the Tour de Turghiu.

59

LAC DE NINO

DURATION	DIFFICULTY	DISTANCE	START/END
4¾hr return	Moderate	11.5km	Maison forestière de Poppaghia
TERRAIN	Mountain trail, rocky terrain		

When first viewed after clambering up the steep, rocky slope, Lac de Nino and its surrounding pastures come across like a vision of a mountain paradise, and the lake is quite rightly considered one of Corsica's most beautiful. But as well as the goal of the lake, this enjoyable and popular hike (suitable for older children; min/max altitude 1076/1762m) also offers a melodic amble through stately forests where semi-wild black pigs forage, and there are glorious views across to Corsica's highest mountain.

GETTING HERE
The walk starts from the Maison forestière de Poppaghia, which is around 11km east of the Col de Verghio on the D84 between Calacuccia and Évisa. You'll need your own car to get here.

STARTING POINT
There's a parking area, picnic benches and a small *accrobranche* (tree-climbing centre) next to the Maison forestière de Poppaghia. There are also information boards giving that day's forest-fire risk level. At times of heightened alert, you might be forbidden from walking here.

01 Follow the yellow paint splodges uphill away from the forestry office and into the impressive **Forêt de Valdu Niellu**. Made up predominately of Corsican black pine, this is the largest montane forest in Corsica. Some of the magisterial trees found here can be 30m high and 300 years old. If you see shadows moving in the undergrowth that will be the **semi-wild pigs** and cattle that wander at will through this forest.

208/CORSICA

02 After around 20 minutes, you will come to a forestry road. Cross straight over and continue marching gently up through the trees. Ten minutes later hop across a small stream.

As you gain altitude the trees slowly start to die away and, behind you, views will start opening out across the valley to mighty **Monte Cinto** (2706m), the highest mountain on the island.

03 The trail, which starts to become a little rockier, crosses over a couple of streams (look for suitable rocks to hop on to) and then emerges onto a small rocky plateau where you'll find the semi-abandoned shepherds' huts known as **Bergerie de Coiga**, 1¼ hours from the start.

04 This next part is where the hard work begins. For the next hour and a bit, the trail climbs steeply up a rocky slope. At times, you might need to use hands and feet to scramble over some of the rocks. Be careful in wet weather as they can be very slippery. Finally, you'll emerge onto the **Bocca à Stazzona** pass (1762m), from where you'll catch your first view of the lake just below (pictured).

05 Descend from the pass to **Lac de Nino**. After the rocky, barren country on the last half of the climb up here, the piercing green pastures, laced through with streams and marshes, are a welcome surprise. Do a complete circuit of the lake, admiring how the colours change with the light, before climbing back up to the Bocca à Stazzona and retracing your route back to the car.

☕ TAKE A BREAK

There's nowhere to get food on the trail. Bring a picnic and tuck in with the view over the lake from the Bocca à Stazzona.

60

LAC DE MELO & LAC DE CAPITELLO

DURATION	DIFFICULTY	DISTANCE	START/END
4hr return	Moderate	6.7km	Parking Bergerie de Grottelle

TERRAIN	Mountain trail

If we had to pick one mountain walk in Corsica that simply cannot be missed then it would be this superb day hike to Lake Melo and its higher altitude twin, Lake Capitello. Although it's relatively short, you will traverse a fascinating range of habitats, from grand old-growth woodland to alpine pastures, before finally arriving in the high-altitude rock and scree wastes of the high mountains. It's in this zone that the two lakes can be found. The lower of the two, Lac de Melo, is saucer round and a peaty-black colour, while Capitello, some 200m higher up, is a richer blue that reflects the stark surrounding mountains.

With some short steep sections, and even a few rock-bolted chains and ladders to haul yourself up, there's just enough challenge in this walk (min/max altitude 1370/1930m) to make it feel like you've achieved something, but it still remains easy enough for children to make it to at least the first of the lakes. All up, if you want to see why Corsica has earned such high regard in the eyes of walkers the world over, then this spectacular walk will show you.

GETTING HERE

The best base for this walk is the lovely mountain town of Corte. There's every possible kind of tourist facility here and much of it is aimed at walkers (there are some decent hiking shops). From Corte, the trailhead is a 15km drive along the D623; a very narrow and tortuous drive (and very busy in summer) to the very end of the Restonica Valley.

In July and August, a shuttle service operated by **Autocars Cortenais** (http://autocars-cortenais.fra) runs from the information point at Chjarasgiolu (4km from Corte) to the trailhead. Return tickets are €15 and departures are at 8am, 9am, 10.30am and noon. Return services are at 1.30pm, 2.30pm, 4pm and 5.30pm.

STARTING POINT

The start point is the Bergerie de Grottelle, which sits at the very end of the road that winds up the Restonica Valley. There's a large car park here (car/motorcycle €6/3) and a huddle of shepherds' huts that sell drinks, cheeses and snacks

To Higher Ground

An exciting add-on to this walk is to go from Lac de Capitello up onto the mountain ridge directly behind the lake, hook up with the famed GR20 route and then drop back down on a steep trail to the Lac de Melo. This semicircular route adds around 2½ hours more onto your overall walk time and takes you to an altitude of 2133m.

In snow-free, clear conditions the route isn't too taxing and there's clear waymarking (look for the yellow waymarkers). From the top, you could even carry on eastward past the Col de Rinoso to descend back down to the valley floor almost opposite the stone shepherds' huts you passed on the way up.

01 This is a well-marked and popular trail so in general route-finding is simple. From the parking, follow the clear but rocky trail heading southwest further up the valley. The icy-blue **Restonica River** will be crashing over the rocks on your left.

02 After 30 minutes, you'll pass a couple of **stone shepherds' huts**. In July and August, the shepherds will whip you up a delicious omelette and sell cheese, coffee and cold drinks.

03 A short way from the shepherds' huts, you'll pass the first of a couple of small **waterfalls** on the opposite side of the river. Look for the shepherd's livestock grazing on the slopes around here.

04 After an hour, the trail, which has been pretty forgiving up until this point, suddenly lurches upwards over giant boulders and bare rock face. These can be very slippery so, at one point, some **chains** were attached to an especially steep bit of rock (pictured). You're only really likely to need them in icy or wet conditions. Just after this, a series of **fixed ladders** run up the rock face next to a waterfall. These you will have to use but there's nothing dangerous about it and the kids will love it.

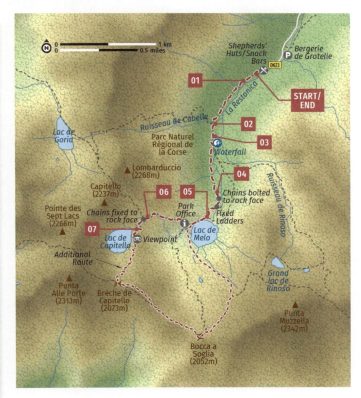

CORSICA/211

05 Wobble off the last of the ladders and there in front of you is the first of the lakes, **Lac de Melo** (1711m). Lodged between great shafts of soaring rock, this dark-coloured lake is quite a sight. For hiking families, this is a good endpoint to your adventure and the grassy pastures around the lake make for an ideal picnic stop. Leave one hour to return to the car (total 2¼ hours).

06 For everyone else follow the path around to the right, skirting around the side of the lake. Walk past a small park office on your left and start climbing; at first only gently but then much more steeply as you aim for a gap in the cliff face below shark-tooth peaks (pictured). There's a fair bit of scrambling over rock and boulder and, once again, there are a couple of **chains** bolted to the mountain in places to help ease you up the trickier and steeper sections (but again these aren't normally strictly necessary). The trail is always clear and obvious though.

07 Two and a half hours from the start and with a final heave-ho, you'll emerge onto a platform of rock, in the centre of which lies the deep blue **Lac de Capitello** (1930m) framed against a ridge of mountains of around 2400m. Be sure to walk to the eastern edge of this small plateau to check out the startling view to the Lac de Melo almost directly below.

To return simply retrace your route back to the parking (leave at least 1¾ hours for the descent).

212/CORSICA

Tackling the GR20

The GR20 long-distance walking path has gained almost mythical status among hardened hikers. Running from north to south across almost the entire length of Corsica's jagged spine, this 180km walk takes an average of 15 days to complete and is considered the hardest of all the GR trails in France.

With near-endless steep ascents and descents and punishing summer sun, it's perhaps no surprise to learn that the majority of people who set out on the trail don't complete it. It's even said that up to 40% of people who start out on the GR20 give up before the end of day one.

If you do want to attempt it, then early June and September are considered the prime periods.

TAKE A BREAK

There's nowhere to buy food and drinks around the lakes but shepherds set up seasonal cafes both in the car park and around a third of the way along the trail. Even so, it's wise to bring a picnic.

Also Try...

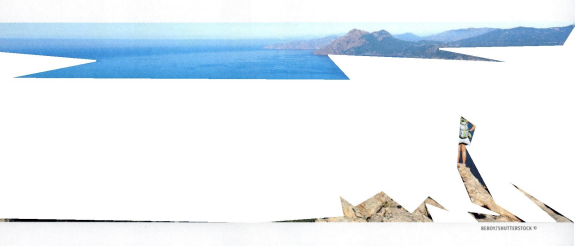

CALANCHE

Just outside the small town of Piana, melted mountains of orange-red granite have created a bizarre landscape of strange rock creatures and faces overlooking a shimmering Mediterranean. It's one of the most memorable landscapes in Corsica and is a very popular place for an easy walk (some might say it's a bit too popular!).

There are three standard, signed walks here, all of which are very short but by easily linking them together, you can come up with a satisfying half-day walk. Start off by following the Chemin de la Châtaigneraie trail, which is the quietest, longest and wildest of the three routes. From this, you can link straight into the Chemin du Château-Fort trail, which takes you to an impressive coastal viewpoint (pictured). Finally, clamber through the Chemin des Muletiers, which heads through a landscape of surreal rock formations.

DURATION 4½hr return
DIFFICULTY Easy
DISTANCE 11km

ÎLES LAVEZZI

So perfect are the white-sand beaches fringed by giant granite boulders, that sailing into a bay on the Îles Lavezzi, a group of small islands off the south coast of Corsica, you could well be forgiven for thinking you'd arrived in the Seychelles.

This walk, which meanders lazily around the main island, might be super short and easy, but it'll likely take you all day to complete because of having to continuously stop and test the waters at each and every beautiful beach. There's a web of sandy trails around the car-free island and walking arrows guide you in the right direction but, in truth, this is one place where it really doesn't matter if you're on the right trail. Just walk. Swim. And enjoy.

DURATION 1½hr return
DIFFICULTY Easy
DISTANCE 4.5km

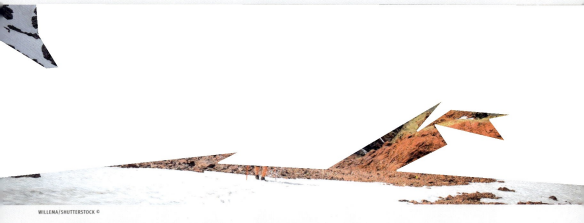

WILLEMA/SHUTTERSTOCK ©

MONTE D'ORO

At 2389m, Monte d'Oro isn't the highest mountain on the island but the circular route to the summit of the mountain is arguably the most spectacular.

Starting from the Gare de Vizzavona, follow trails through dense beech woodland higher and higher until trees turn to mountain meadows and mountain meadows turn to rock moonscapes. The thrilling route runs along a ridge to the Bocca di Porco, then up to the summit before a whirlwind steep descent on the other side and back through more woodland via the Cascade des Anglais.

DURATION 9hr return
DIFFICULTY Hard
DISTANCE 16km

MONTE SAN PETRONE

East and slightly away from the main knuckle of Corsican mountains, Monte San Petrone (1767m) has wonderful views from the summit. On a clear day they take in much of the east coast of the island, the fortress-like central mountains and most of the Cap Corse peninsula.

The walk begins from the Col de Prato and spends much of the time in the shade of Mediterranean woodland and, higher up, beech forest, before arriving at the rocky summit topped by a big cross. It's a good goal with older children.

DURATION 5hr return
DIFFICULTY Medium
DISTANCE 13km

MONTE CINTO

At 2706m, Monte Cinto is the summit of Corsica.

There are a couple of routes up the mountain. All are long and very challenging, but perhaps the most satisfying, varied and manageable for the average mountain walker is the southeast route starting from close to the small village of Lozzi. You can also shave a good 2½ hours off the walk by starting from a parking area, Capella a sa Lisei, at the end of a long bumpy piste, but doing so means you miss out on some delightful scenery (pictured).

DURATION 8hr return
DIFFICULTY Hard
DISTANCE 16km

Language

The sounds used in spoken French can almost all be found in English. There are a couple of exceptions: nasal vowels (represented in our pronunciation guides by 'o' or 'u' followed by an almost inaudible nasal consonant sound 'm', 'n' or 'ng'), the 'funny' *u* sound ('ew' in our guides) and the deep-in-the-throat *r*. Bearing these few points in mind and reading our pronunciation guides below as if they were English, you'll be understood just fine. The markers (m) and (f) indicate the forms for male and female speakers respectively.

To enhance your trip with a phrasebook, visit **lonelyplanet.com**. Lonely Planet iPhone phrasebooks are available through the Apple App store.

BASICS

Hello.
Bonjour. — bon·zhoor

Goodbye.
Au revoir. — o·rer·vwa

How are you?
Comment allez-vous? — ko·mont a·lay·voo

I'm fine, thanks.
Bien, merci. — byun mair·see

Please.
S'il vous plaît. — seel voo play

Thank you.
Merci. — mair·see

Excuse me.
Excusez-moi. — ek·skew·zay·mwa

Sorry.
Pardon. — par·don

Yes./No.
Oui./Non. — wee/non

Good luck
Bonne chance — bon shaw·ns

I don't understand.
Je ne comprends pas. — zher ne kom·pron pa

Do you speak English?
Parlez-vous anglais? — par·lay·voo ong·glay

ON THE TRAIL

hiking *randonnée* ran·donay

trail *sentier* son·ti·ay

summit *sommet* so·may

mountain hut
cabane de montagne ca·ban de mon·tan·ya

I'd like to buy/hire…
Je voudrais acheter louer… zher voo·dray ashe·tay loo·way…

hiking poles
bâtons de randonée — ba·ton de ran·donay

hiking boots
bottes de randonnée — botu de ran·donay

raincoat
imperméable — em·per·mee·abler

backpack
havresac — a·vresak

I have a blister.
J'ai une ampoule. — jay ewn em·pooler.

How is the weather today?
Comment est la météo d'aujourd'hui? ko·mont ay la meteo o·zhoor·dwee

Is it OK if I take a break here?
Puis-je me reposer ici? pwee·zher meh re·po·say ee·see

EATING & DRINKING

…, please.
…, s'il vous plaît. — … seel voo play

A coffee *un café* un ka·fay

A table for two *une table pour deux* — ewn ta·bler poor der

Two beers *deux bières* der bee·yair

I'm a vegetarian.
Je suis végétarien/ végétarienne. (m/f) — zher swee vay·zhay·ta·ryun/ vay·zhay·ta·ryen

Cheers!
Santé! — son·tay

That was delicious!
C'était délicieux! — say·tay day·lee·syer

The bill, please.
L'addition, s'il vous plaît. — la·dee·syon seel voo play

EMERGENCIES

Help!
Au secours! — o skoor

Call the police!
Appelez la police! — a·play la po·lees

Call a doctor!
Appelez un médecin! — a·play un mayd·sun

I'm sick.
Je suis malade. — zher swee ma·lad

I'm allergic to …
Je suis allergique … — zher swee a·lair·zheek …

I'm lost.
Je suis perdu/ perdue. (m/f) — zhe swee pair·dew

Where are the toilets?
Où sont les toilettes? — oo son lay twa·let

216/LANGUAGE

Signs

Entrée	Entrance
Femmes	Women
Fermé	Closed
Hommes	Men
Interdit	Prohibited
Ouvert	Open
Renseignements	Information
Sortie	Exit
Toilettes/WC	Toilets

TRANSPORT & DIRECTIONS

boat	*bateau*	ba·to
bus	*bus*	bews
plane	*avion*	a·vyon
train	*train*	trun

I want to go to...
Je voudrais aller à...
zher voo·dray a·lay a...

Where's ?
Où est...?   oo ay...

What's the address?
Quelle est l'adresse?   kel ay la·dres

Can you show me (on the map)?
Pouvez-vous m'indiquer (sur la carte)?
poo·vay·voo mun·dee·kay (sewr la kart)

Does it stop at (Amboise)?
Est-ce qu'il s'arrête à (om·bwaz)?
es·kil sa·ret a (*Amboise*)?

At what time does it leave/arrive?
À quelle heure est-ce qu'il part/arrive?
a kel er es kil par/a·reev

Can you tell me when we get to...?
Pouvez-vous me dire quandnous arrivons à...?
poo·vay·voo mer deer kon noo za·ree·von a...

I want to get off here.
Je veux descendre ici.
zher ver day·son·drer ee·see

first	*premier*	prer·myay
last	*dernier*	dair·nyay
next	*prochain*	pro·shun

a ... ticket	*un billet...*	un bee·yay...
1st-class		
de première classe		der prem·yair klas
2nd-class		
de deuxième classe		der der·zyem klas
one-way		
simple		sum·pler
return		
aller et retour		a·lay ay rer·toor
aisle seat		
côté couloir		ko·tay kool·war
window seat		
côté fenêtre		ko·tay fe·ne·trer
delayed	*en retard*	on rer·tar
cancelled	*annulé*	a·new·lay
platform	*quai*	kay
ticket office	*guichet*	gee·shay
timetable	*horaire*	o·rair
train station	*gare*	gar
at the corner	*au coin*	o kwu
in front of	*devant*	der·von
left	*gauche*	gosh
next to...	*à côté de...*	a ko·tay der...
opposite...	*en face de...*	on fas der...
right	*droite*	drwat
straight ahead	*tout droit*	too drwa

DRIVING & CYCLING

I'd like to hire a...
Je voudrais louer...
zher voo·dray loo·way...

car	*une voiture*	ewn vwa·tewr
child seat	*siège-enfant*	syezh·on·fon
diesel	*diesel*	dyay·zel
bicycle	*un vélo*	un vay·lo
helmet	*casque*	kask
petrol/gas	*essence*	ay·sons
mechanic		
mécanicien		may·ka·nee·syun
service station		
station-service		sta·syon·ser·vees

Is this the road to ...?
C'est la route pour?...
say la root poor . . .

(How long) Can I park here?
(Combien de temps) Est-ce que je peux stationner ici?
(kom·byun der tom) es·ker zher per sta·syo·nay ee·see

The car/motorbike has broken down (at...).
La voiture/moto est tombée en panne (à...).
la vwa·tewr/mo·to ay tom·bay on pan (a...)

I have a flat tyre.
Mon pneu est à plat.
mom pner ay ta pla

I've run out of petrol.
Je suis en panne d'essence.
zher swee zon pan day·sons

I've lost my car keys.
J'ai perdu les clés de ma voiture.
zhay per·dew lay klay der ma vwa·tewr

ACCOMMODATION

Do you have any rooms available?
Est-ce que vous avez des chambres libres?
es·ker voo za·vay day shom·brer lee·brer

How much is it per night/person?
Quel est le prix par nuit/personne?
kel ay ler pree par nwee/per·son

campsite	*camping*	kom·peeng
dorm	*dortoir*	dor·twar
guest house	*pension*	pon·syon
hotel	*hôtel*	o·tel
youth hostel		
auberge de jeunesse		o·berzh der zher·nes

a ... room
une chambre... ewn shom·brer...

single	*à un lit*	a un lee
double	*avec un grand lit*	a·vek un gron lee
twin	*avec des lits jumeaux*	a·vek day lee zhew·mo

with (a)...	*avec...*	a·vek . . .
air-con		
climatiseur		klee·ma·tee·zer
bathroom		
une salle de bains		ewn sal der bun
window		
fenêtre		fe·nay·trer

LANGUAGE/**217**

Behind the Scenes

Send us your feedback

We love to hear from travelers – your comments help make our books better. We read every word,and we guarantee that your feedback goes straight to the authors. Visit **lonelyplanet.com/contact** to submit your updates and suggestions. We may edit, reproduce and incorporate your comments in Lonely Planet products such as guidebooks, websites and digital products, so let us know if you don't want your comments reproduced or your name acknowledged. For a copy of our privacy policy visit lonelyplanet.com/privacy.

ACKNOWLEDGEMENTS

Cover photograph Chèvres Trail at Puy de Dôme, Auvergne, Hervé Lenain/Alamy Stock Photo ©

Digital Model Elevation Data U.S. Geological Survey Department of the Interior/USGS U.S. Geological Survey

Photographs pp6-11
Hemis/Alamy Stock Photo ©; LAURENT DARD/AFP/Getty Images ©; Stuart Butler/lonely planet ©; JordiCarrio, Jon Chica, Jon Ingall, Julia Kuznetsova, DaLiu/shutterstock ©

WRITER THANKS

STUART BUTLER

Thanks to COVID-19, this was the most complicated book I have ever worked on, and I would like to thank my fellow writers and everyone in-house at LP – especially Darren O'Connell and Daniel Bolger – for keeping the project afloat. For joining meon so many walks, thanks go to my wife and children. Thanks also to thank Simon Mahomo and Oliver Fitzjones for their companionship on many a trail.

OLIVER BERRY

A big thank you to everyone who helped me with my research, including Fabien Latour, Yves Martigny, Agnès Caron, Sophie Dupont, Jean Robarte and Aurelie Martin. Back home, thanks to Rosie Hillier, and to everyone in the LP team putting the project together, especially commissioning editor Dan Bolger. *Un grand merci à tous!*

STEVE FALLON

A number of people helped me on this book, including staff at both Brittany and Normandy Tourism, in particular Fran Lambert. Thanks to friends and contacts for assistance, ideas, hospitality and/or laughs along the way, including Brenda Turnndige, Olivier Cirendini, Caroline Guilleminot and Chew Terrière. As always, I'd like to dedicate my share of the book to my husband Michael Rothschild.

ANITA ISALSKA

Big thanks to Vanessa Michy, Laure Chapuis and Janet Darne for sharing their knowledge while I walked, ate and scribbled my way around the Auvergne. Thank you also to my parents who were graciously hospitable during the great 2020 lockdown. *Bisous* to Normal Matt, who cheered me on during the write-up.

NICOLA WILLIAMS

Sincere thanks to the fantastic colleagues I worked with on this title, including Stuart Butler and Chris Pitts, and commissioning editor Daniel Bolger. Out on the trail would not have been nearly as much fun without mountain-mad family and friends who scuttled up snowy peaks, scary ladders and slippery rock faces with me: Sally Dibden, Lynne England, Lucie Albertone and Matthias, Niko, Mischa and Kaya Lüfkens.

THIS BOOK

This Lonely Planet guidebook was researched and written by Stuart Butler, Oliver Berry, Steve Fallon, Anita Isalska and Nicola Williams.

This guidebook was produced by:

Senior Product Editor Daniel Bolger

Product Editor Claire Rourke

Book Designer Virginia Moreno

Assisting Editors Janet Austin, Andrea Dobbin

Cartographers Julie Dodkins, Anthony Phelan

Cover Researcher & Design Ania Bartoszek

Product Development Imogen Bannister, Liz Heynes, Anne Mason, Dianne Schallmeiner, John Taufa, Juan Winata

Design Development Virginia Moreno

Cartographic Series Designer Wayne Murphy

Thanks to Victoria Harrisson, Karen Henderson, Kate Kiely, Anne Mason, Genna Patterson, Angela Tinson

By Difficulty

EASY

Dinan: Up & Down Town 30
La Côte de Granit Rose 32
Thiepval Loop.. 52
Beaumont-Hamel
   Newfoundland Memorial 54
Lac de Roselend &
   Lac de la Gittaz 68
Grand Balcon Nord 70
Brantôme Circuit 98
Lac Chambon & Murol Circuit 100
Beynac Castle Loop 102
The Chemin de Halage......................... 104
Wetlands of the Camargue 124
Lac du Lauzanier................................... 126
Gorges d'Héric 148
Plateau de Bellevue 168
Cascade des Anglais 198
Capu Pertusato & Bonifacio 200
Sentier des Douaniers......................... 202
Vallée du Tavignano............................204

MODERATE

Giverny Impressions 34
Grouin: Up to a Point 36
Circling the Ile d'Ouessant...................38
Baie St-Jean.. 56
Lochnagar Crater 58
Lac Blanc..74
Pic des Mémises 76
Chalets de Bise to Lac de Darbon........ 78
Arbois to Pupillin....................................80
Cirque de Baume-les-Messieurs.......... 82
Pilgrimage Around Rocamadour........106
Stevenson's Journey 108
Climbing Puy de Dôme 110
Ascent to Puy de Sancy 112
Castles of the Dordogne..................... 114
Port-Miou, Port-Pin & En-Vau 128
Roussillon Ramble 130
Cap Roux.. 132
The Blanc-Martel Trail 134
Gordes Loops 136
Cirque de Mourèze 150
Roc des Hourtous.................................152
Pic St-Loup 154

Cirque de Navacelles 156
Refuge des Oulettes de Gaube............170
Lac d'Ayous Circuit............................... 172
Brèche de Roland 174
Cirque de Troumouse 176
Lac Vert 178
Lac d'Oo & Lac Saussat 180
Pic du Tarbesou &
   the Blue & Black Lakes....................182
Capo Rosso...206
Lac de Nino...208
Lac de Melo & Lac de Capitello 210

HARD

Omaha Beach...40
Pointes du Raz & Van 44
Tête de la Maye.......................................86
Lac des Vaches &
   Col de la Vanoise 88
Les Eaux Tortes 140
Mont Aigoual 158
Marcadau Valley &
   the Cardinquère Lakes 184
Col & Pic de Madamète 188

Index

A

accessible travel 16-17
accommodation
  Central France 97
  Corsica 197
  Côte d'Azur 123
  French Alps 67
  Jura 67
  language 217
  Languedoc-Roussillon 147
  Pyrenees, the 167
  Somme, the 51
Aiguille de la Grande Sassière 92
Albert 50
Amiens 50
Arbois to Pupillin 80-1
Arles 122
Armistice Memorial Circuit, the 62
Puy de Sancy 112-13

B

Bagnères-de-Luchon 166
Baie St-Jean 56-7
Barcelonnette 122
Battle of the Somme 52-3, 54-5, 58-61
Bayeux 28
Bayeux Tapestry 43
beaches 32, 39, 40, 40-3, 135, 202, 203, 214,
  see also coastal trails
Beaumont-Hamel Newfoundland Memorial
  10, 54-5
Besançon 66
Beynac Castle Loop 102-3
birdwatching 36-7, 56-7, 62
Blanc-Martel Trail, the 8, 134-5
Bonifacio 196
Boulogne-Sur-Mer 50
Brantôme 96
Brantôme Circuit 98-9
Brèche de Roland 9, 174-5
Brittany 26-47
  planning 29

C

cable cars 70, 74-5
Cadouin Abbey 118
Calanche 214
camping 18
Canal du Midi, the 162
Cancale 36-7

Cannes 122
Cap Blanc-Nez 63
Cap Roux 132-3
Capo Rosso 206-7
Capu Pertusato & Bonifacio 200-1
Carcassonne: La Bastide to the Cité 163
Carnac Megaliths 47
Cascade des Anglais 198-9
Cassis 122
castles 8, 102-3, 114-17
Cauterets 166
cemeteries (war) 43, 52, 55, 59, 60
Central France 94-119
  planning 97
Chalets de Bise to Lac de Darbon 78-9
Chamonix 66
Chemin de Halage, the 104-5
children, travel with 14-15, see also fami-
  ly-friendly trails
Circuit de la Roche Trouée 143
Cirque de Baume-les-Messieurs 82-5
Cirque de Gavarnie 192
Cirque de Mourèze 150-1
Cirque de Navacelles 156-7
Cirque de Troumouse 176-7
Cirque des Évettes 93
Cirque du Fer-à-Cheval 93
city escape trails 12
climate 18, see also individual locations
coastal trails 13
  Baie St-Jean 56-7
  Calanche 214
  Cap Blanc-Nez 63
  Cap Roux 132-3
  Capo Rosso 206-7
  Capu Pertusato & Bonifacio 200-1
  Côte d'Albâtre 46
  Grouin 36-7
  Île de Batz 47
  Île d'Ouessant 38-9
  Îles Lavezzi 214
  La Côte de Granit Rose 32-3
  Le Hourdel 63
  Les Crocs 62
  Mont St-Michael 46
  Omaha Beach 40-1
  Pointes du Raz & Van 44-5
  Port-Miou, Port-Pin & En-Vau 128-9
  Presqu'île de Crozon 47
  Sentier des Douaniers 202-3
  Sentier du Littoral 143

Col & Pic de Madamète 188-91
Corsica 194-215
  planning 196-7
Corte 196
Côte d'Albâtre 46
Côte d'Azur 120-43
  planning 122-3

D

D-Day 41-2
Dinan 30-1
disabilities, travellers with 16-17
Dordogne, Castles of the 8, 114-17

E

Eaux-Bonnes 166

F

family-friendly trails
  Arbois to Pupillin 80-1
  Beaumont-Hamel Newfoundland Memorial
    54-5
  Beynac Castle Loop 102-3
  Brantôme Circuit 98-9
  Calanche 214
  Camargue 124-5
  Canal du Midi, the 162
  Cap Blanc-Nez 63
  Capu Pertusato & Bonifacio 200-1
  Carcassonne: La Bastide to the Cité 163
  Cascade des Anglais 198-9
  Chemin de Halage, the 104
  Cirque de Gavarnie 192
  Cirque de Mourèze 150-1
  Cirque de Troumouse 177
  Cirque du Fer-à-Cheval 93
  Gorges d'Héric 148-9
  Grand Balcon Nord 70
  Île de Batz 47
  La Côte de Granit Rose 32
  Lac Chambon & Murol Circuit 100-1
  Lac d'Allos 143
  Lac de Nino 208-9
  Lac d'Oo & Lac Saussat 180-1
  Lac du Lauzanier 126-7
  Lac Vert 179
  Plateau de Bellevue 168-9
  Puy de Dôme 110-11
  Refuge des Oulettes de Gaube 170
  Roussillon Ramble 130-1

220/INDEX

Sentier des Douaniers 202-3
Thiepval Loop 52-3
Vallée du Tavignano 205
Wetlands of the Camargue 124-5
family travel 14-15, *see also* family-friendly
trails
Faÿ 63
festivals & events
Brittany 29
Central France 97
Corsica 197
Côte d'Azur 123
French Alps 67
Jura 67
Languedoc-Roussillon 147
Lille 51
Normandy 29
Pyrenees, the 167
Somme, the 51
forest trails
Beynac Castle Loop 102-3
Blanc-Martel Trail, the 134-5
Cap Roux 132-3
Cascade des Anglais 198-9
Cirque de Baume-les-Messiers 82-3
Cirque de Mourèze 150-1
Cirque de Navacelles 156-7
Dinan 30
Dordogne, Castles of the 114-17
Lac de Nino 208-9
Lac Pavin 119
Lac Vert 178-9
Signal St-Pierre 162
French Alps 64-93
planning 66-7

G

Giverny 28, 34-5
glaciers 71, 72, 170
Gordes 122, 136-9
Gorges d'Héric 148-9
GR5 93
GR10 192
GR20 211, 213
GR70 162
Grand Balcon Nord 7, 70-3
Grouin 11, 36-7

H

historical trails 13, 40-3
Armistice Memorial Circuit 62
Beaumont-Hamel Newfoundland Memorial
54-5
Beynac Castle Loop 102-3
Cadouin Abbey 118
Carcassonne: La Bastide to the Cité 163

Carnac Megaliths 47
Cirque de Baume-les-Messiers 82-5
Faÿ 63
Gordes Loops 136-7
Lochnagar Crater 58-61
Signal St-Pierre 162
Stevenson's Journey 108-9
Thiepval Loop 52-3
Vallée des Merveilles 142
Vézère Panoramas 118

I

Île de Batz 47
Île d'Ouessant 38-9
Îles Lavezzi 214
islands 37, 38-9, 46, 47, 214

J

Jura 64-93
planning 66-7

L

La Côte de Granit Rose 32-3
Lac Blanc 74-5
Lac Chambon & Murol Circuit 100-1
Lac d'Allos 143
Lac de Melo & Lac de Capitello 11, 210-13
Lac de Nino 208-9
Lac de Roselend & Lac de la Gittaz 68-9
Lac des Vaches & Col de la Vanoise 88-91
Lac d'Oo & Lac Saussat 180-1
Lac du Lauzanier 126-7
Lac Pavin 119
Lac Vert 178-9
lake trails
Chalets de Bise to Lac de Darbon 78-9
Col & Pic de Madamète 188-91
Lac Blanc 74-5
Lac Chambon & Murol Circuit 100-1
Lac d'Allos 143
Lac d'Ayous Circuit 172
Lac de Melo & Lac de Capitello 210-13
Lac de Nino 208-9
Lac de Roselend & Lac de la Gittaz 68-9
Lac des Vaches & Col de la Vanoise 88-91
Lac d'Oo & Lac Saussat 180-1
Lac du Lauzanier 126-7
Lac Pavin 119
Lac Vert 178-9
Le Cézallier 119
Marcadau Valley & the Cardinquère Lakes
184-7
Néouvielle Lake Circuit 193
Pic du Tarbésou & the Blue & Black Lakes
182-3

landscapes 20
language 216-17
Languedoc-Roussillon 144-63
planning 146, 147
Le Cézallier 119
Le Hourdel 63
Le Mont-Dore 97
Le Puy-en-Velay 96
Les Crocs 62
Les Eaux Tortes 140-1
lighthouses 32, 39, 124, 201
Lille 48-63
planning 50-1
Lochnagar Crater 58-61
Luz St-Sauveur 166

M

Macinaggio 196
Marcadau Valley & the Cardinquère Lakes
6, 184-7
memorials (war) 42, 43, 49, 52-3, 55, 62, 63
Monbazillac Vineyards 119
Monet, Claude 34-5
Mont Aigoual 10, 158-61
Mont Aigoual Observatory 160
Mont Blanc 72, 92
Mont Canigou 163
Mont Cinto 215
Mont St-Michel 36-7, 40, 46
Monte d'Oro 215
Monte San Petrone 215
Montpellier 146
mountain trails
Aiguille de la Grande Sassière 92
Blanc-Martel Trail, the 134-5
Brèche de Roland 174-5
Calanche 214
Cascade des Anglais 198-9
Chalets de Bise to Lac de Darbon 78-9
Cirque de Gavarnie 192
Cirque des Évettes 93
Cirque de Troumouse 176-7
Cirque du Fer-à-Cheval 93
Col & Pic de Madamète 188-91
GR5 93
GR10 192
Grand Balcon Nord 70-3
Lac Blanc 74-5
Lac d'Allos 143
Lac d'Ayous Circuit 172
Lac de Melo & Lac de Capitello 210
Lac de Nino 208-9
Lac de Roselend & Lac de la Gittaz 68-9
Lac des Vaches & Col de la Vanoise 88
Lac d'Oo & Lac Saussat 180-1
Les Eaux Tortes 140-1

INDEX/221

Marcadau Valley & the Cardinquère Lakes 184-7
Mont Aigoual 158-61
Mont Blanc 92
Mont Canigou 163
Mont Cinto 215
Monte d'Oro 215
Monte San Petrone 215
Néouvielle Lake Circuit, the 193
Pic des Mémises 76-7
Pic des Trois Seigneurs 193
Pic du Tarbésou & the Blue & Black Lakes 182-3
Pic St-Loup 154-5
Plateau de Bellevue 168-9
Puig Carlit 193
Puy de Sancy 112-13
Refuge des Oulettes de Gaube 170-1
Sentier Imbut 142
Sommet de Finiels 163
Tête de la Maye 86-7
Vallée du Tavignano 204-5
Moustiers Ste-Marie 122
Murol 96
Musée des Phares et des Balises 39
museums 39, 42, 43, 52-3, 146

N

national parks 18, 23-4, *see also* individual locations
Néouvielle Lake Circuit, the 193
Nîmes 146
Normandy 26-47
  planning 29
Normandy American Cemetery and Memorial 42-3

O

Omaha Beach 40-3

P

packing tips 19
Paimpol 28
Perpignan 146
Piana 196
Pic des Mémises 76-7
Pic des Trois Seigneurs 193
Pic du Tarbésou & the Blue & Black Lakes 182-3
Pic St-Loup 154-5
pilgrim trails 23, 106-7, 118
planning, *see also individual locations*
  accessible travel 16-17
  highlights 6-11

travel with children 14-15
  walking essentials 18-19
Plateau de Bellevue 168-9
Pointes du Raz & Van 7, 44-5
Port-Miou, Port-Pin & En-Vau 128-9
Presqu'île de Crozon 47
Provence 120-43
Puig Carlit 193
Puy de Dôme 110-11
Puy de Sancy 112-13
Pyrenees, the 164-93
  planning 166-7

Q

Quimper 28

R

Refuge des Oulettes de Gaube 170-1
resources
  accessible travel 17
  Brittany 29
  Central France 97
  Corsica 197
  Côte d'Azur 123
  French Alps 67
  Jura 67
  Languedoc-Roussillon 147
  Lille 51
  Normandy 29
  Pyrenees, the 167
  Somme, the 51
  walking essentials 19
responsible walking 18
Roc des Hourtous 152-3
Rocamadour 96, 106-7
Roussillon 122, 130-1

S

safety 19, 141
Sarlat-la-Canéda 96
Sentier des Douaniers 202-3
Sentier des Ocres 131
Sentier du Littoral 143
Sentier Imbut 142
signage 19
Signal St-Pierre 162
skiing 72
snow shoeing 25
Somme, the 48-63
  planning 51
Sommet de Finiels 163
St-Cirq-Lapopie 96
Stevenson, Robert Louis 108-9, 160, 162
Stevenson's Journey 108-9

St-Malo 28, 36-7
swimming 32, 56-7, 75, 128-9, 134-5, 148-9, 200-1, 202-3, 214

T

Tête de la Maye 86-7
Thiepval Loop 52-3
transport
  Central France 97
  Corsica 197
  Côte d'Azur 123
  language 217
  Languedoc-Roussillon 147
  Pyrenees, the 167
travel seasons 18, 29, 50-1, 66-7, 97, 122-3, 146, 166-7, 196-7

V

Vallée des Merveilles 142
Vallée du Tavignano 204-5
Vanoise National Park 17
Vézère Panoramas 118
Village des Bories 139
village trails 13
  Brantôme Circuit 98-9
  Capu Pertusato & Bonifacio 200-1
  Castles of the Dordogne 114-17
  Chemin de Halage, the 104-5
  Cirque des Évettes 93
  Dinan 30-1
  Giverny 34-5
  Gordes Loops 136-9
  Monbazillac Vineyards 119
  Roussillon Ramble 130-1
  Vézère Panoramas 118
von Richthofen, Manfred 59

W

war cemeteries 43, 52, 55, 59, 60
war memorials 42, 43, 49, 52-3, 55, 62, 63
waymarking 19
wetlands (Camargue) 124-5
wildlife 12, 24, 91, 185
wildlife trails
  Camargue 124-5
  Chalets de Bise to Lac de Darbon 78-9
  Circuit de la Roche Trouée 143
  Grouin 36-7
  Lac d'Ayous Circuit 172-3
  Lac du Lauzanier 126-7
  Le Hourdel 63
  Pointes du Raz & Van 44-5
  Puy de Sancy 112-13
wineries 80-1, 119

OLIVER BERRY

Oliver Berry is a writer and photographer from southwest England. He has worked on more than 30 guidebooks for Lonely Planet, covering destinations from Cornwall to the Cook Islands. He is also a regular contributor to many newspapers and magazines. His writing has won several awards, including the Guardian Young Travel Writer of the Year and the TNT Magazine People's Choice Award. His latest work is published at www.oliverberry.com.

My favourite walk It's far from easy going, but for me the epic walk to Mont Aigoual (p158) offers some of the finest views of one of France's loveliest corners, the Cévennes. Hills, forests, ridges, traditional villages and a top-of-the-world lookout – this walk has them all. And at the end of the day, your aching legs will make you feel like you've earned them.

STEVE FALLON

A native of Boston, Massachusetts, Steve lived in Hong Kong for more than a dozen years and Budapest for three years, before moving to London in 1994. He has written or contributed to more than a hundred Lonely Planet titles. Steve is a qualified London Blue Badge Tourist Guide. Visit his website at www.steveslondon.com.

My favourite walk The Grouin: Up to a Point walk (p36) to the stormy headland offers everything – from views over islands to the sea and even to Mont St-Michel, as well as WWII-era relics and a plethora of local birdlife.

ANITA ISALSKA

Anita is a travel journalist and digital content strategist. After several merry years as a staff writer and editor – a few of them in Lonely Planet's London office – Anita now works freelance between California, the UK and any French mountain lodge with wi-fi. Anita specialises in Eastern and Central Europe, Australia, France and her adopted home, San Francisco. Read about her on www.anitaisalska.com.

My favourite walk The Chemin des Chèvres to the top of Puy de Dôme (p110) is a classic, thanks to volcanic views and a quaint train ride back down. This trail sparked my long love affair with the Auvergne.

NICOLA WILLIAMS

Be it walking, trail running, cross-country or alpine skiing, the French Alps have been the weekend playground of British writer Nicola Williams for over a decade. From her home in a village on the southern shore of Lake Geneva in Haute-Savoie, she has researched and written more than 50 guidebooks for Lonely Planet and covers France as a destination expert for the *Daily Telegraph*. Catch her hard at work on the road or up a mountain on Twitter and Instagram at @tripalong.

My favourite walk It really is hard to pinpoint just one, but it's Lac des Vaches & Col de la Vanoise (p88). It is a reasonably challenging walk, full of surprises and exhilarating moments, leading walkers through every possible alpine landscape: from pea-green flower fields at lower altitudes to heartachingly bleak, desolate moraines and awe-inspiring, ice-blue glaciers up high.

Our Story

A beat-up old car, a few dollars in the pocket and a sense of adventure. In 1972 that's all Tony and Maureen Wheeler needed for the trip of a lifetime – across Europe and Asia overland to Australia. It took several months, and at the end – broke but inspired – they sat at their kitchen table writing and stapling together their first travel guide, Across Asia on the Cheap. Within a week they'd sold 1500 copies. Lonely Planet was born.

Today, Lonely Planet has offices in the US, Ireland and China with a network of over 2000 contributors in every corner of the globe. We share Tony's belief that 'a great guidebook should do three things: inform, educate and amuse'.

Our Writers

STUART BUTLER

Stuart has been writing for Lonely Planet for a decade and, during this time, he's come eye to eye with gorillas in the Congolese jungles, met a man with horns on his head who could lie in fire, huffed and puffed over snow bound Himalayan mountain passes, interviewed a king who could turn into a tree, and had his fortune told by a parrot. When not on the road for Lonely Planet he lives on the beautiful beaches of Southwest France with his wife and two young children.

Today, as well as guidebook writing work, Stuart writes about conservation and environmental issues (mainly in eastern and southern Africa), wildlife watching and hiking. He also works as a photographer and was a finalist in both the 2015 and 2016 Travel Photographer of the Year Awards. In 2015 he walked for six weeks with a Maasai friend across a part of Kenya's Maasai lands in order to gather material for a book he is writing (see: www.walkingwiththemaasai.com). His website is www.stuartbutlerjournalist.com.

My favourite walk Having walked so many different trails throughout France for this book it's hard to choose a single favourite. However, living at the foot of the western Pyrenees, these mountains have a special place in my heart and no walk showcases them quite like Marcadau Valley & Cardinquère Lakes (p184). I was also bowled over by the coastal walks in Brittany, in particular Pointes du Raz & Van (p44).

 MORE WRITERS

STAY IN TOUCH LONELYPLANET.COM/CONTACT

IRELAND Digital Depot, Roe Lane (off Thomas St), Digital Hub, Dublin 8, D08 TCV4, Ireland

Although the authors and Lonely Planet have taken all reasonable care in preparing this book, we make no warranty about the accuracy or completeness of its content and, to the maximum extent permitted, disclaim all liability arising from its use.

All rights reserved. No part of this publication may be copied, stored in a retrieval system, or transmitted in any form by any means, electronic, mechanical, recording or otherwise, except brief extracts for the purpose of review, and no part of this publication may be sold or hired, without the written permission of the publisher. Lonely Planet and the Lonely Planet logo are trademarks of Lonely Planet and are registered in the US Patent and Trademark Office and in other countries. Lonely Planet does not allow its name or logo to be appropriated by commercial establishments, such as retailers, restaurants or hotels. Please let us know of any misuses: lonelyplanet.com/ip.